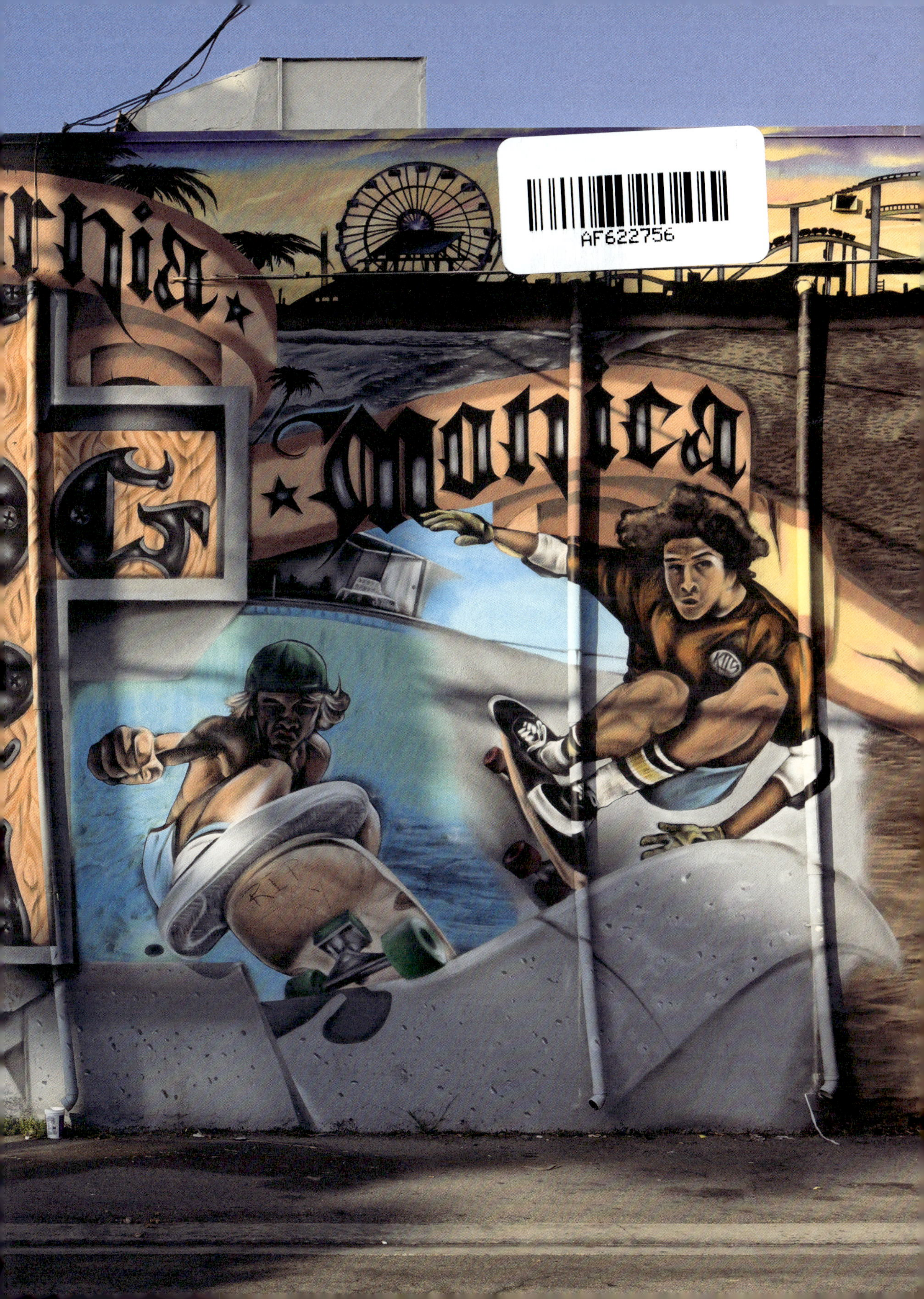
Monica

DOTAN SAGUY

DOG TOWN

THE PUPS OF VENICE BEACH AND THEIR HUMANS

KEHRER

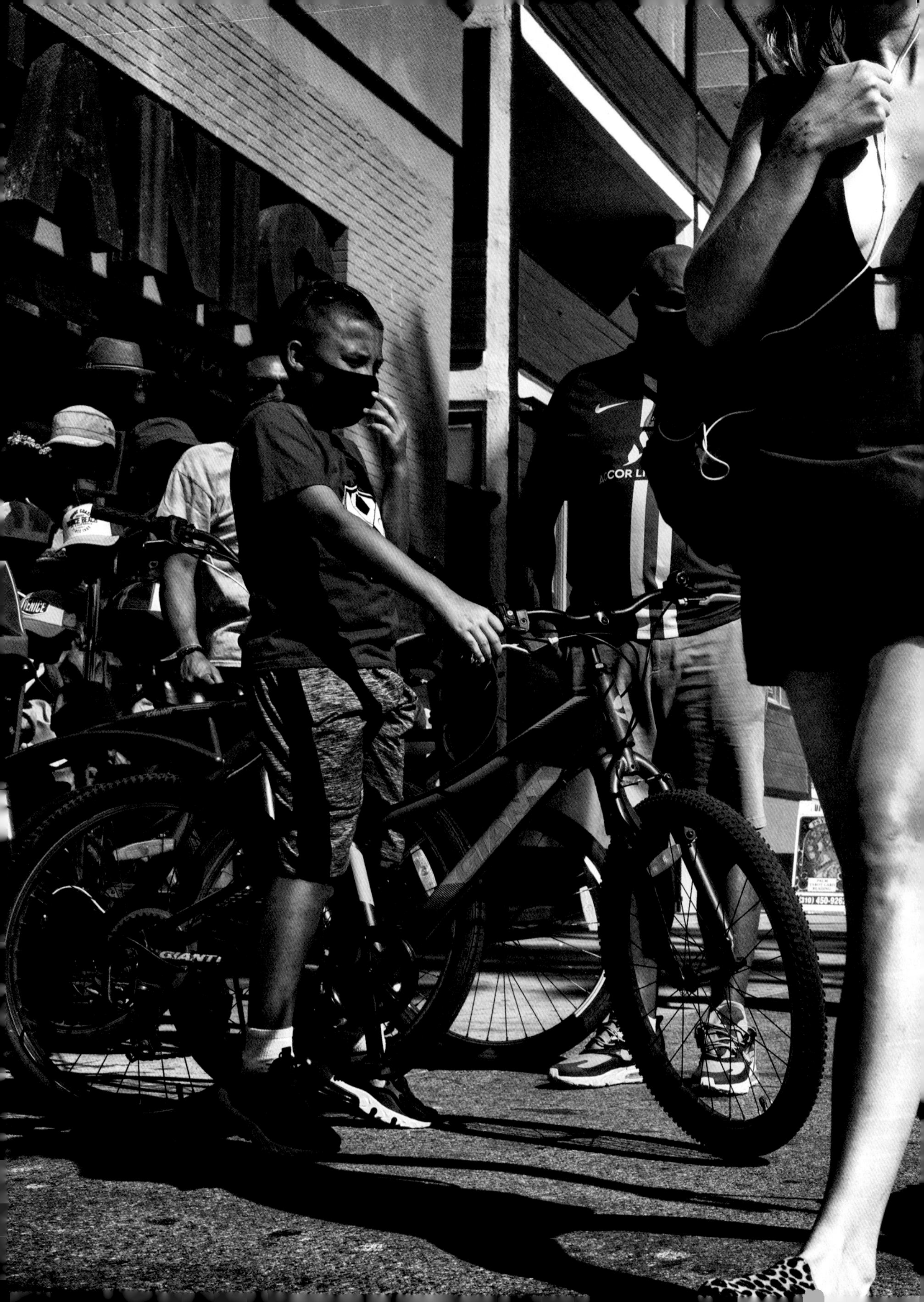
VENICE
GIANT

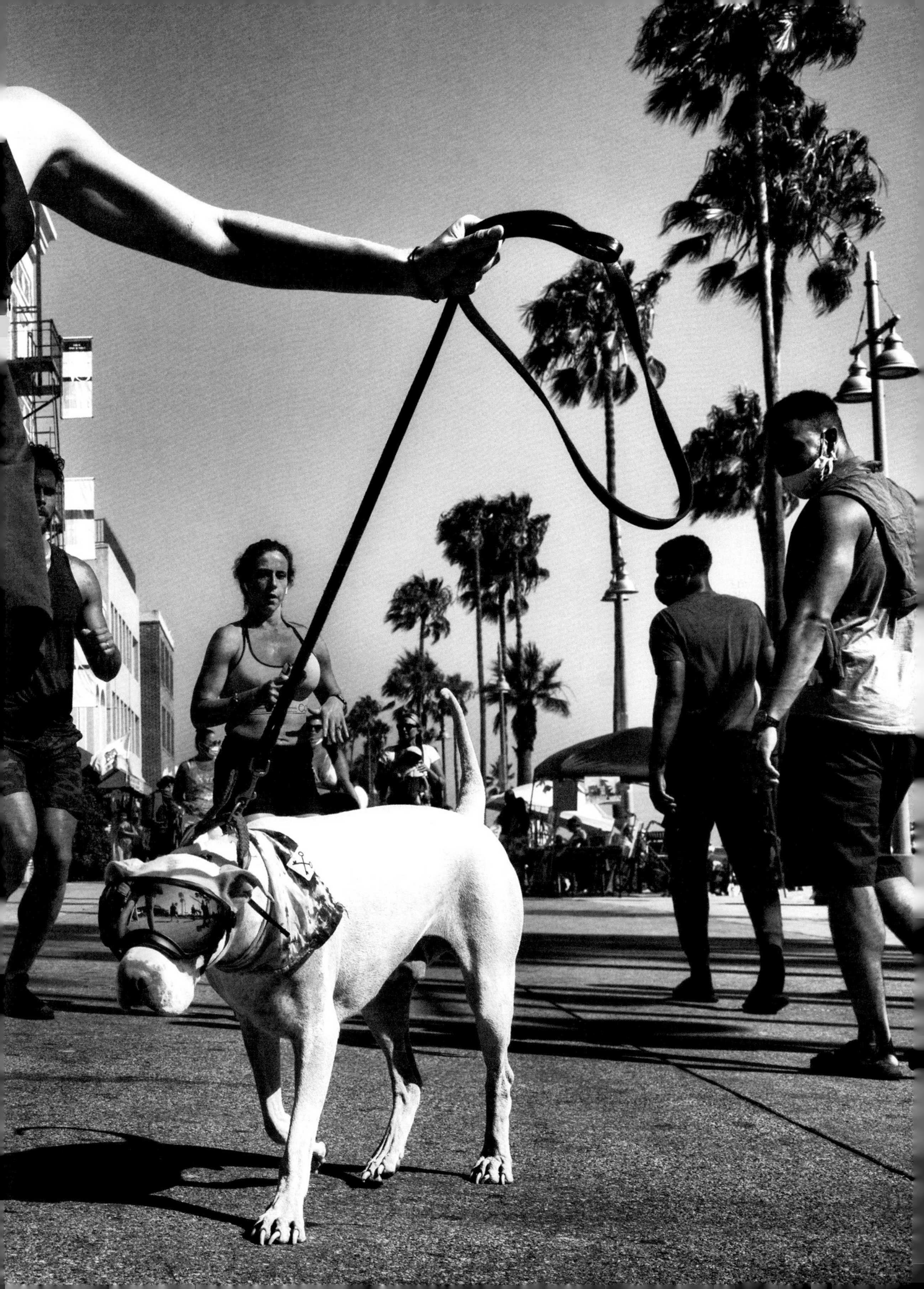

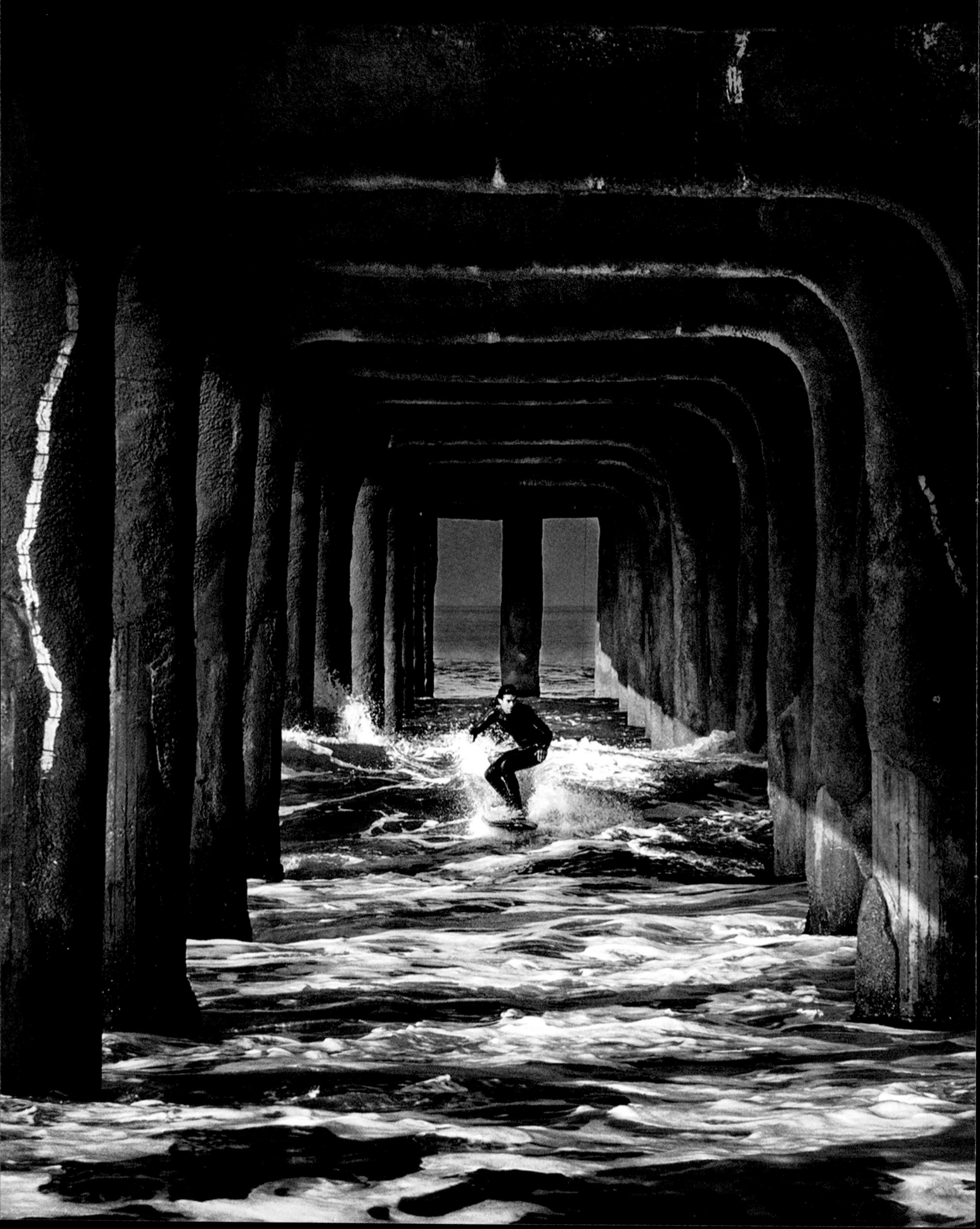

A BIT OF DOGTOWN HISTORY

"Dogtown" is the nickname for an area that includes Venice Beach and part of coastal Santa Monica near Los Angeles, California. Where the nickname comes from is anybody's guess. Whether you ask Google, AI bots, or long-time Venice residents, no one seems to know for sure where the moniker came from. Was it because the area had been home to a large stray dog population back in the 1970s, the rough environment of run-down storefronts lining the shore or the rebellious surfers and skateboarders of that era?

Regardless, the nickname "Dogtown" stuck and remains intimately associated with the iconic Zephyr surf and skateboard team—better known as the "Z-Boys"—who emerged from this rough neighborhood in the mid-70s and went on to take the skateboarding world by storm.

It all started in the early 1970s, when the abandoned Pacific Ocean Park (POP) pier, an amusement park left vacant years earlier, became a gathering spot for young rebellious teenagers from this working-class neighborhood. They were irresistibly attracted by the challenge of surfing a dangerous part of the dilapidated pier structure they affectionately called "the cove."

Those young daredevils developed a surfing technique of quick turns, to slalom between the snapped off and decayed pier pilings sporadically sticking out of the ocean. One mistake and you could break your surfboard or much worse: get impaled. It was a fiercely guarded playground exclusively reserved for a select group of local outcasts who didn't want anyone from the outside cutting them off. It was dangerous. It was violent. It was "dog eat dog."

Left page: "Surfer 'shooting' the Manhattan Beach pier, 2015. Although I made this photograph 10 miles south of Dogtown and 40 years after its heyday, this is the closest I've personally felt to the surfing style of that era."

As the surf was not always up, however, skateboarding also became a popular afternoon activity among this group. Right around the same time two major developments collided into a perfect storm of opportunity for the Z-Boys. First, the invention of grippy polyurethane wheels enabled the young surfers to replicate their quick low turns on asphalt. And second, a major drought struck Southern California, forcing residents to let their private swimming pools dry out. This combination prompted the Z-Boys to start skating the empty private pools of surrounding upscale neighborhoods, inventing new skateboarding moves that we still take for granted today—at least until the cops showed up and everybody split. The rest is history.

Ironically, the last time the Z-boys skated together—before their respective pro careers tore the group apart—was by invitation to a posh North Santa Monica estate. The wealthy owner's son, who was dying of brain cancer, pleaded with his dad to empty their swimming pool for the Z-boys to skate in. The dying wish was granted and the Dogtown skateboard prodigies skated there for several days surrounded by the family's dogs, earning the pool the nickname of the "dog bowl."

Today, the Dogtown spirit endures on the streets of Venice Beach, with names like Jay Adams, Tony Alva, and Stacy Peralta seared into the collective consciousness. Since then, a new generation of skateboarders has taken over, their community skate park pools replacing the trashed private swimming pools of the 1970s, and still often surrounded by dogs—as the images in this book bear witness to.

As I documented in my first photobook, *Venice Beach, the Last Days of a Bohemian Paradise* (Kehrer Verlag, 2018), the boardwalk has gentrified quite a bit since the Dogtown days. However, the area has nevertheless managed to retain a lot of its character, edginess, and bohemian spirit. It is hands down the most diverse and inclusive coastal community in Southern California. It is where Los Angeles working-class families go to the beach for a picnic on a warm weekend afternoon. If you're curious about what I mean, just drop by the Venice Beach drum circle on a Sunday afternoon and dance barefoot in the sand with a hodgepodge of people from all walks of life: blue collar workers, bankers, homeless people, engineers, etc. Everyone is welcome and everyone dances to the same entrancing beat.

WHY A BOOK ABOUT DOGS?

Those who know my street and documentary photography work may wonder: why dogs? Dogs have been a big part of my personal life. I grew up with a boxer rescue named Gus and now my six-year-old Goldendoodle Beau sometimes accompanies me on my street photography adventures.

Canines were already well represented in my 2018 book *Venice Beach*, but after completing that body of work I decided that dogs were so central to Venice—and to my heart—that they deserved their own photography project.

As you will see through the pages of this book, dogs contribute greatly to the unique character of Venice Beach. Whether they are learning to skateboard, wearing funny outfits, taking a shower, or dancing with their human counterparts, they seem to enjoy taking part in every aspect of this chaotically festive yet inclusive, loving community.

And what a treat they are to photograph! You can make friends with them in an instant, they don't have any inhibitions, they are completely transparent with their emotions, and they don't mind being photographed in embarrassing situations! That last quality was once famously pointed out by the father of candid dog photography, Elliott Erwitt.

IN HOMAGE TO ELLIOTT ERWITT

Without a doubt, my biggest inspiration for this work was Elliott Erwitt. Sadly, on November 29 2023, just as I was putting the finishing touches to this introduction, Mr. Erwitt passed away at the age of 95.

I take a lot of pictures of dogs because I like dogs, because they don't object to being photographed, and because they don't ask for prints.

– Elliott Erwitt

Back in 2018, I went to a talk Mr. Erwitt gave in Century City, Los Angeles. He was already 90 years old, using a walker and looking quite frail. Nevertheless, he started his presentation with a mischievous smile by displaying this portrait of himself at 5 years old in a child's sailor outfit. He went on to explain that the host had requested a portrait of him to advertise the talk, so he had sent them this one because they hadn't specified whether it had to be recent. This irreverent humoristic detail captures the ageless spirit of Mr. Erwitt so well that I decided to use it. There's no doubt in my mind that it is the one he would have picked again himself.

Mr. Erwitt's career was too long and his oeuvre too broad to describe here. He photographed many important people at key moments in history, such as Marilyn Monroe, Che Guevara, Jack Kerouac, Richard Nixon and Jacqueline Kennedy, but if you had asked Mr. Erwitt which body of work gave him the most pleasure, he would have undoubtedly pointed to the many books he published on dogs. His empathy for our canine friends was palpable on every page and his humor irresistible. I hope this humble homage to Mr. Erwitt's work would have earned his approval and most importantly that it will entertain you.

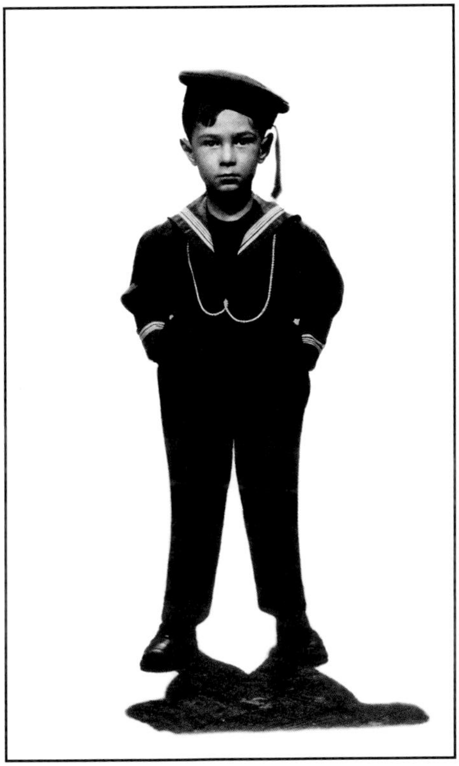

Elliott Erwitt
1928–2023

age 5
Milan, Italy, 1933

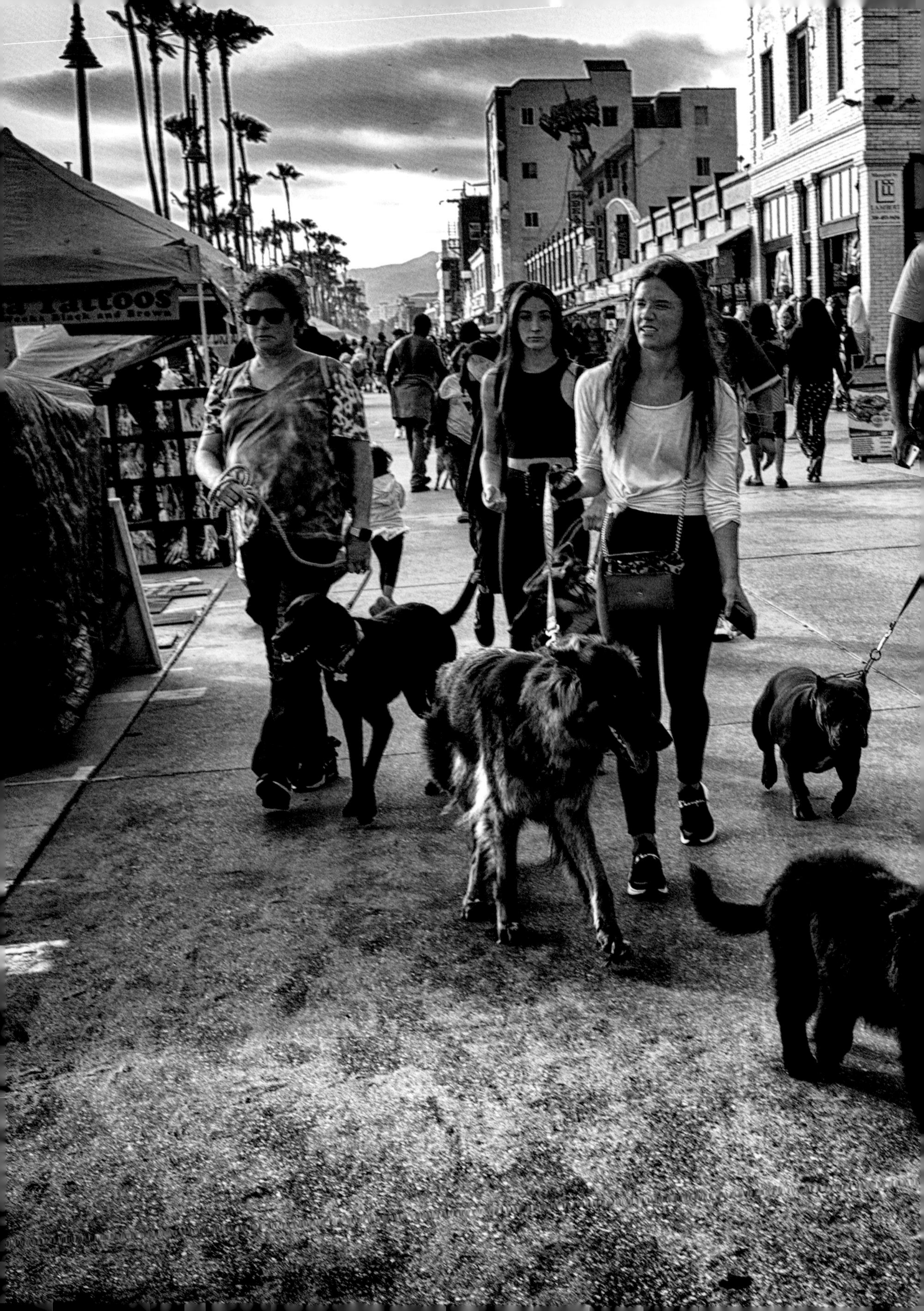
Tattoos

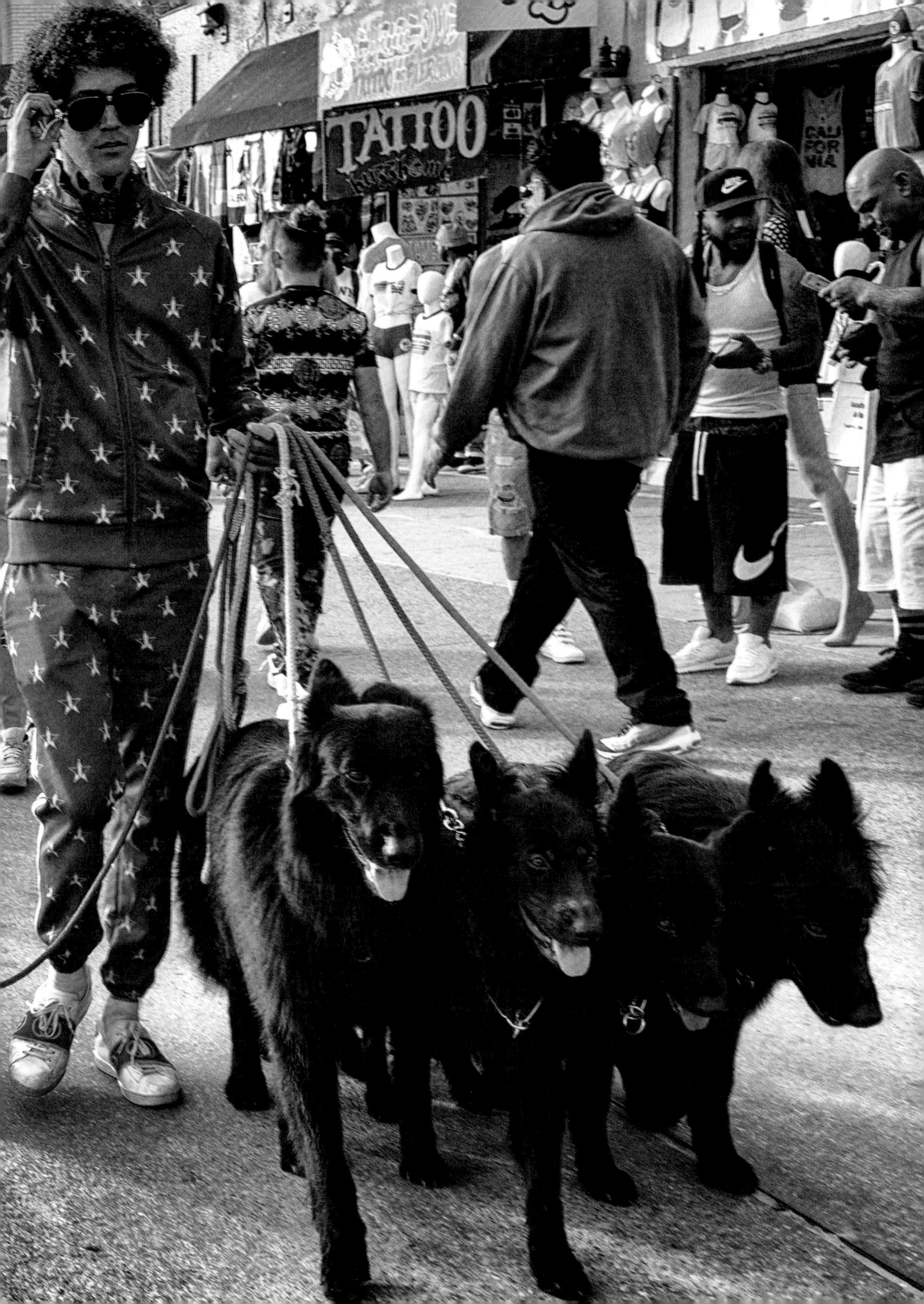
TATTOO
CALI
FOR
NIA
NIKE

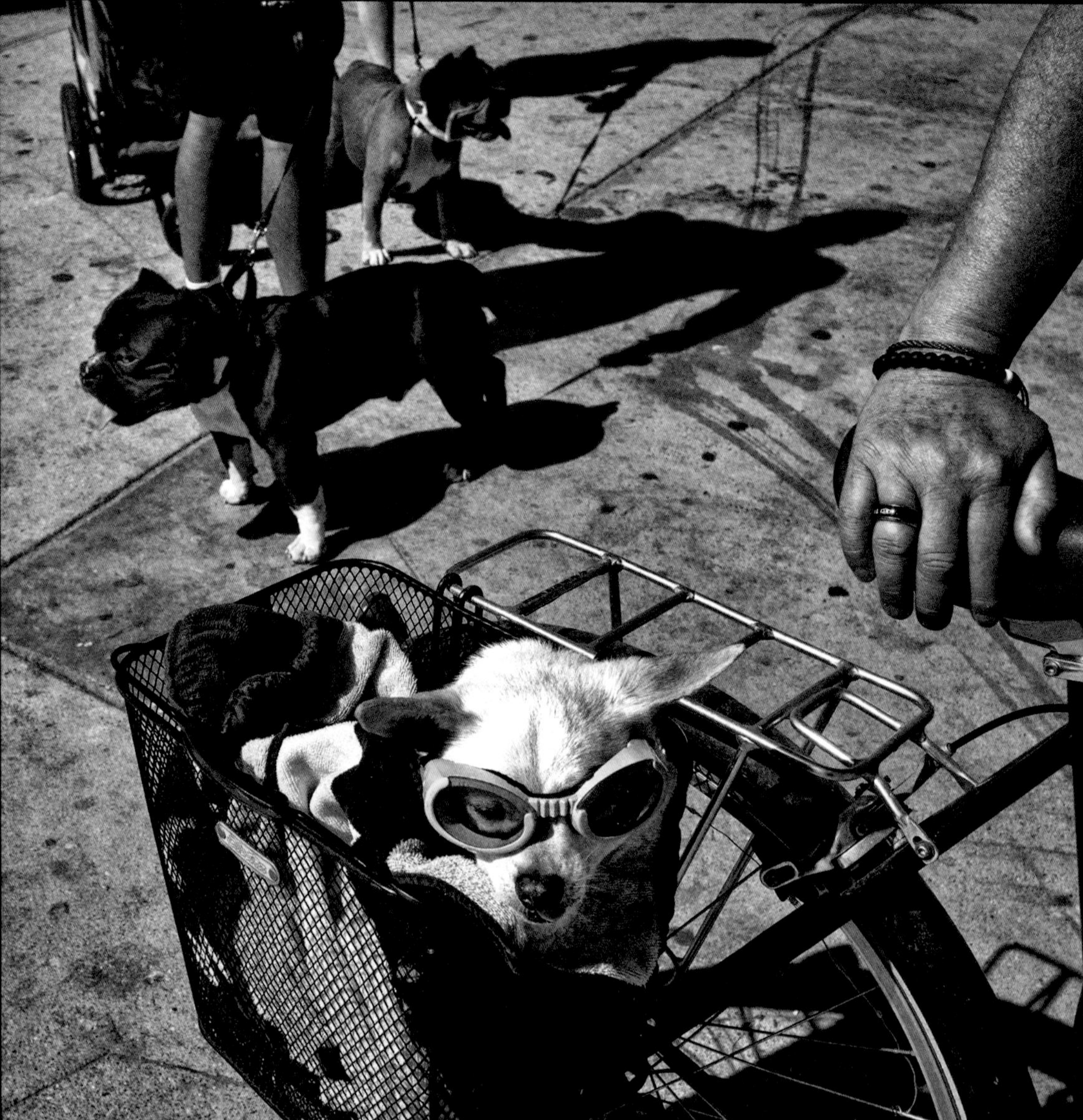

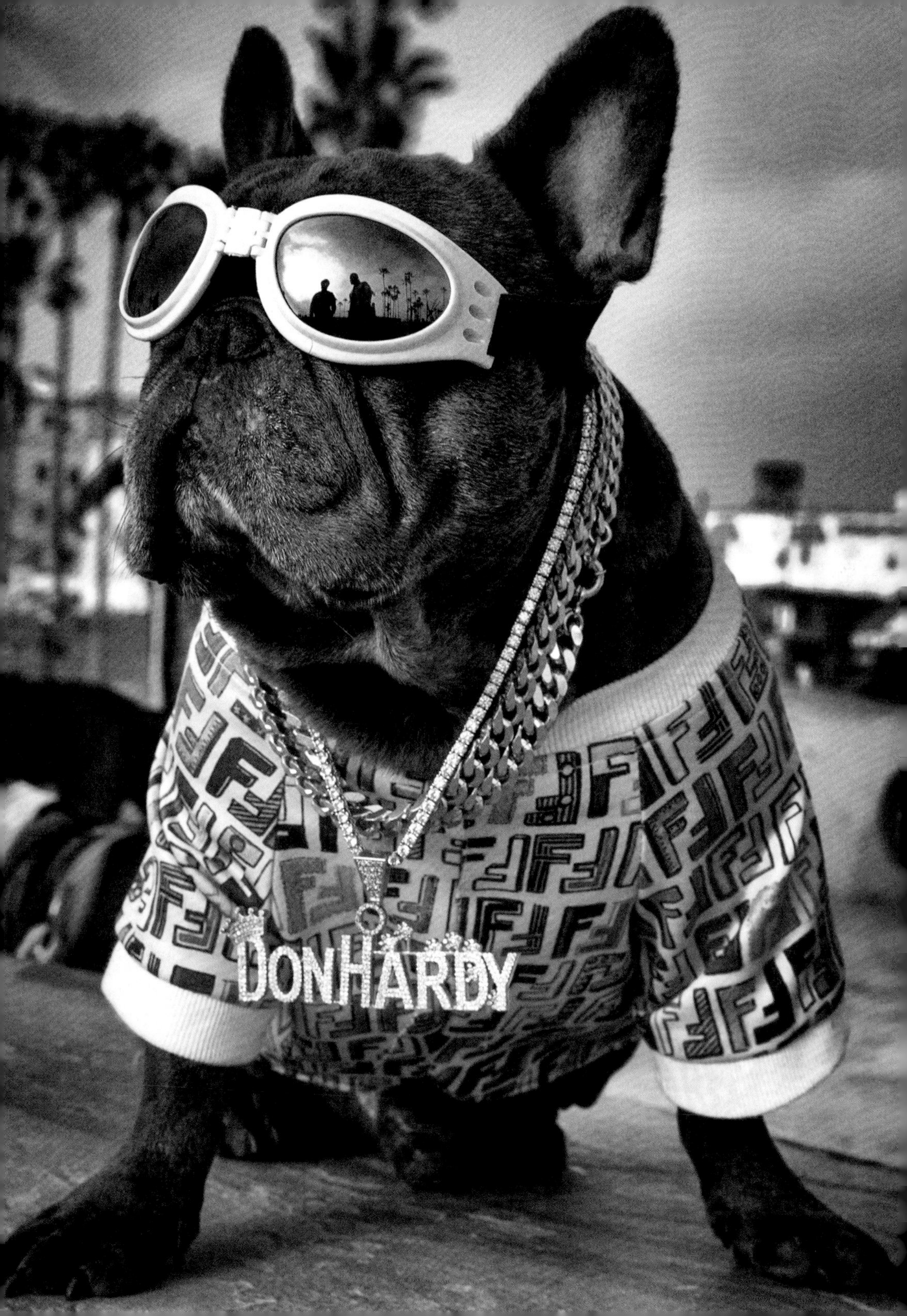
DONHARDY

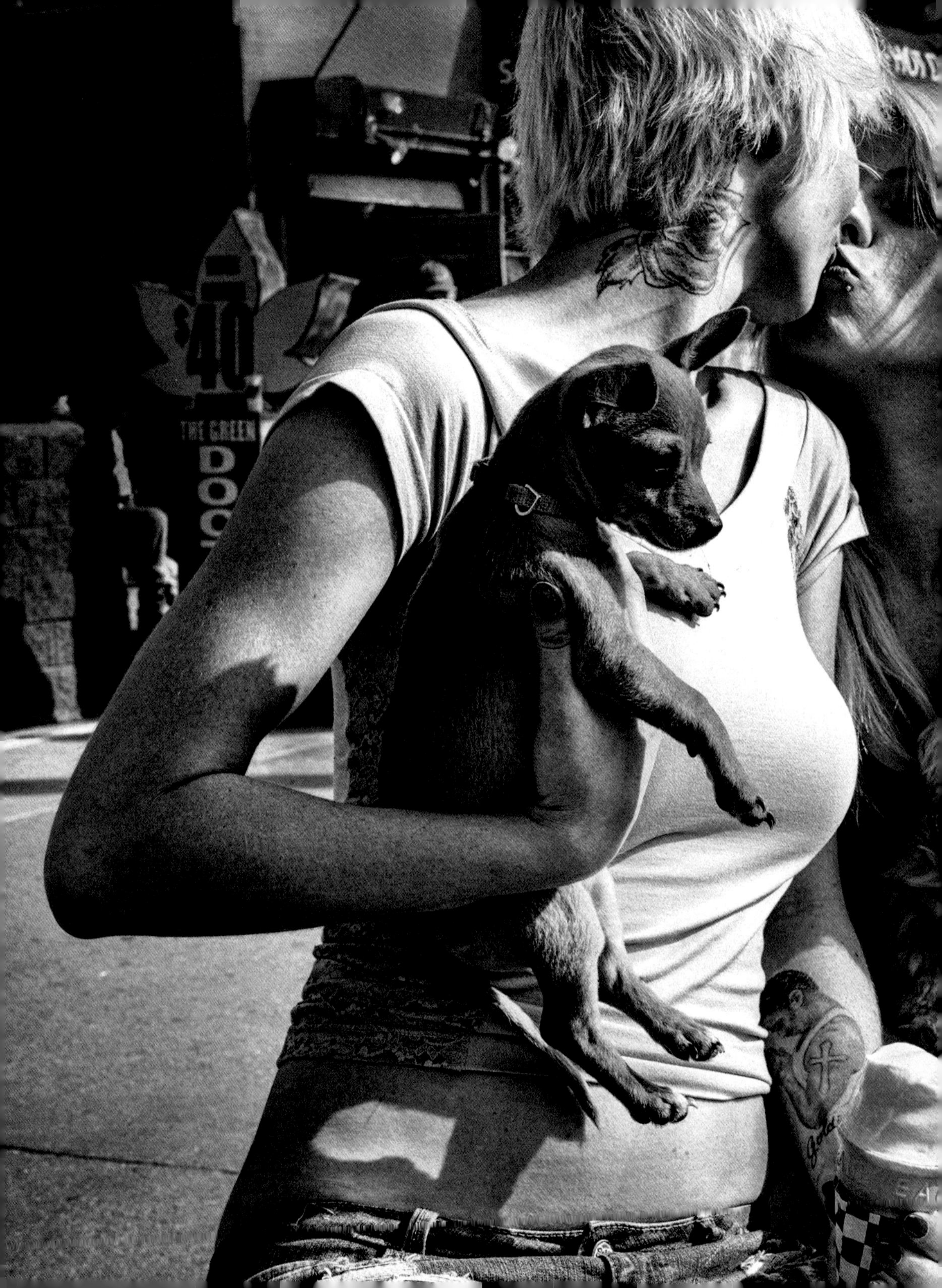
$40
THE GREEN

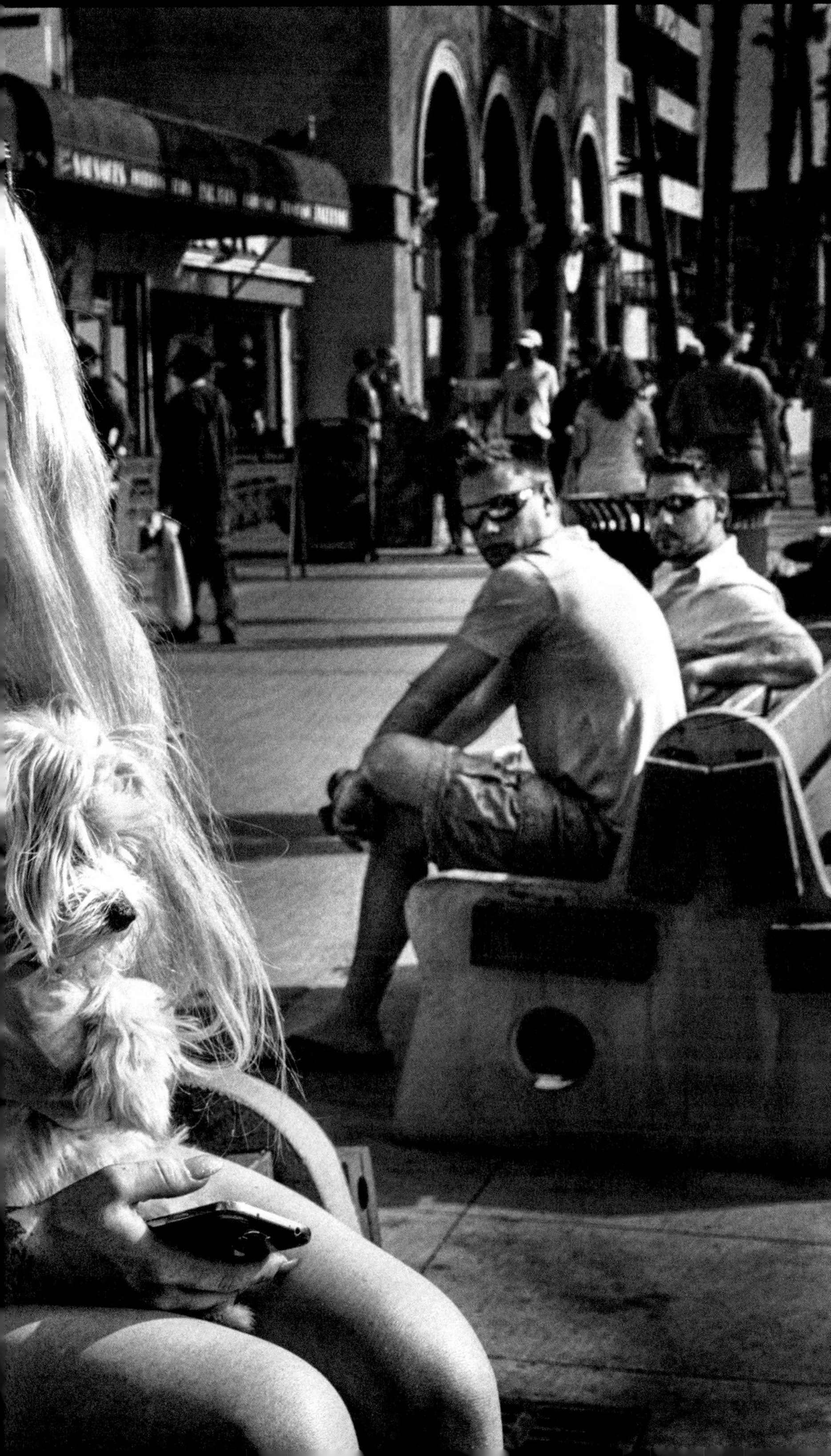

POP

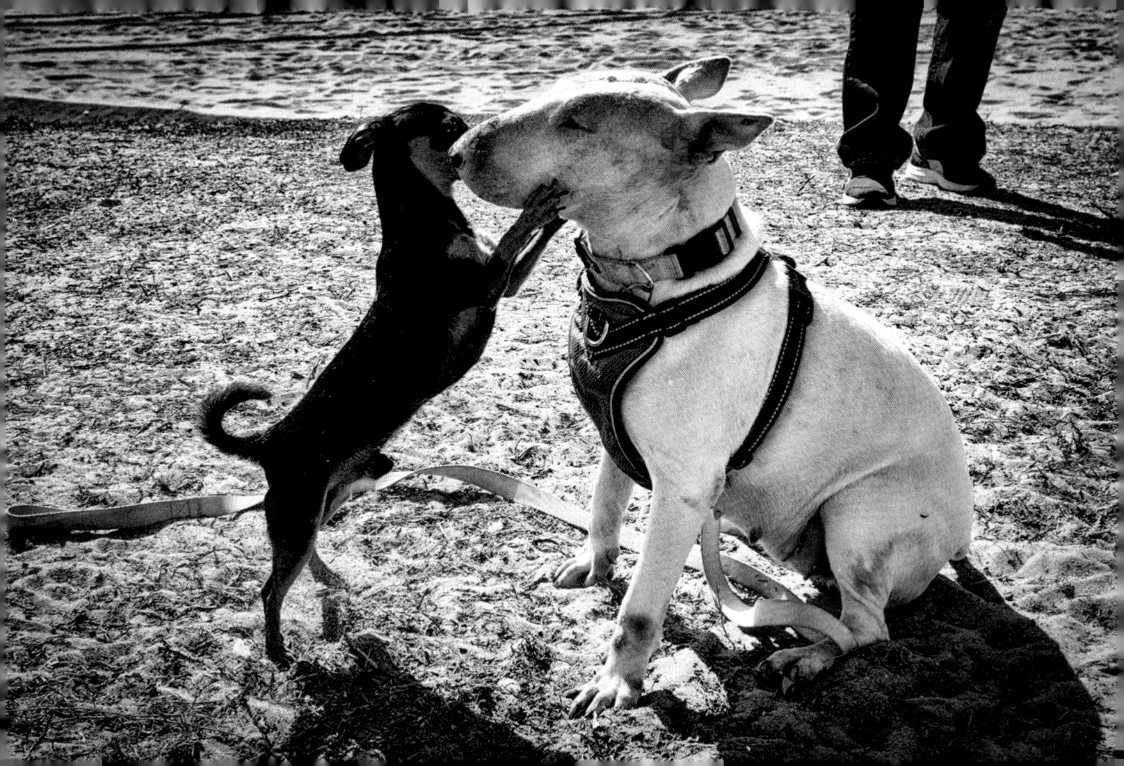

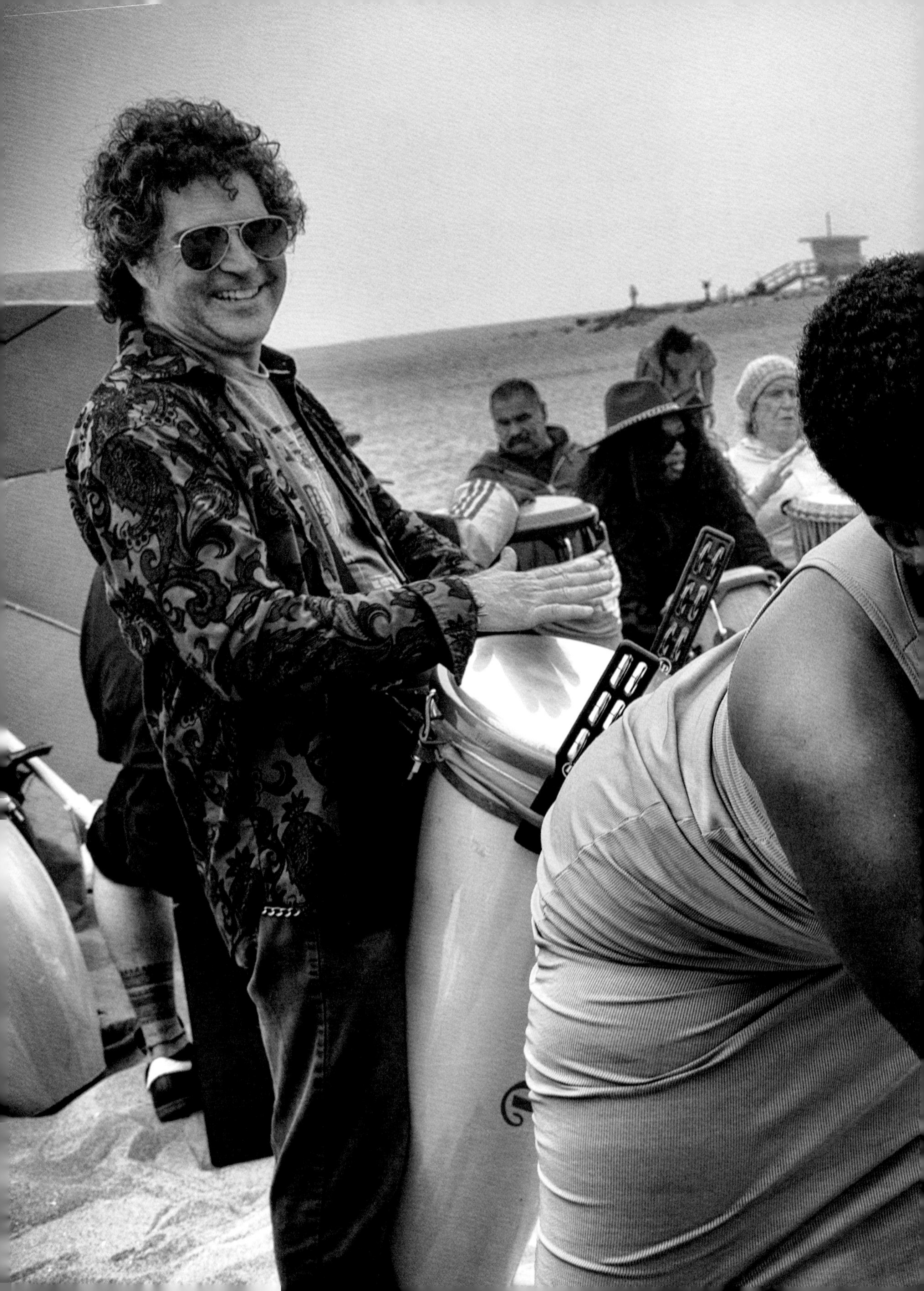

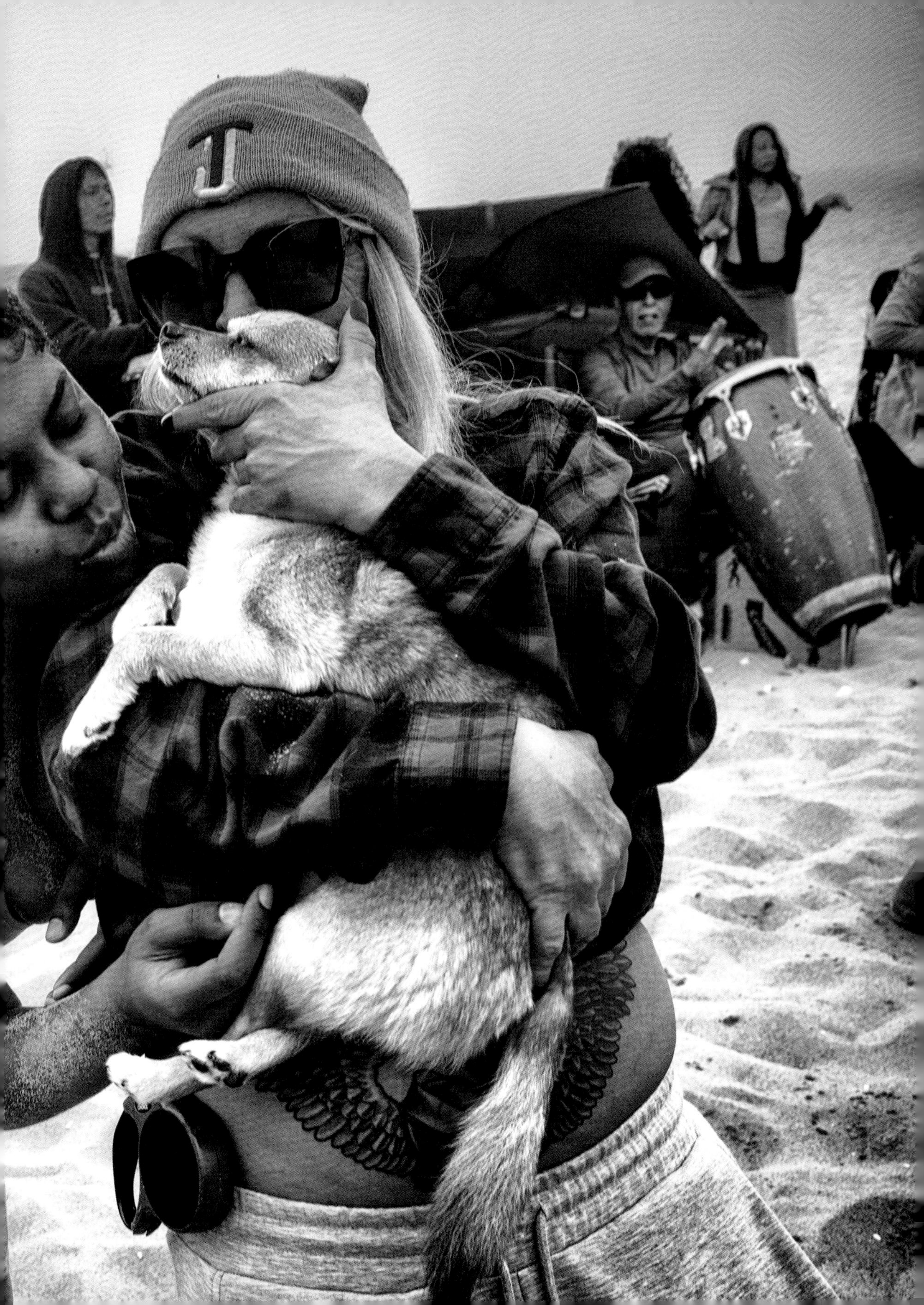

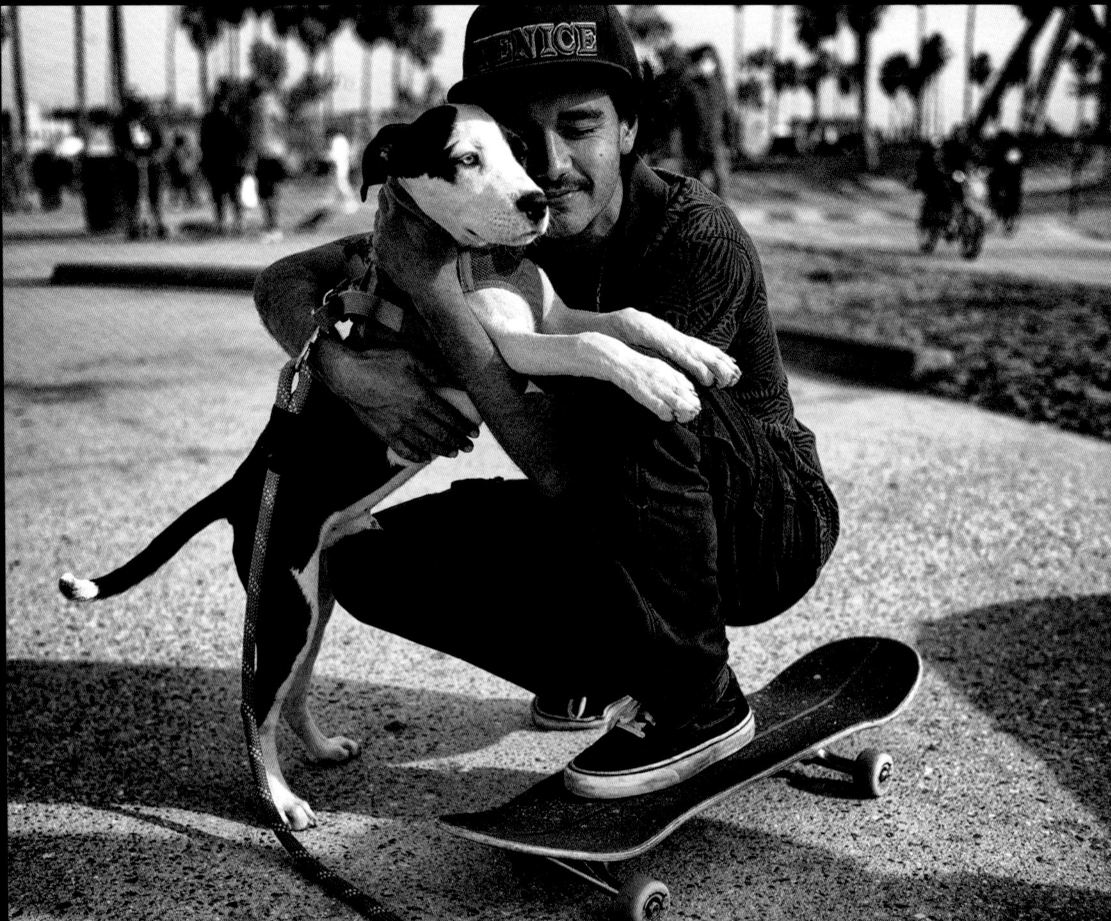

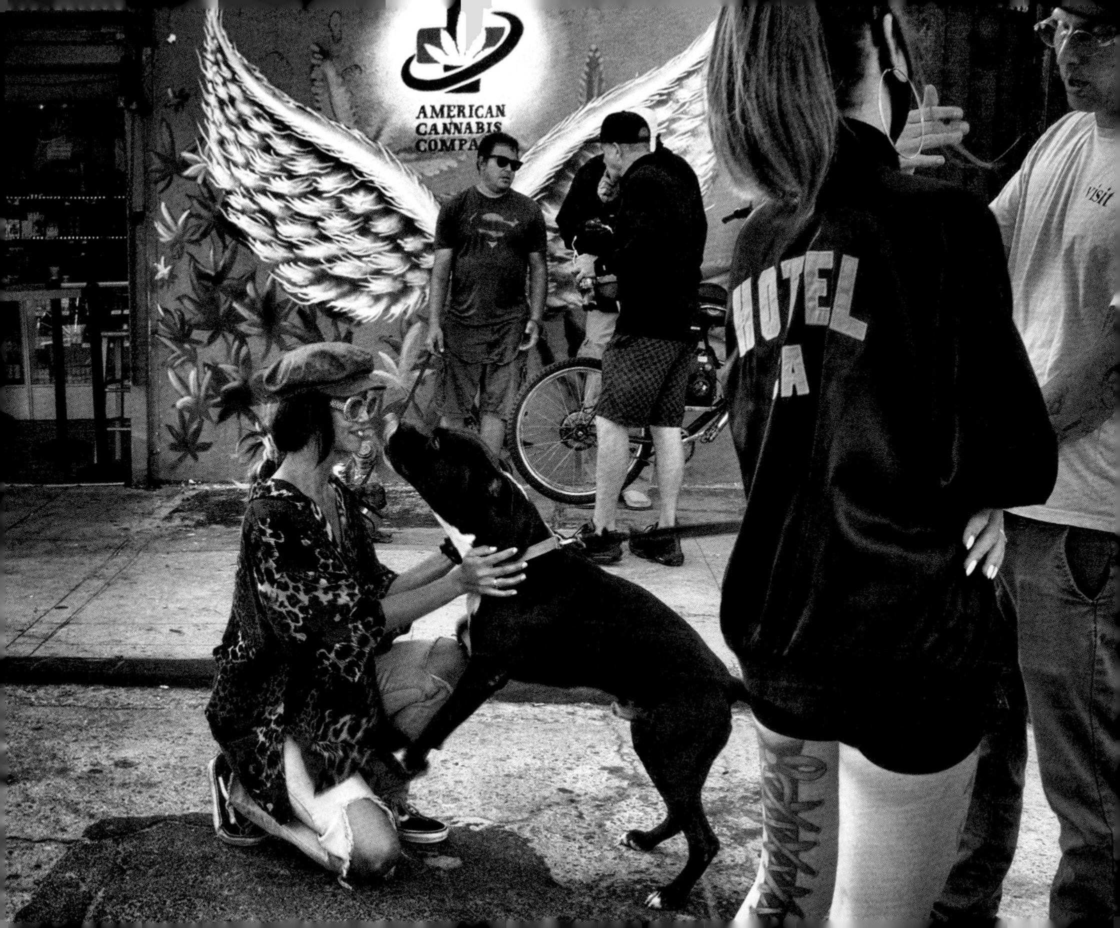
AMERICAN
CANNABIS
HOTEL
visit

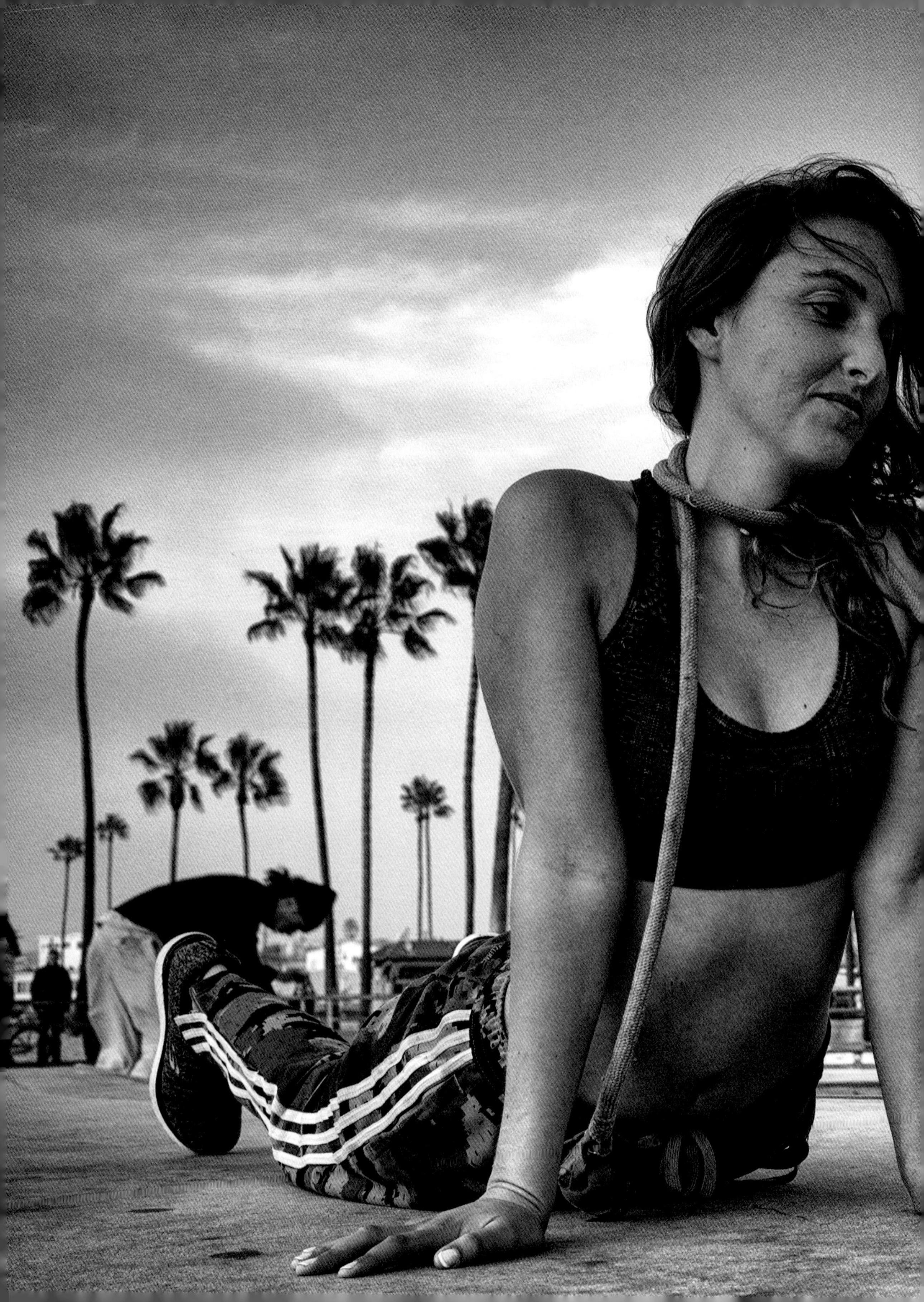

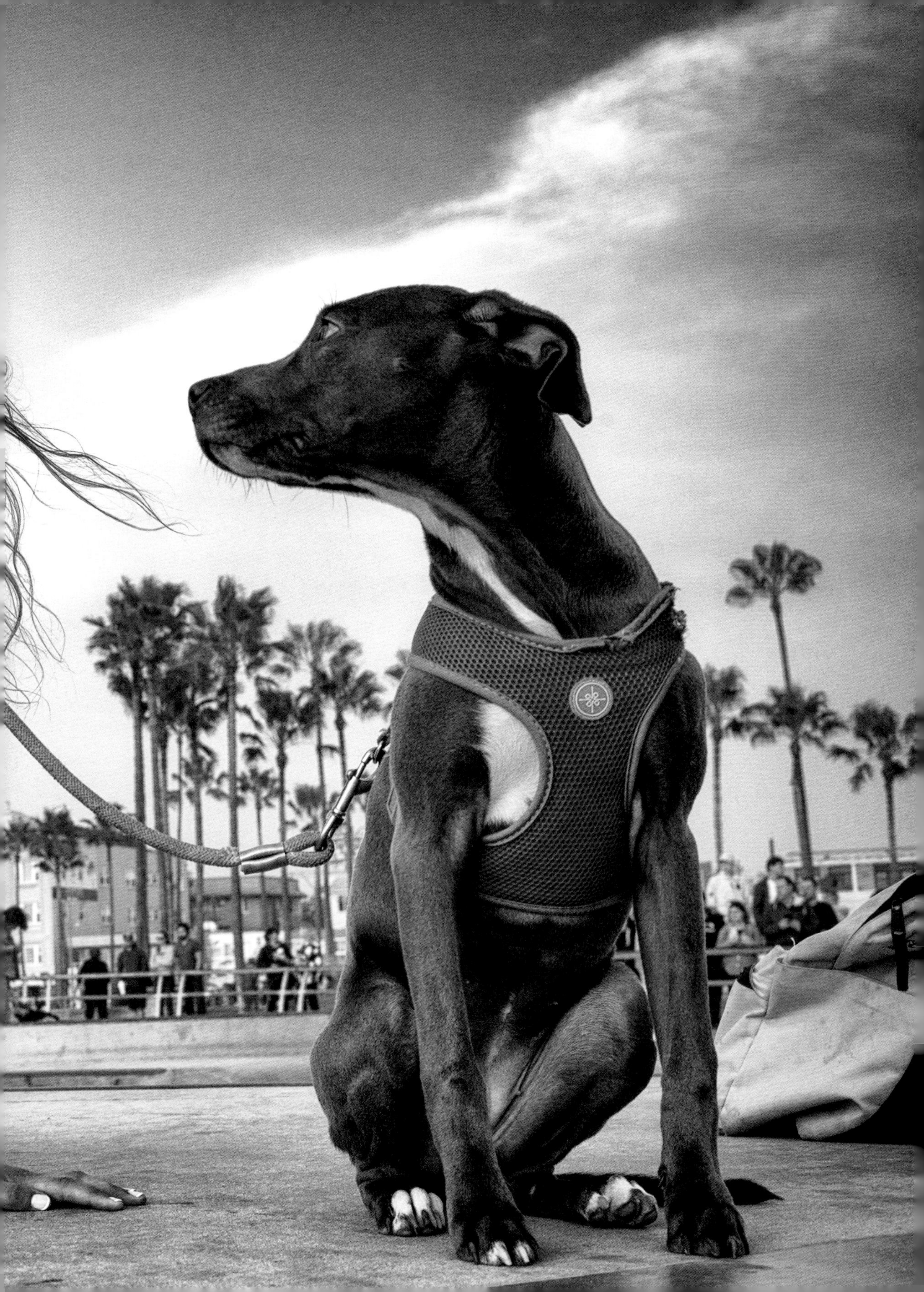

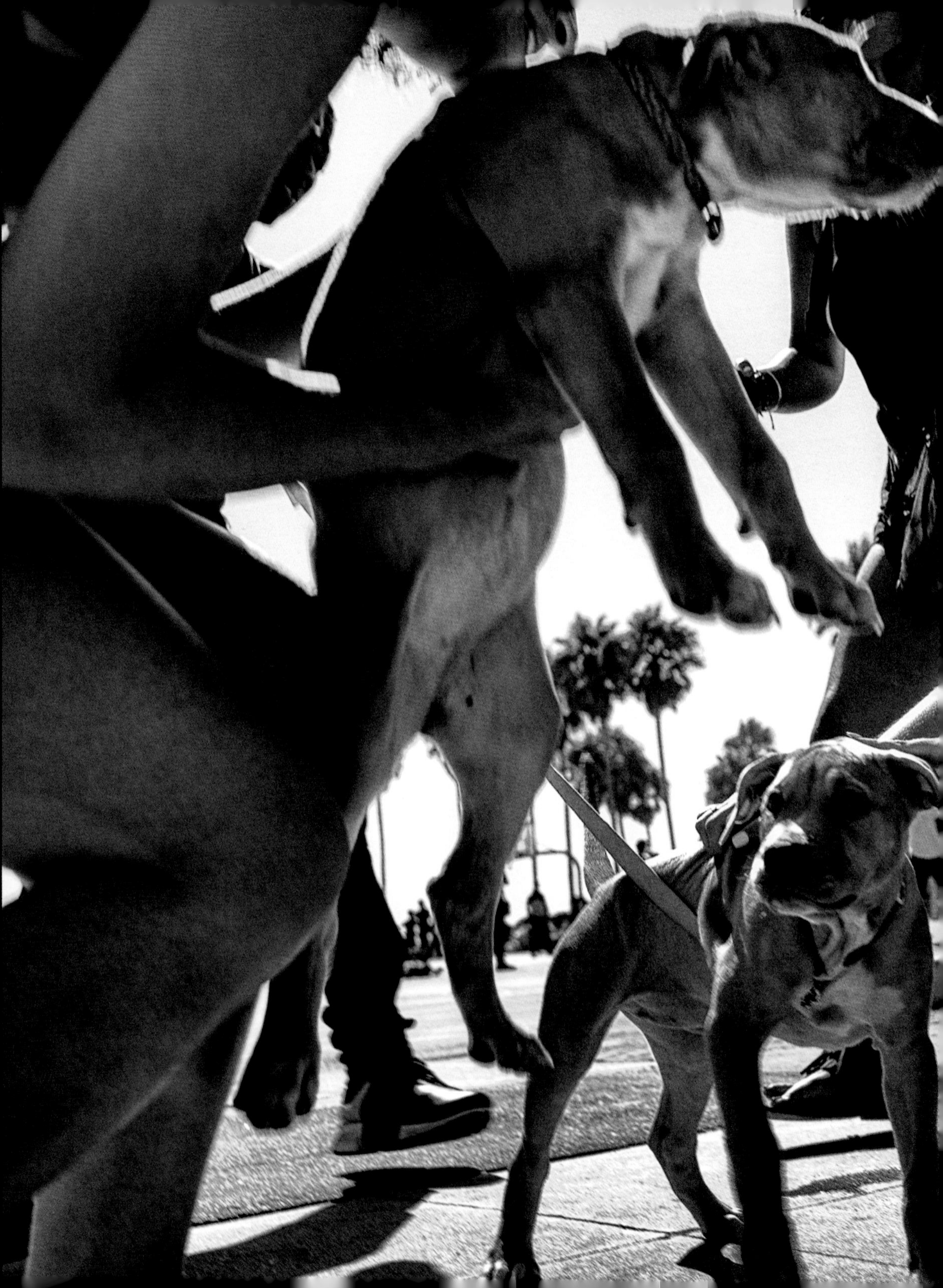

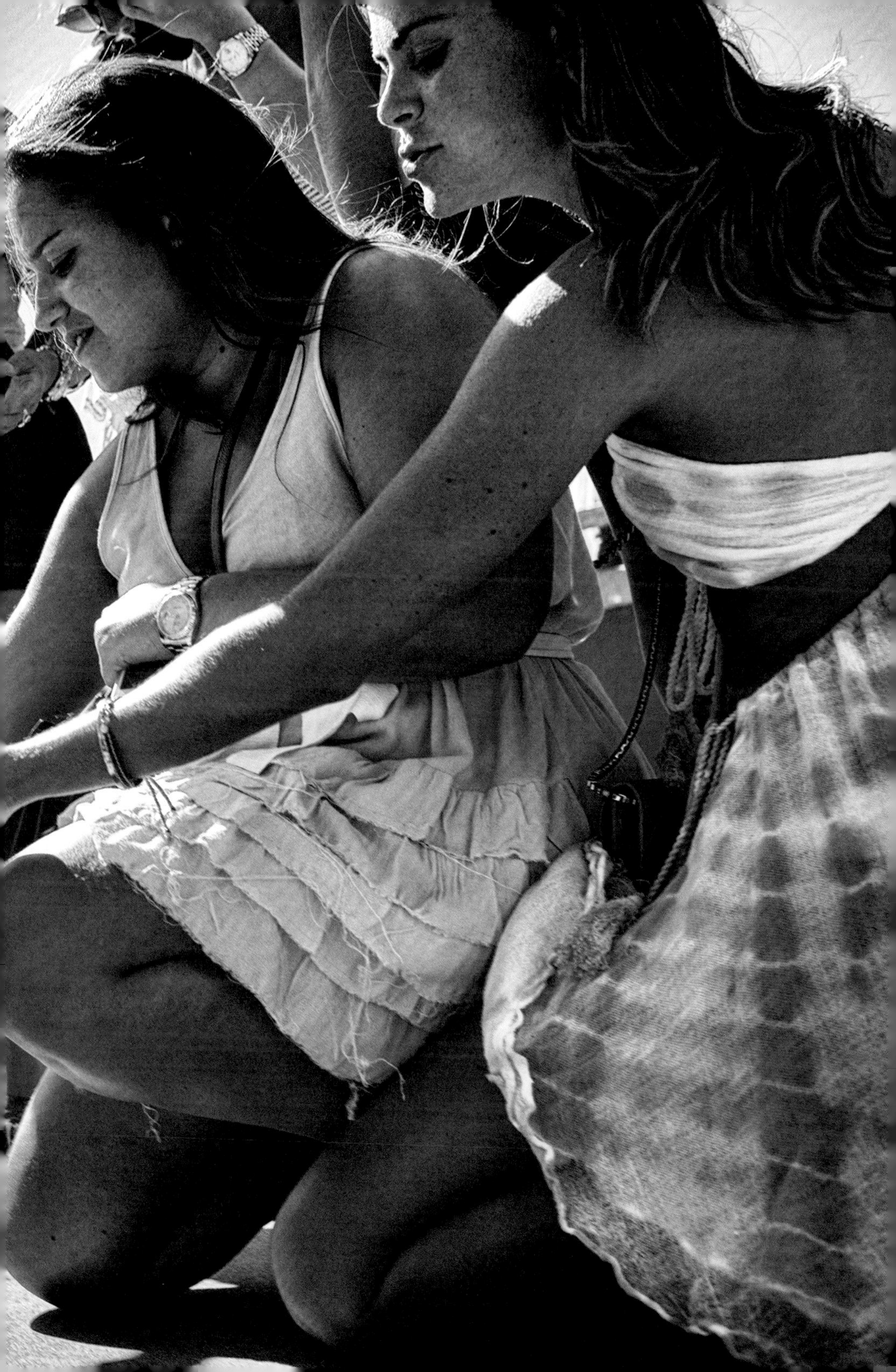

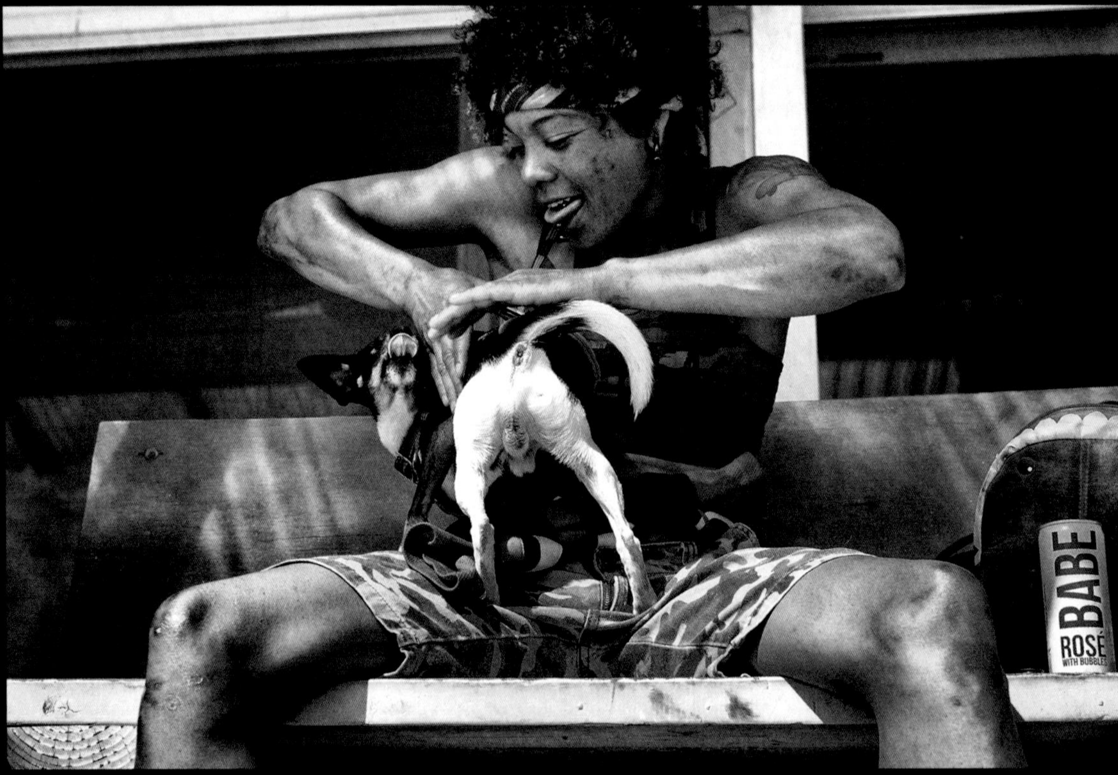
BABE
ROSÉ
WITH BUBBLES

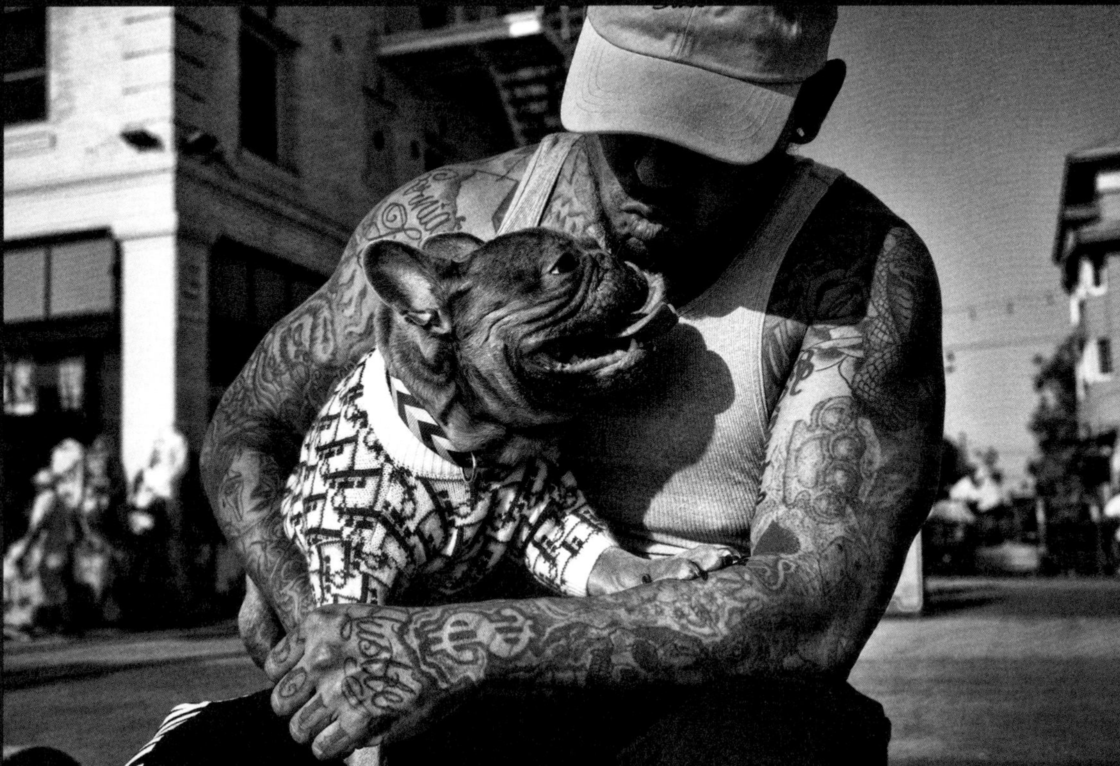

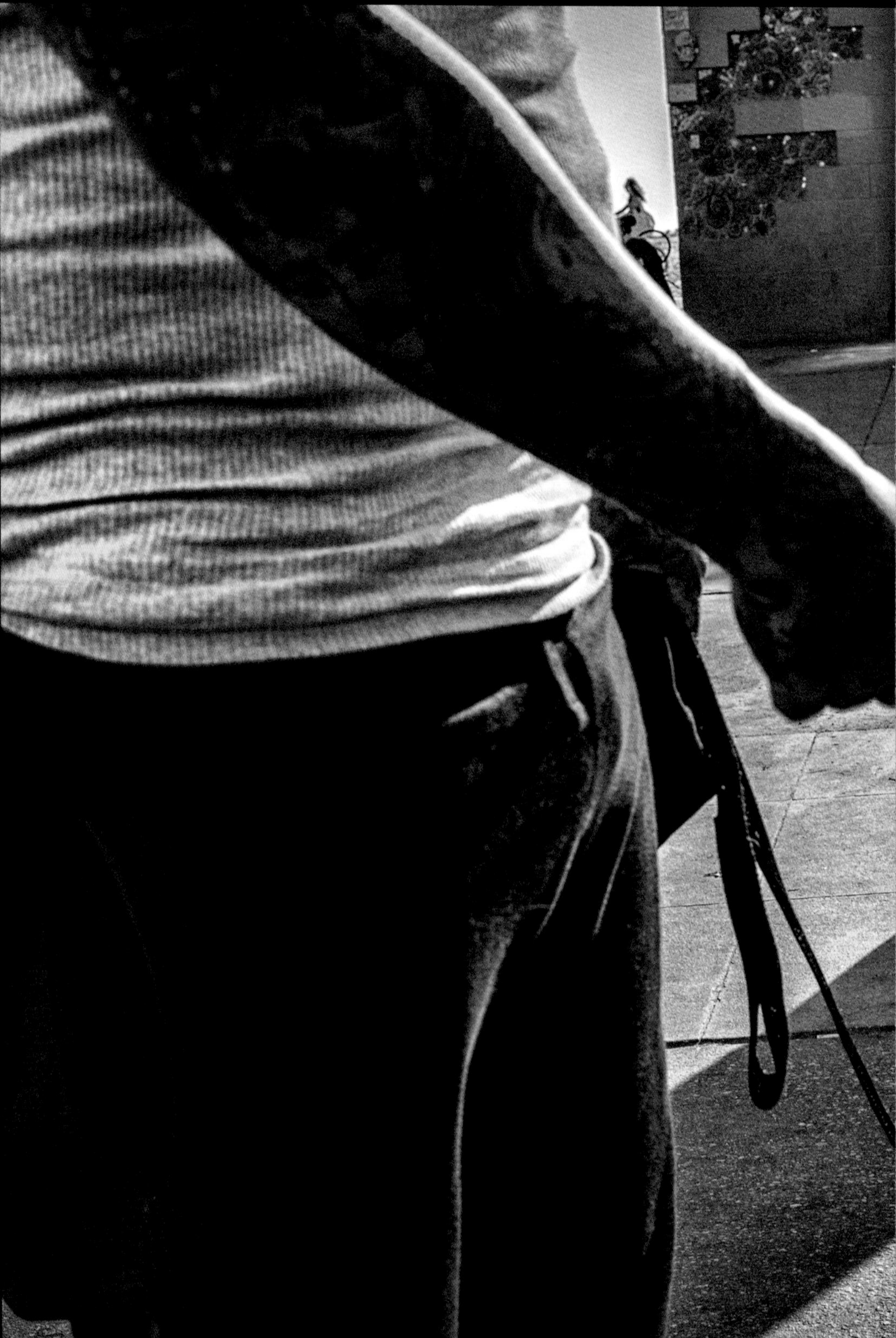

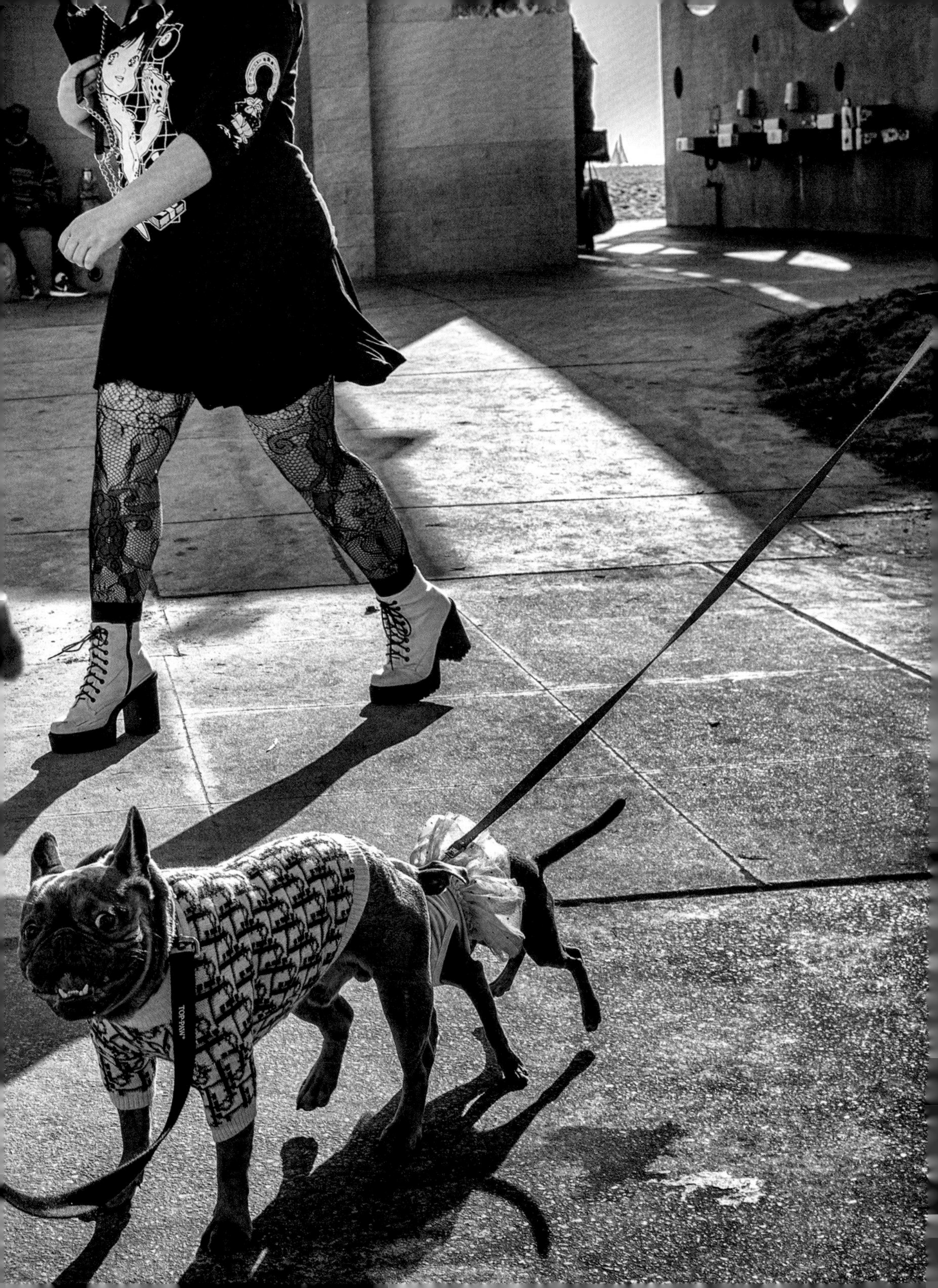
TOP-PAW

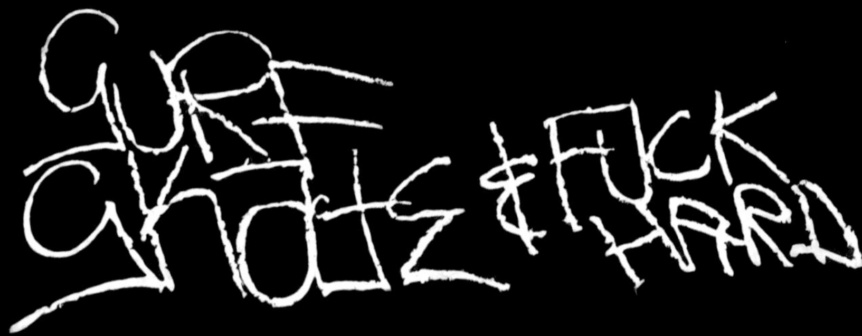
& FUCK HARD

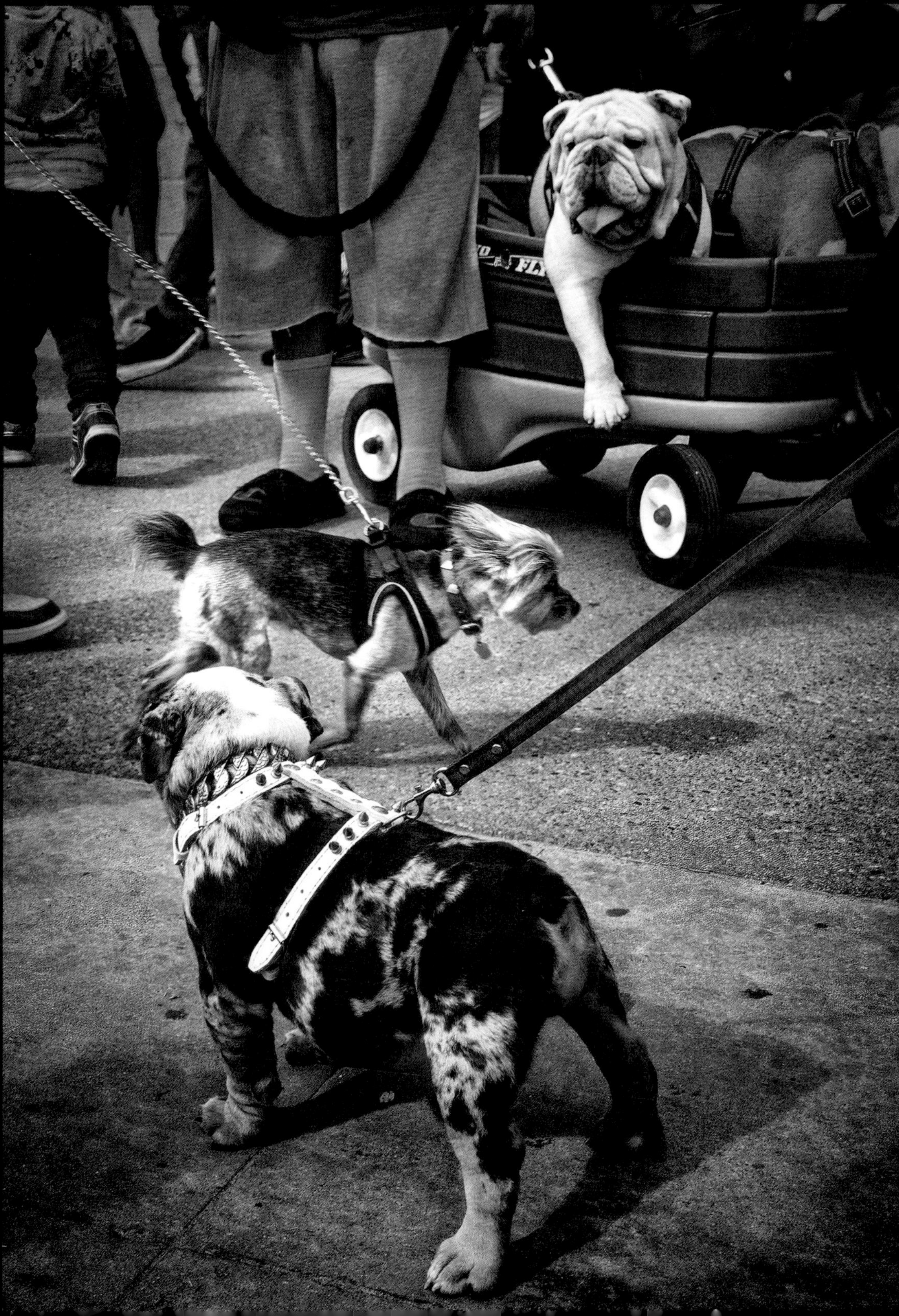

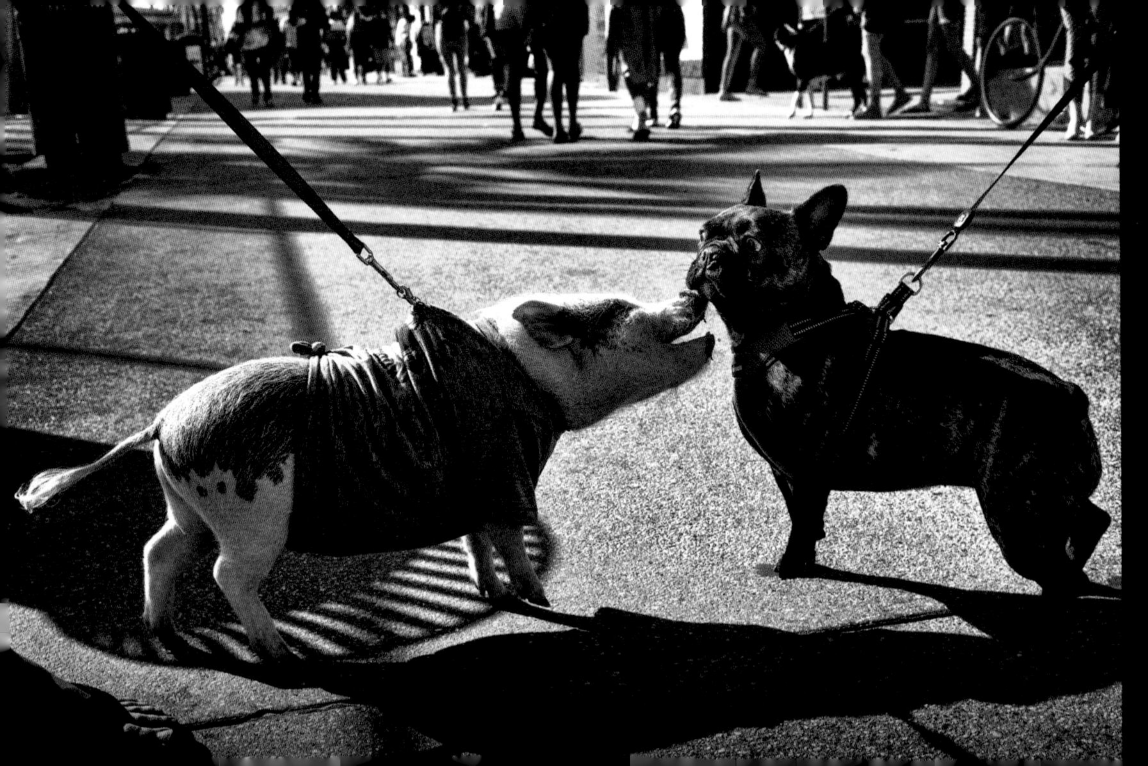

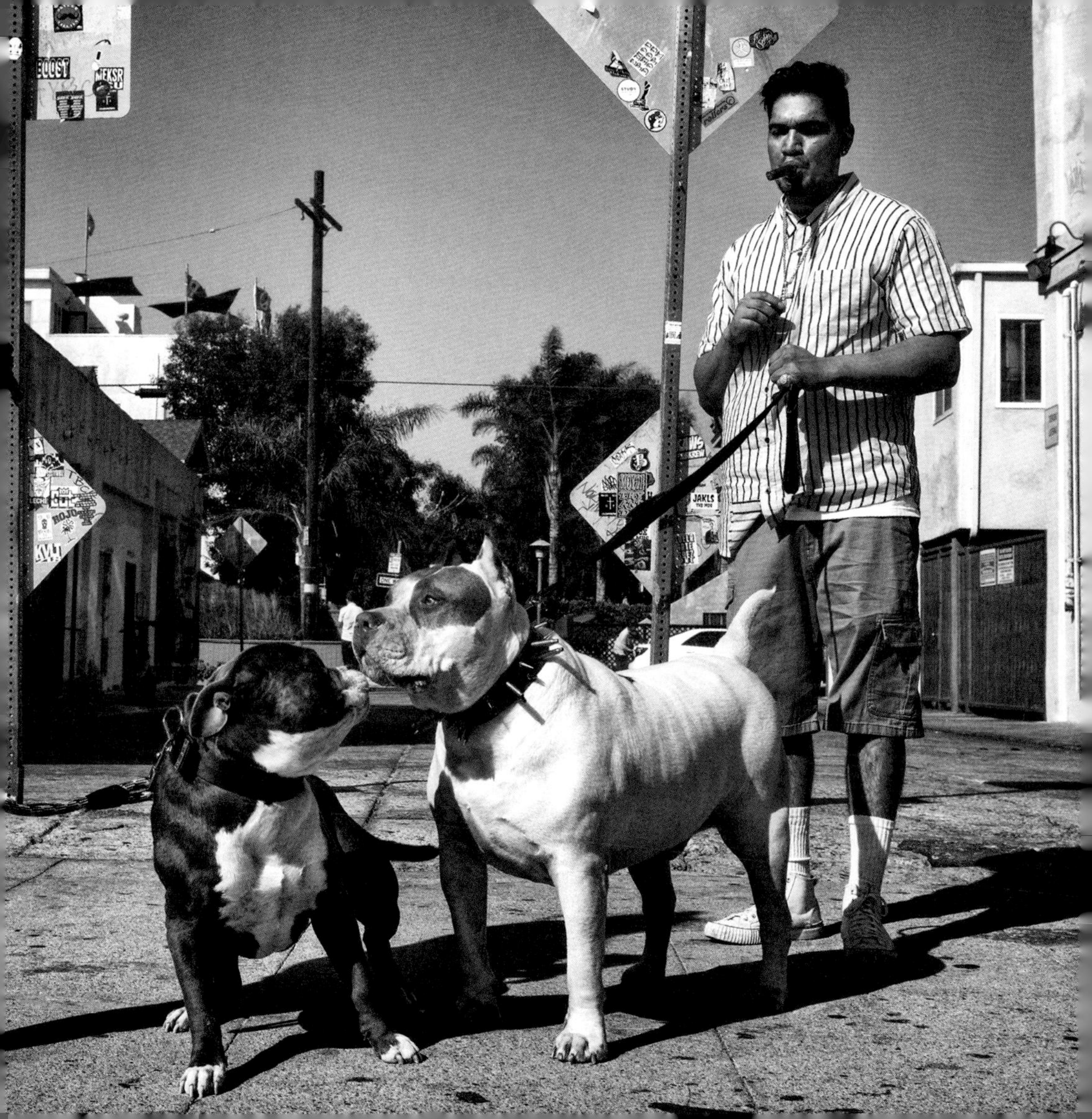
JAKLS

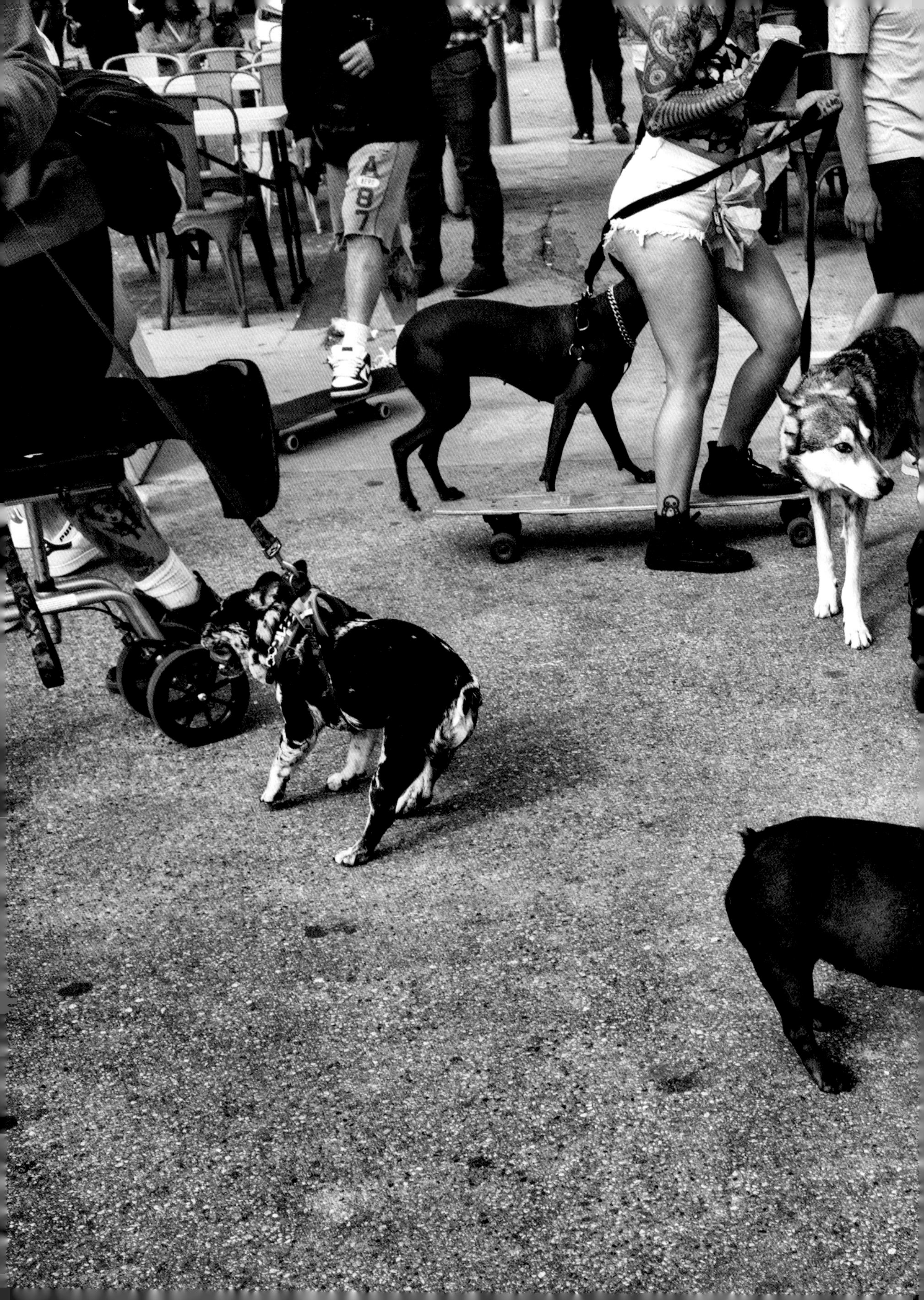

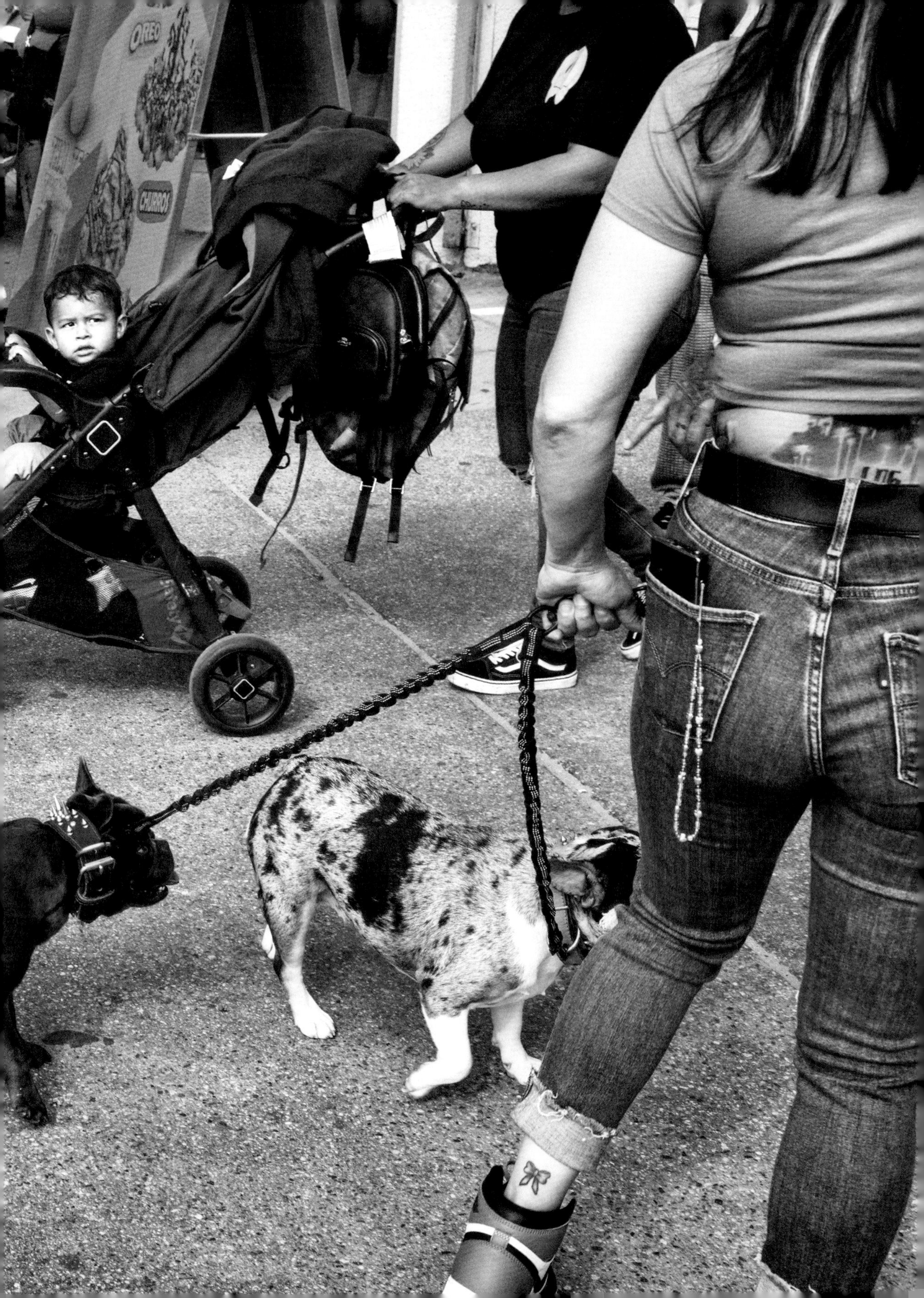
OREO
CHURROS

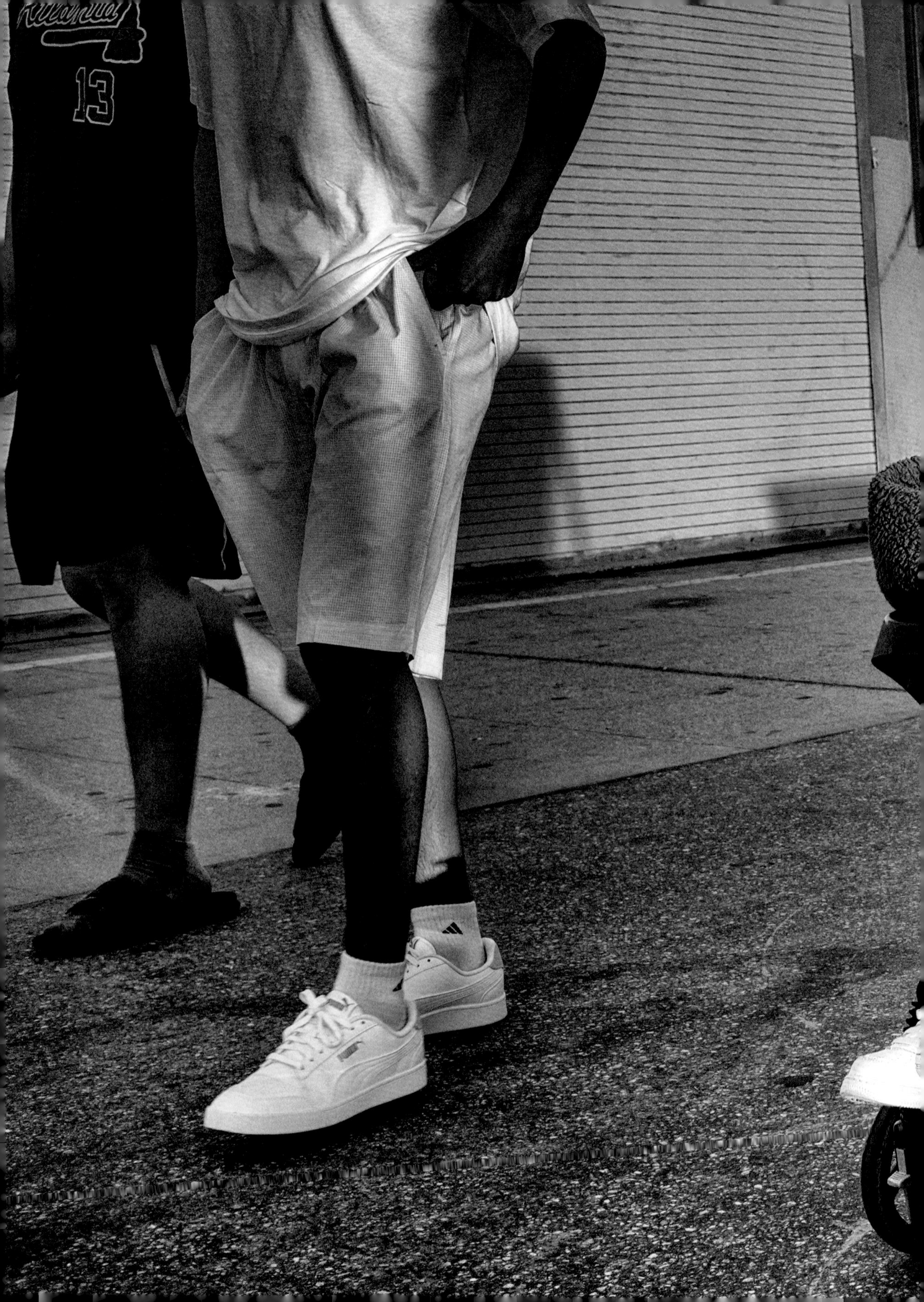
13

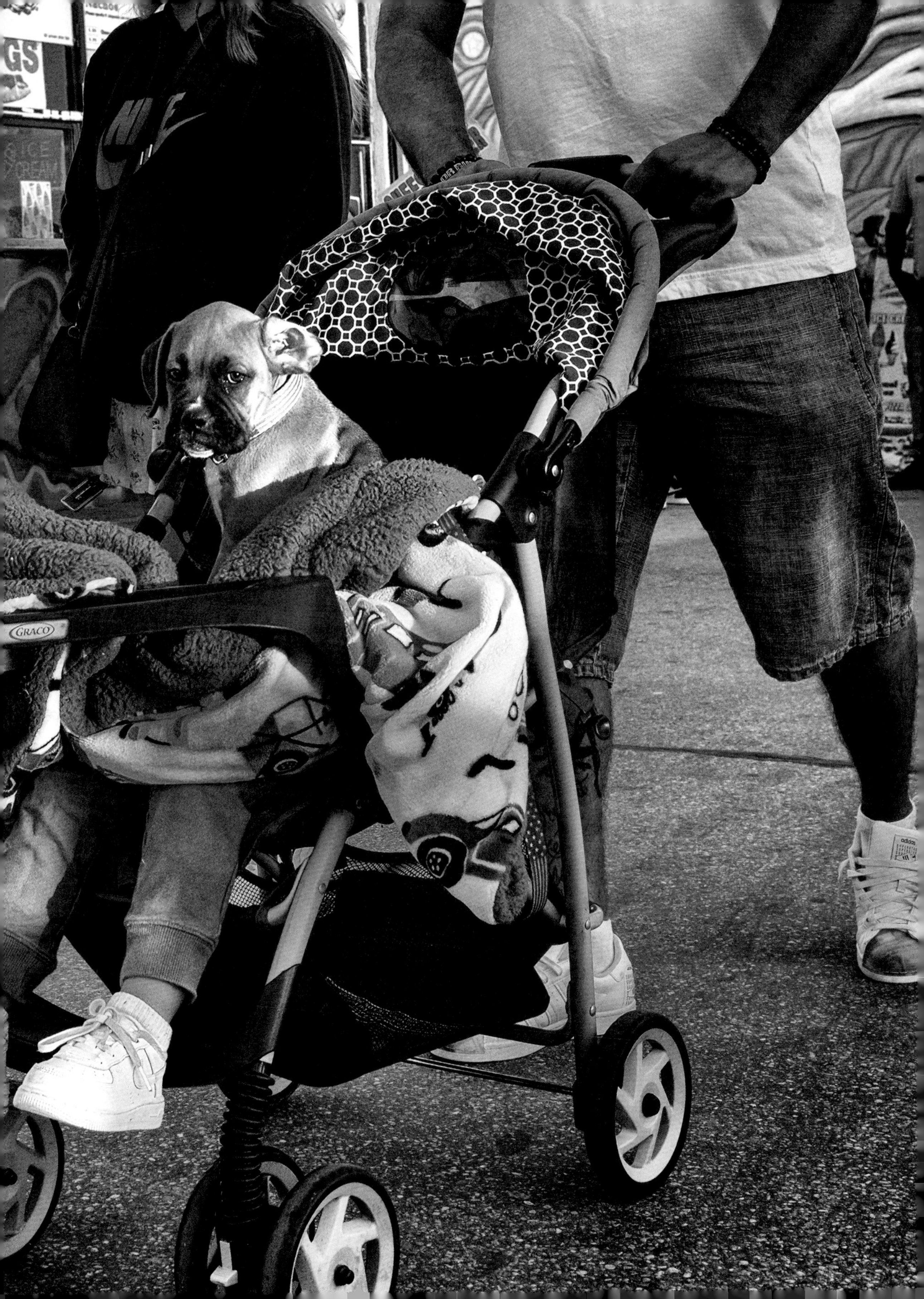
GRACO

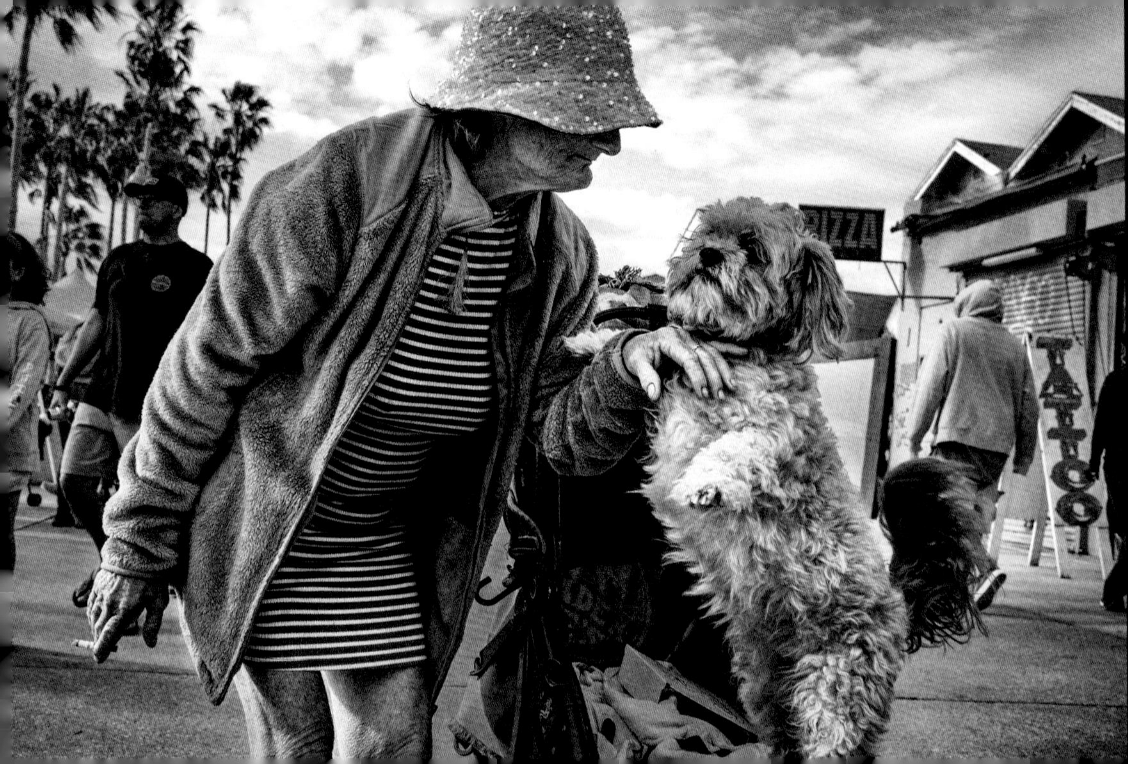

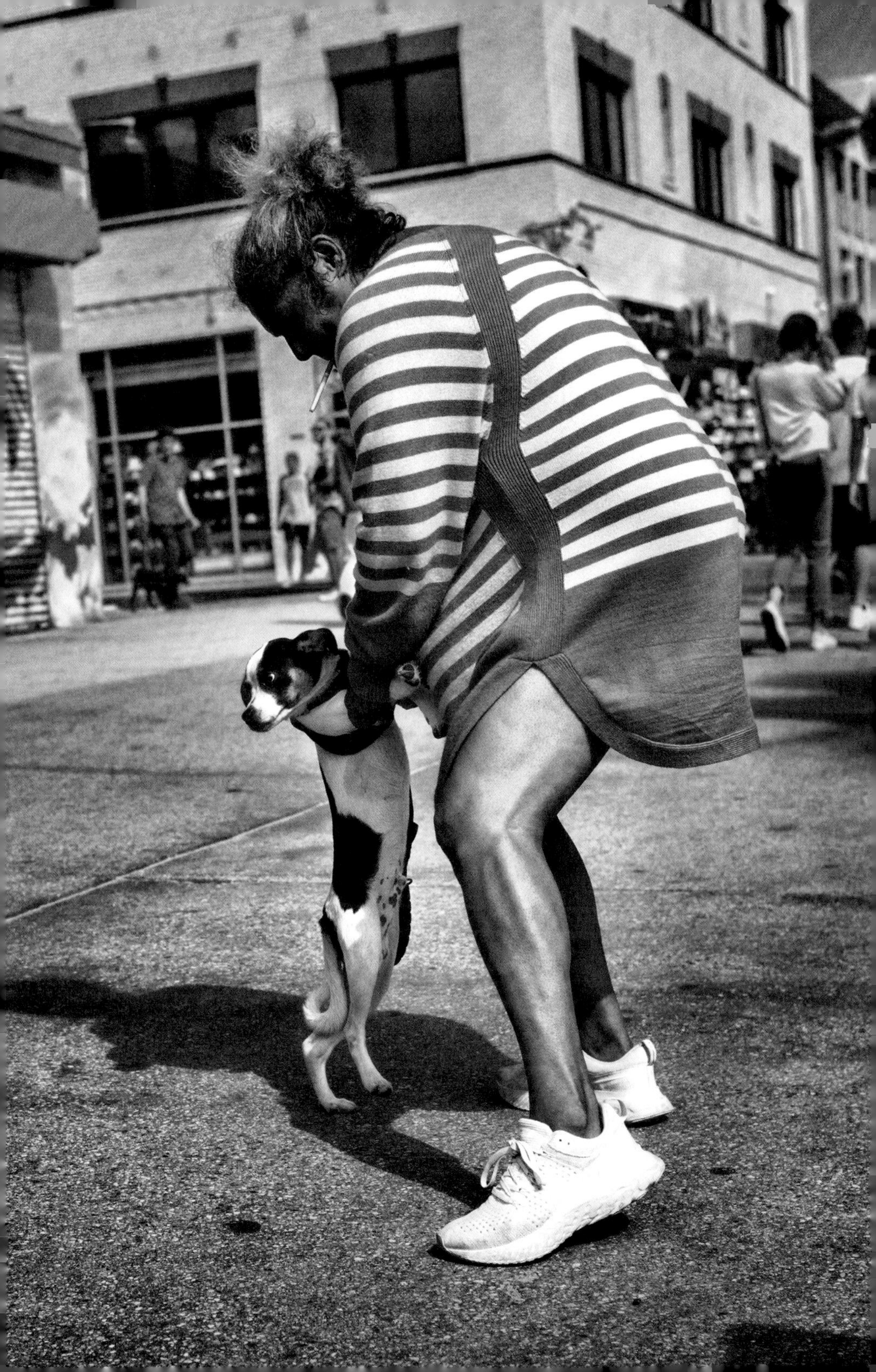

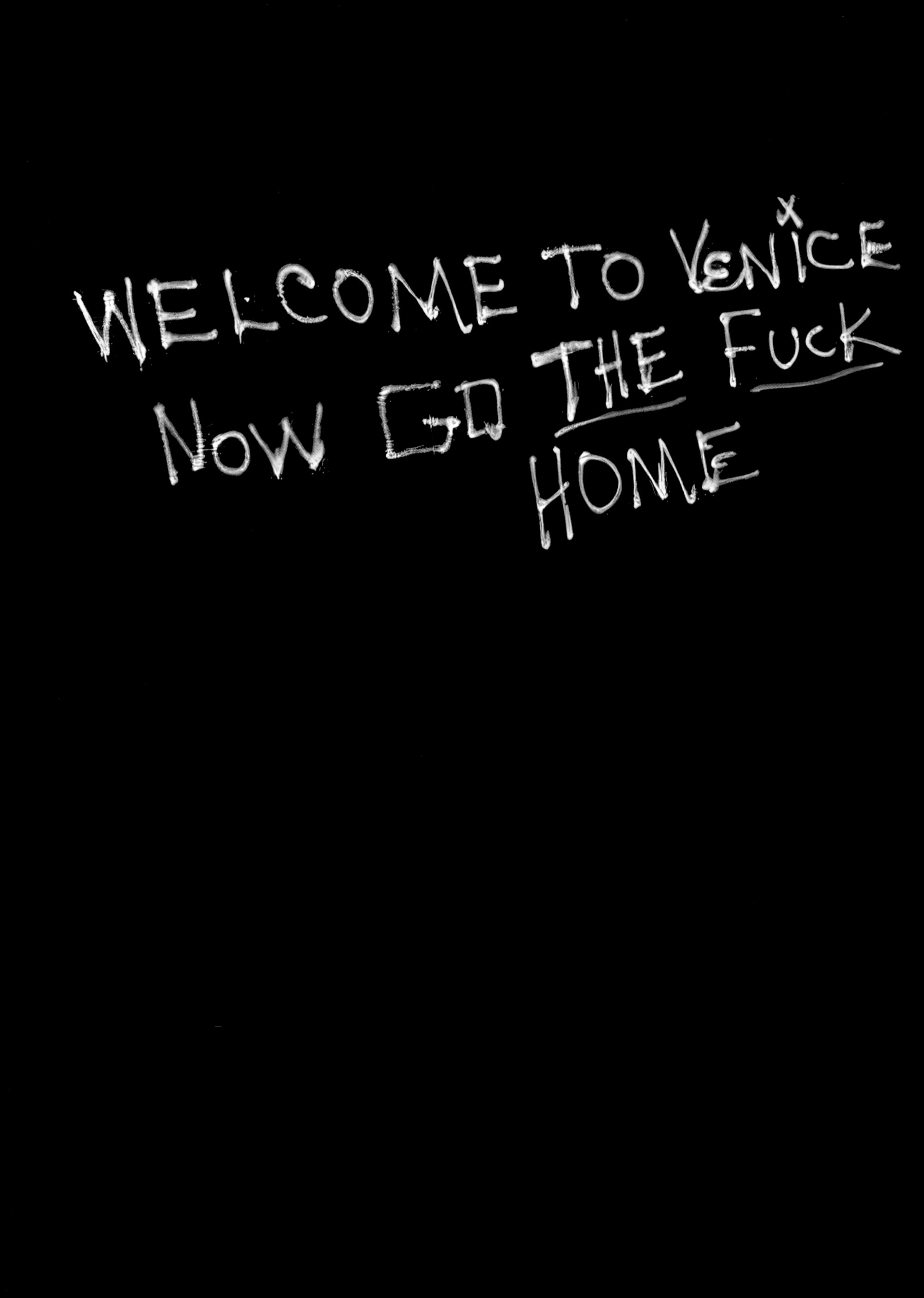
WELCOME TO VENICE
NOW GO THE FUCK
HOME

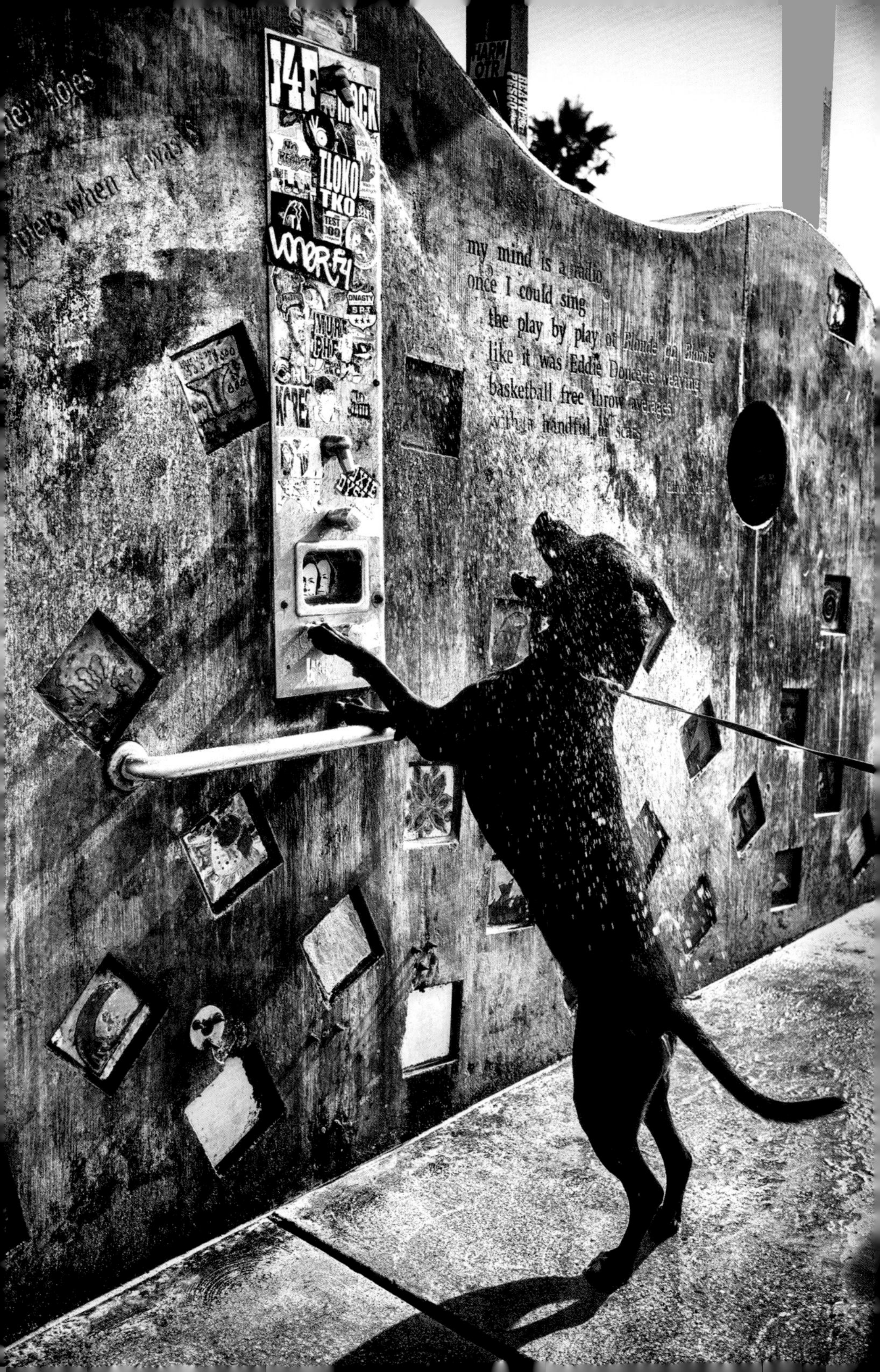
my mind is a radio
once I could sing
the play by play of Blonde on Blonde
like it was Eddie Doucette weaving
basketball free throw averages
within a handful of scars

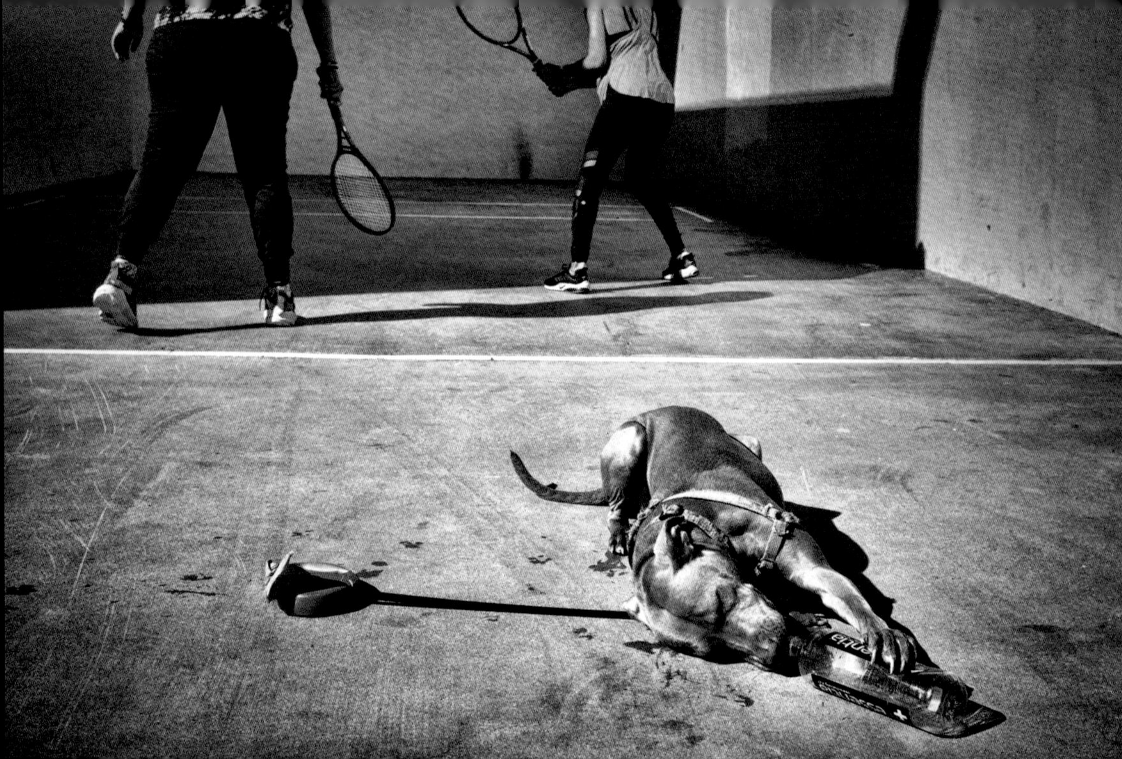

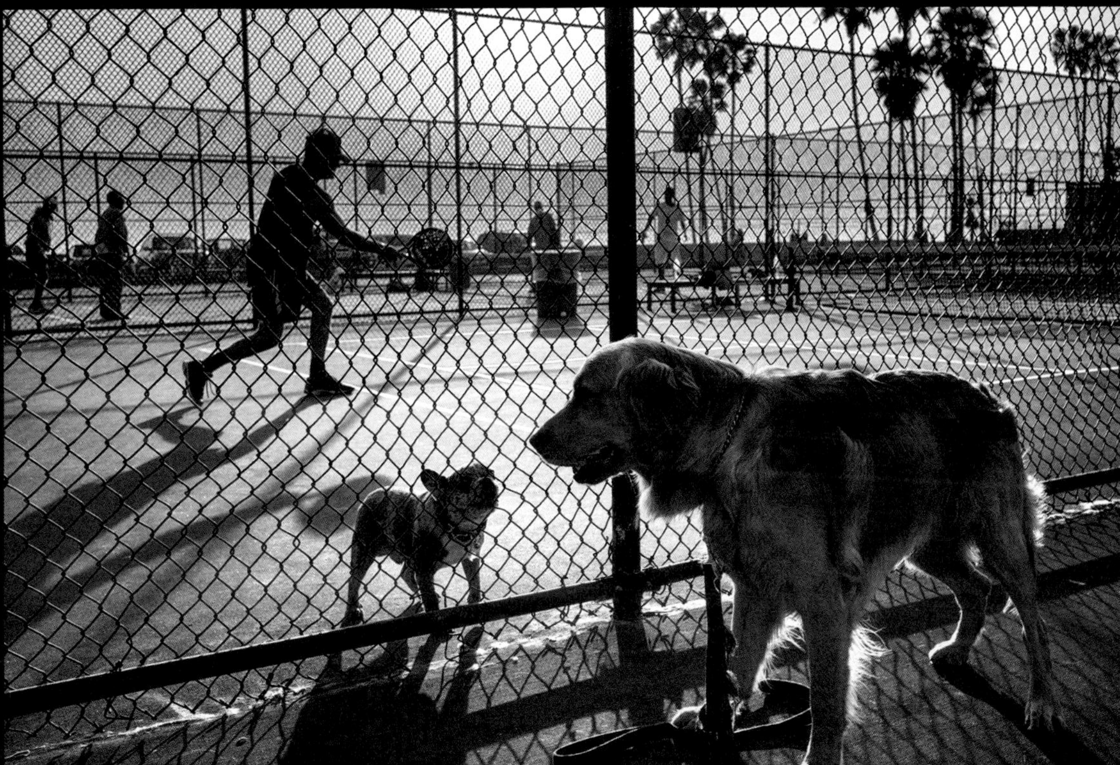

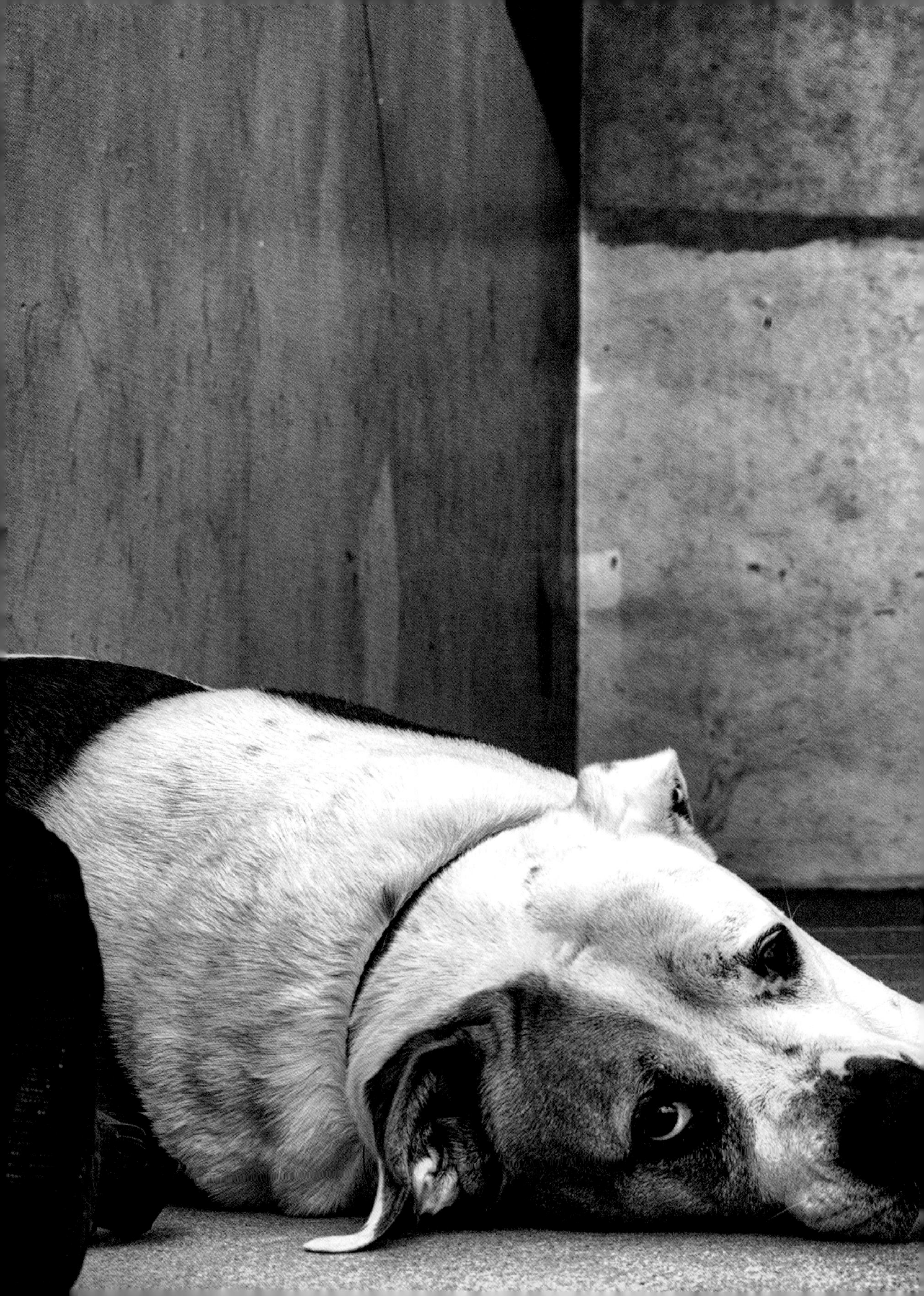

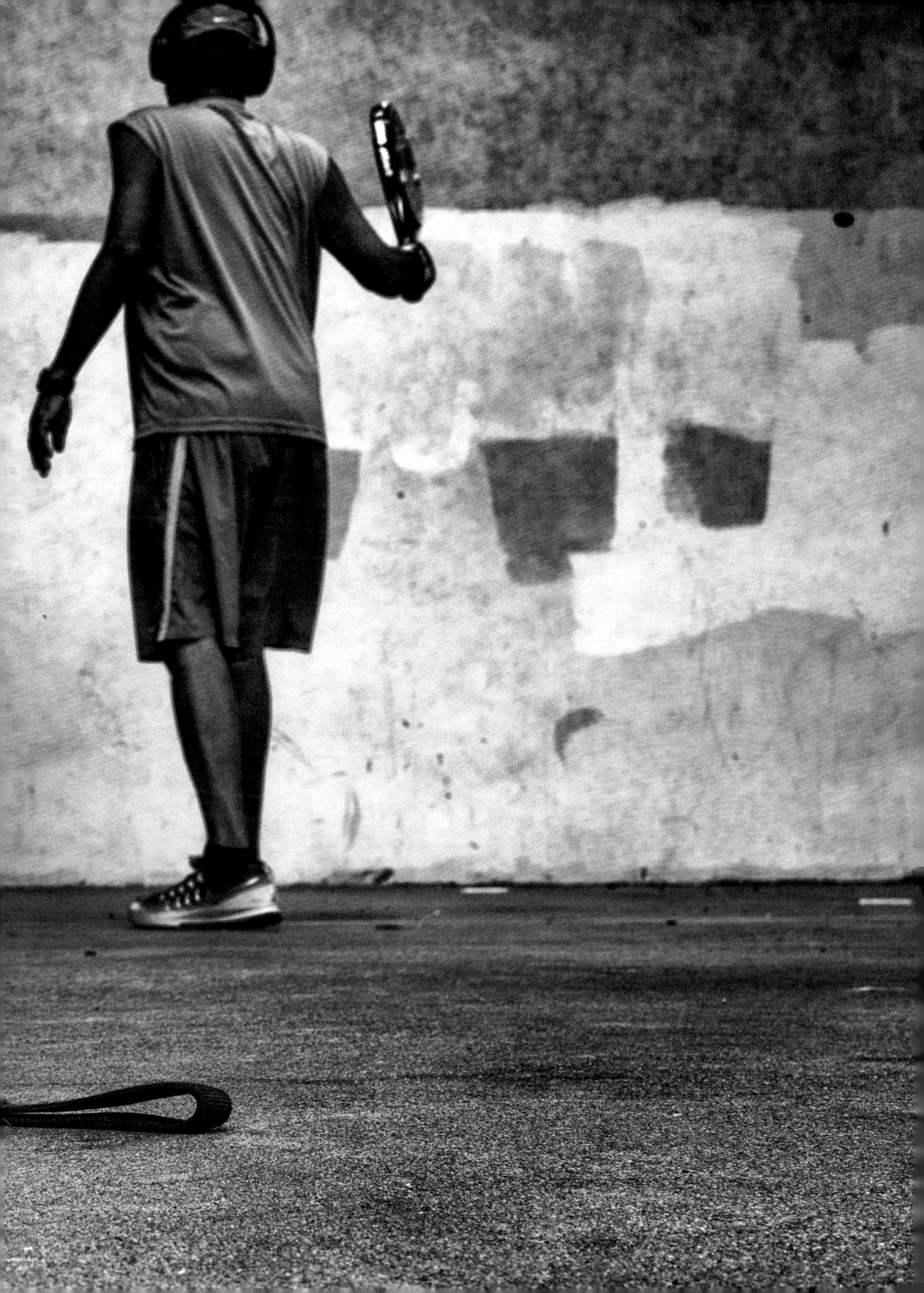

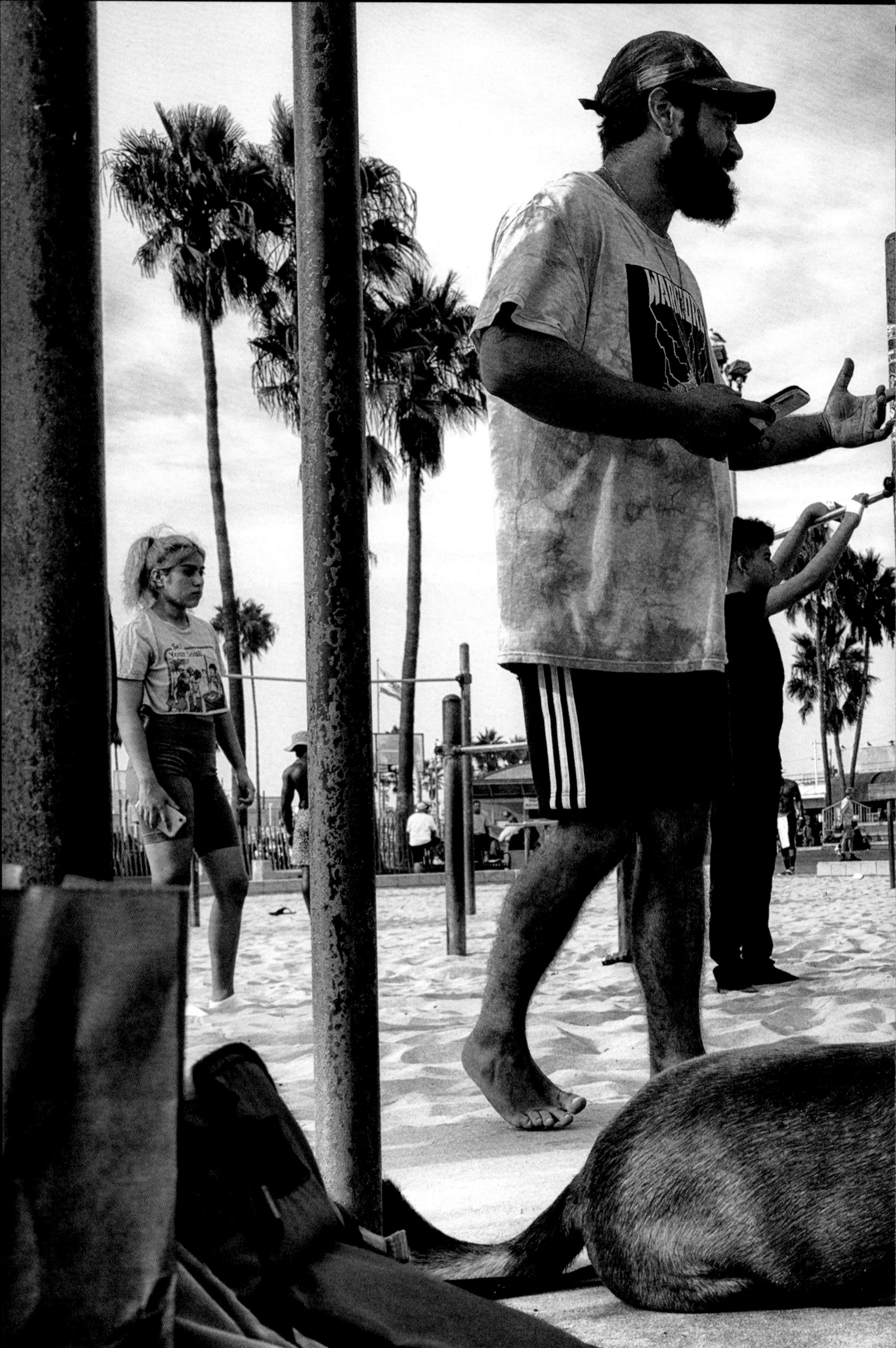

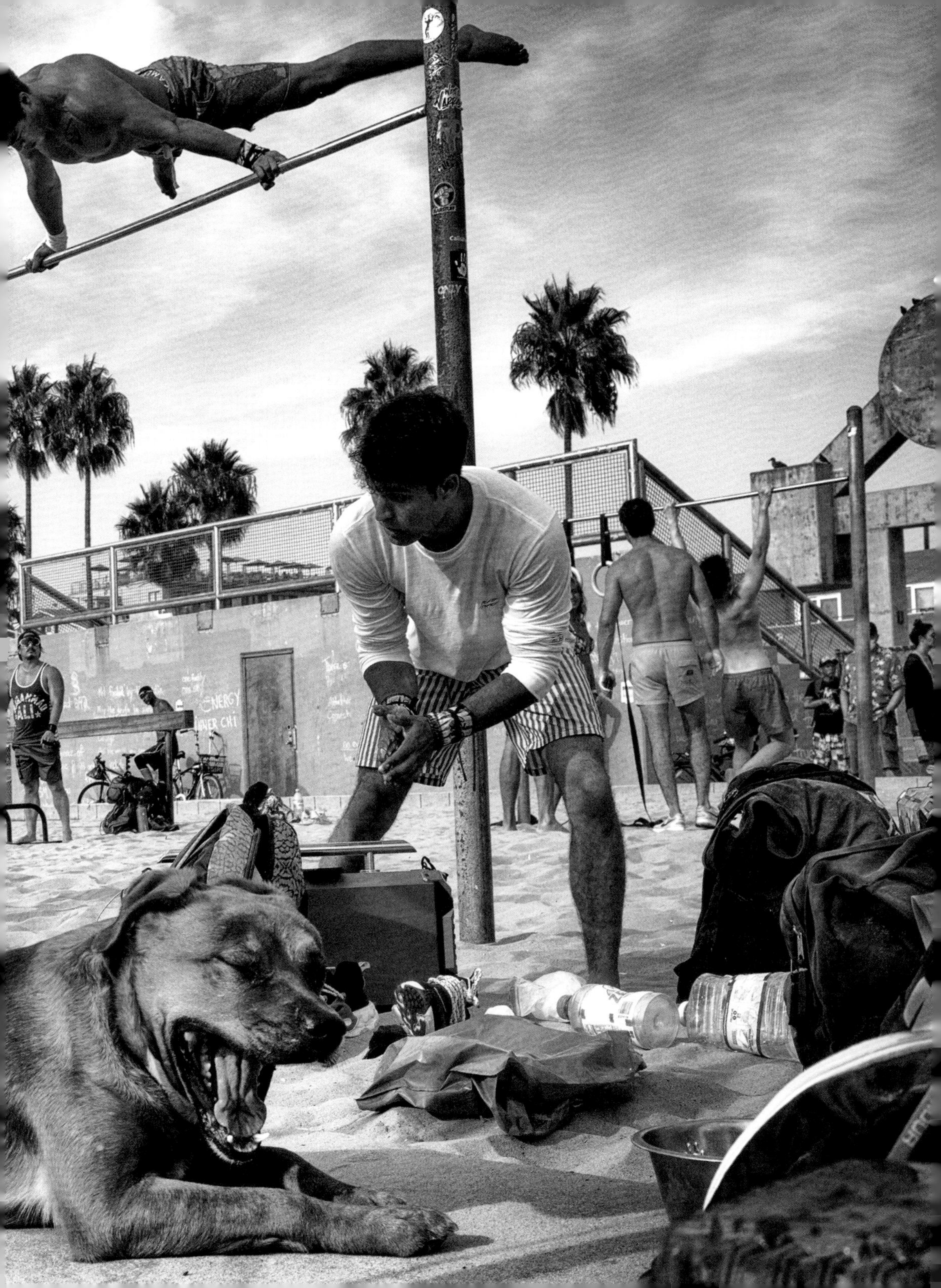

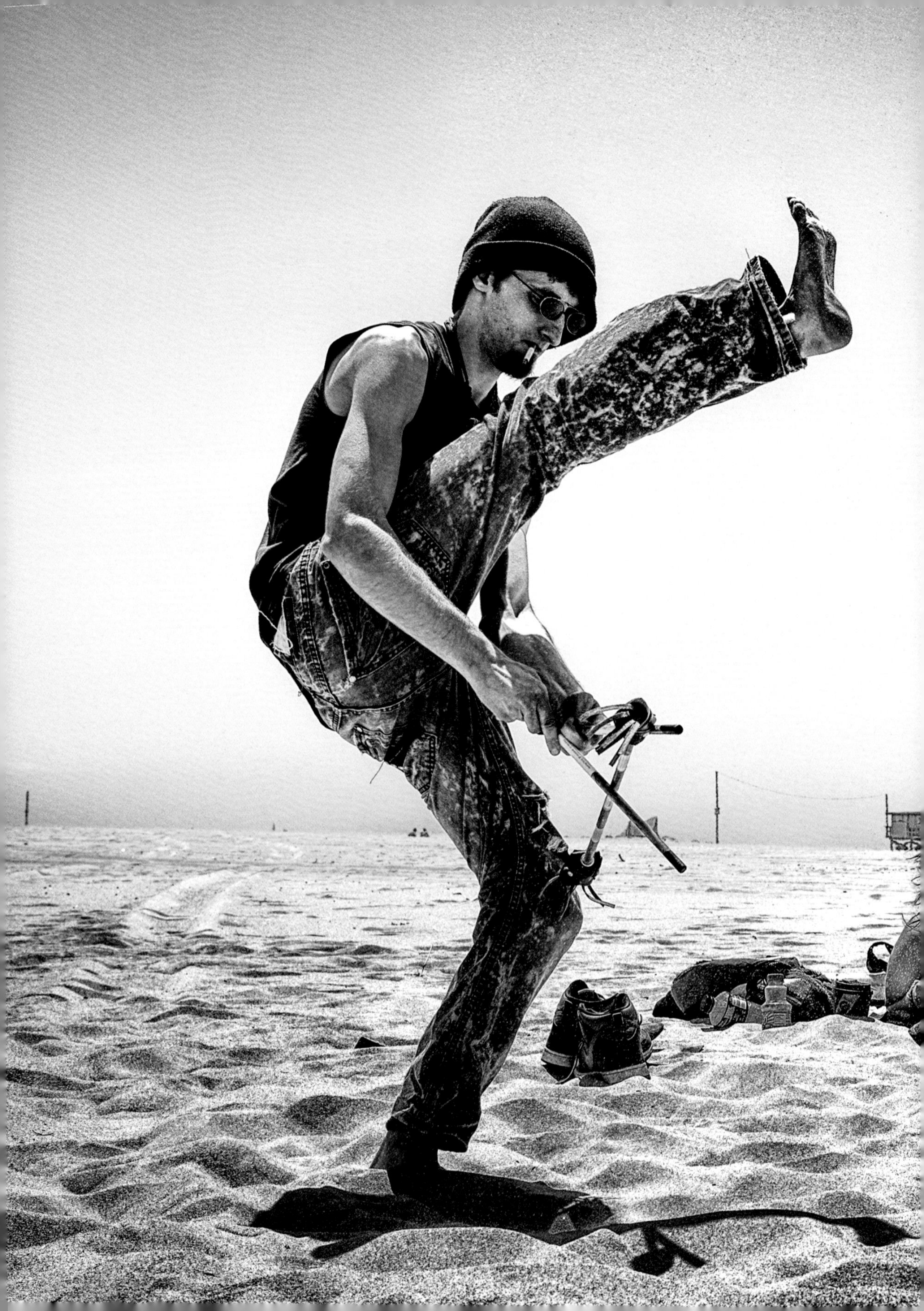

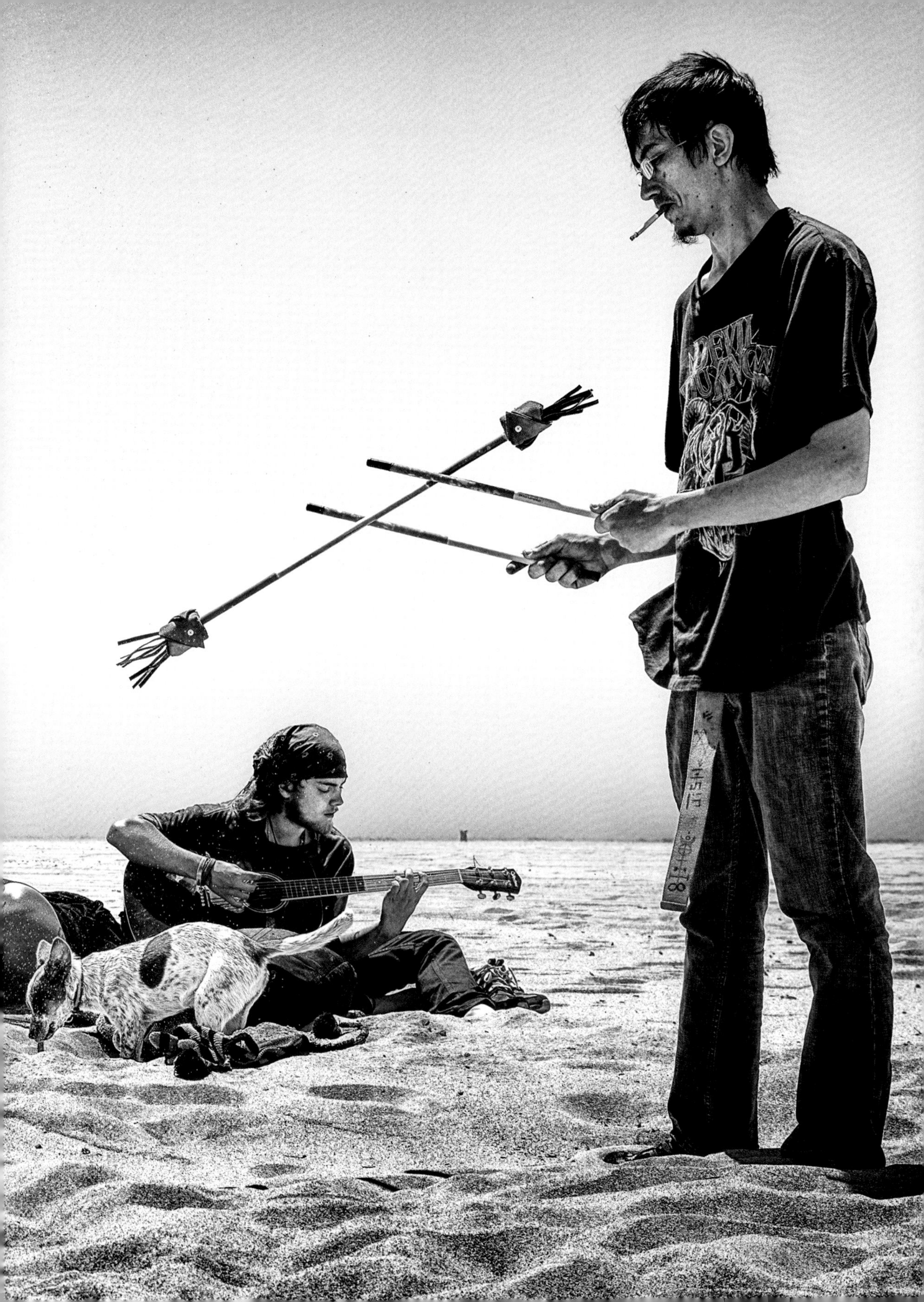

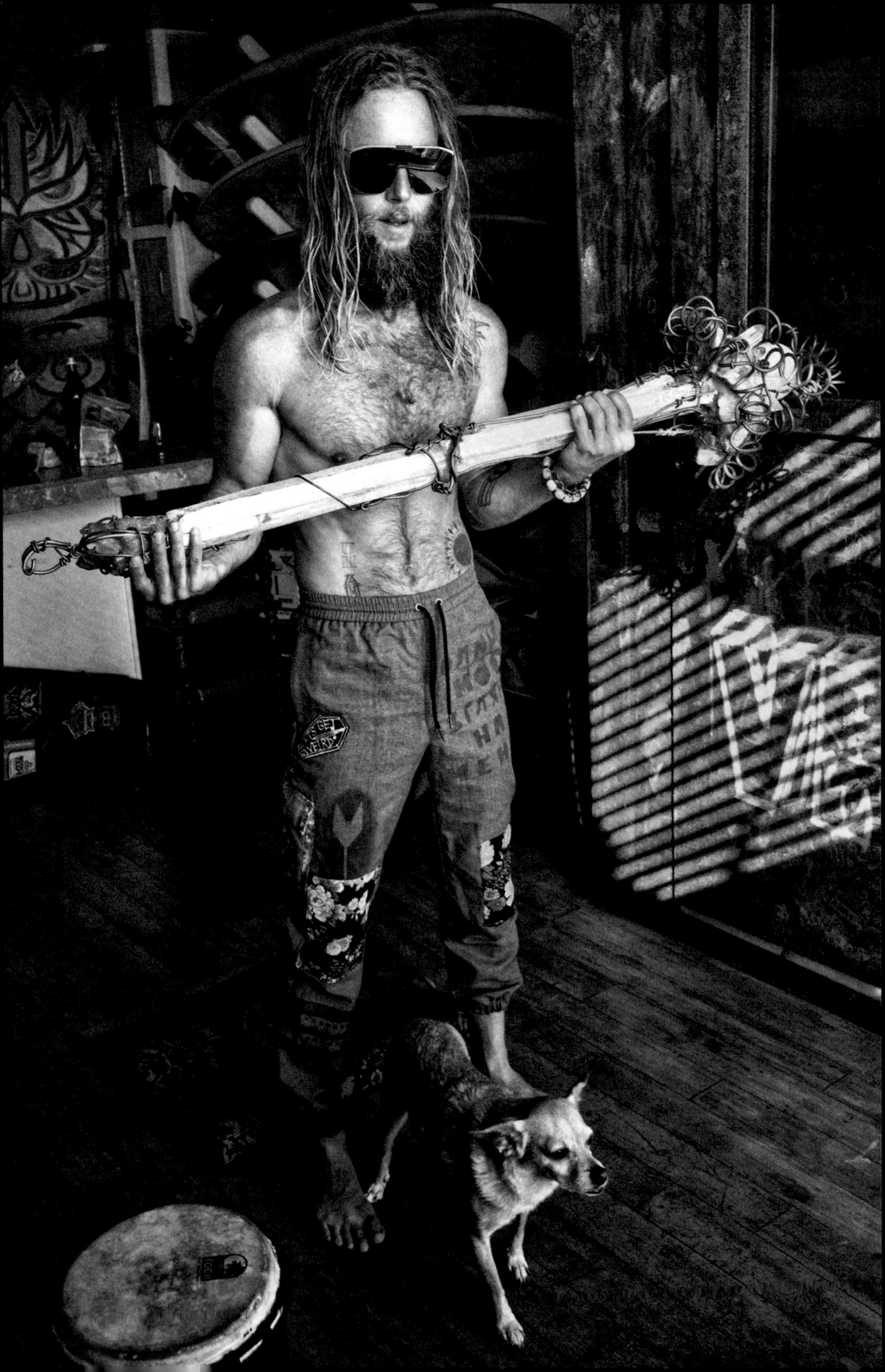

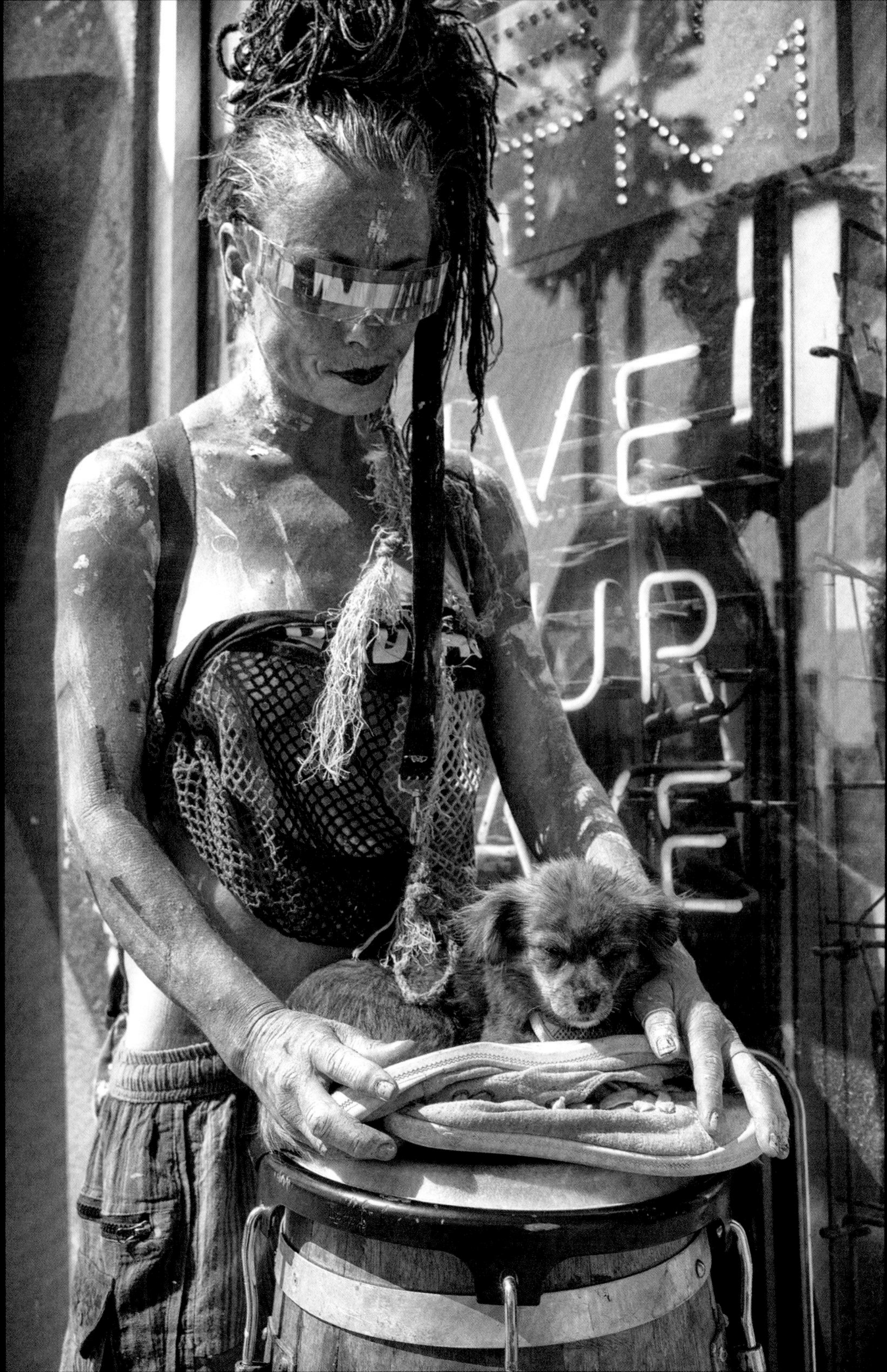

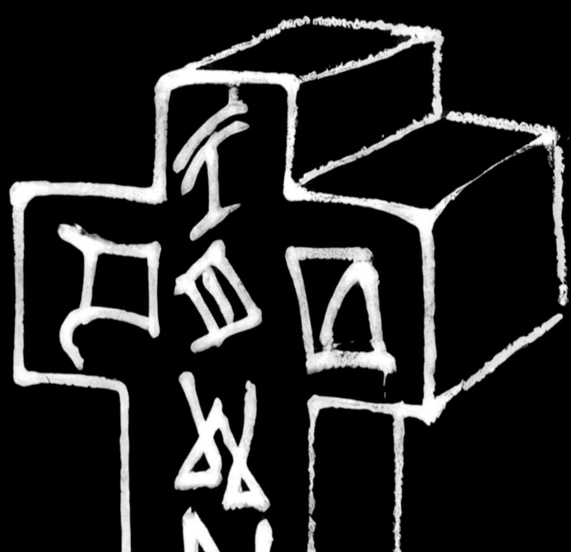

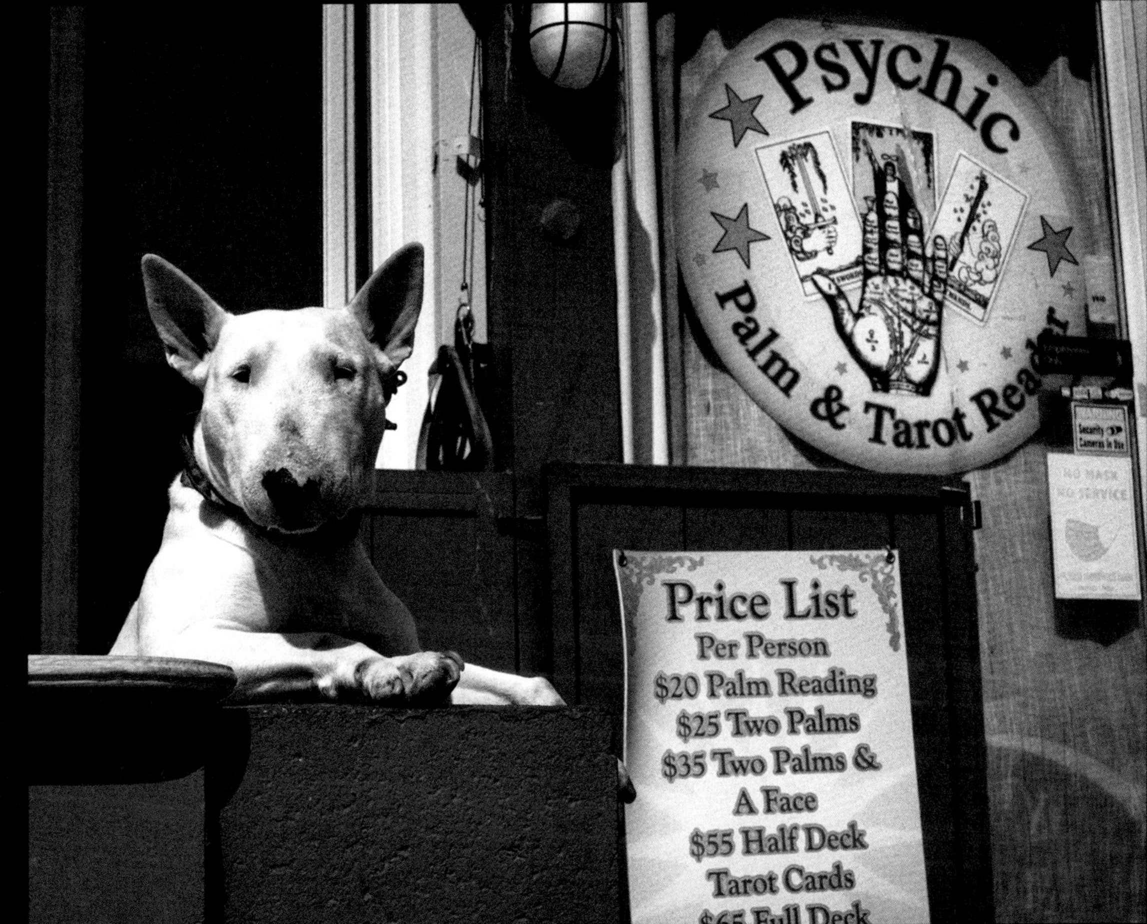
Psychic
Palm & Tarot Rea
Price List
Per Person
$20 Palm Reading
$25 Two Palms
$35 Two Palms &
A Face
$55 Half Deck
Tarot Cards
NO MASK
NO SERVICE

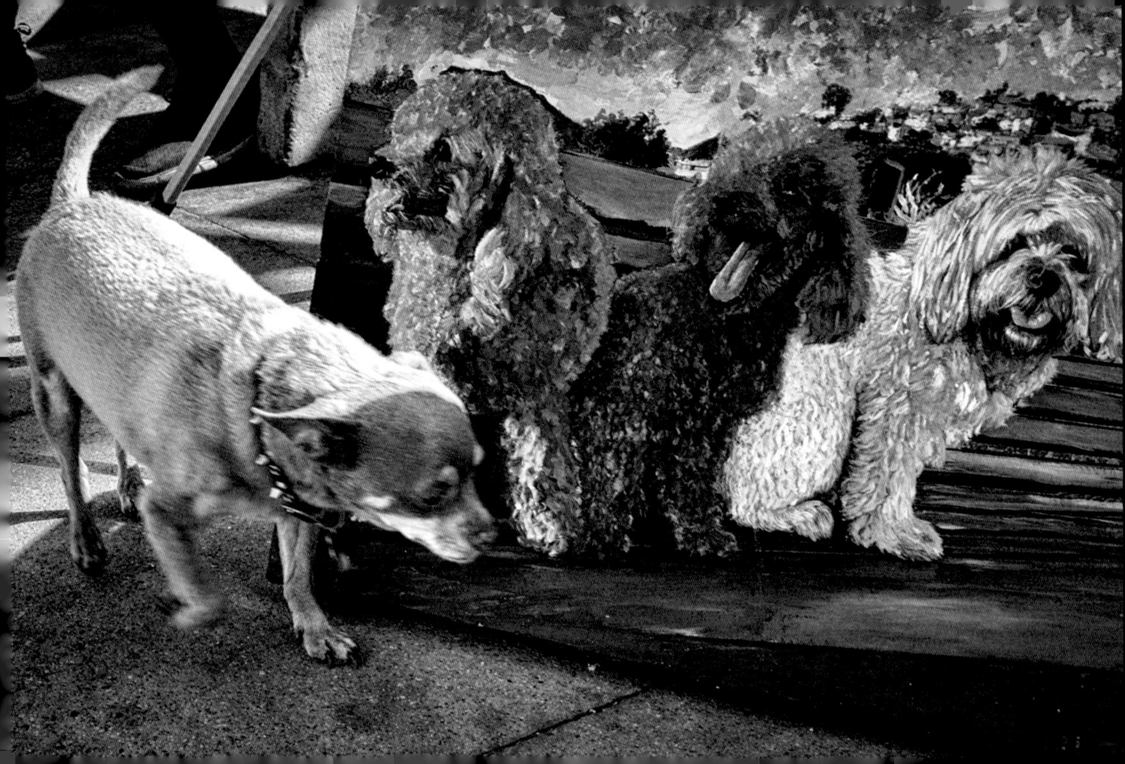

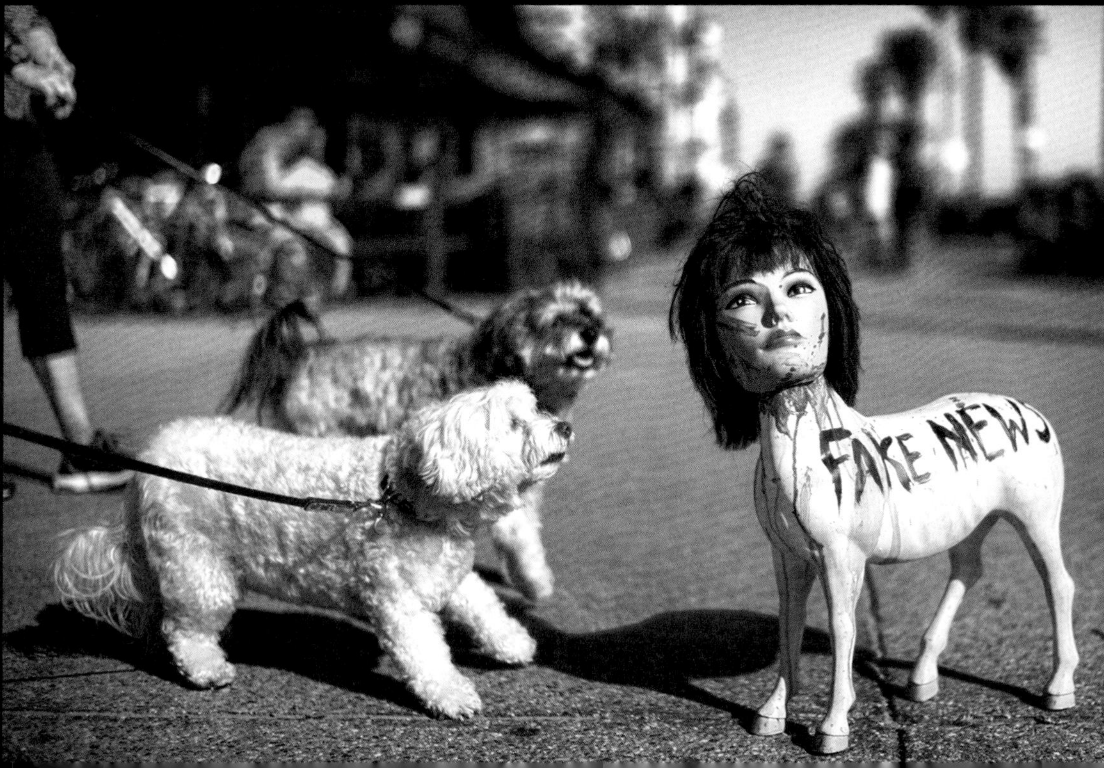
FAKE NEWS

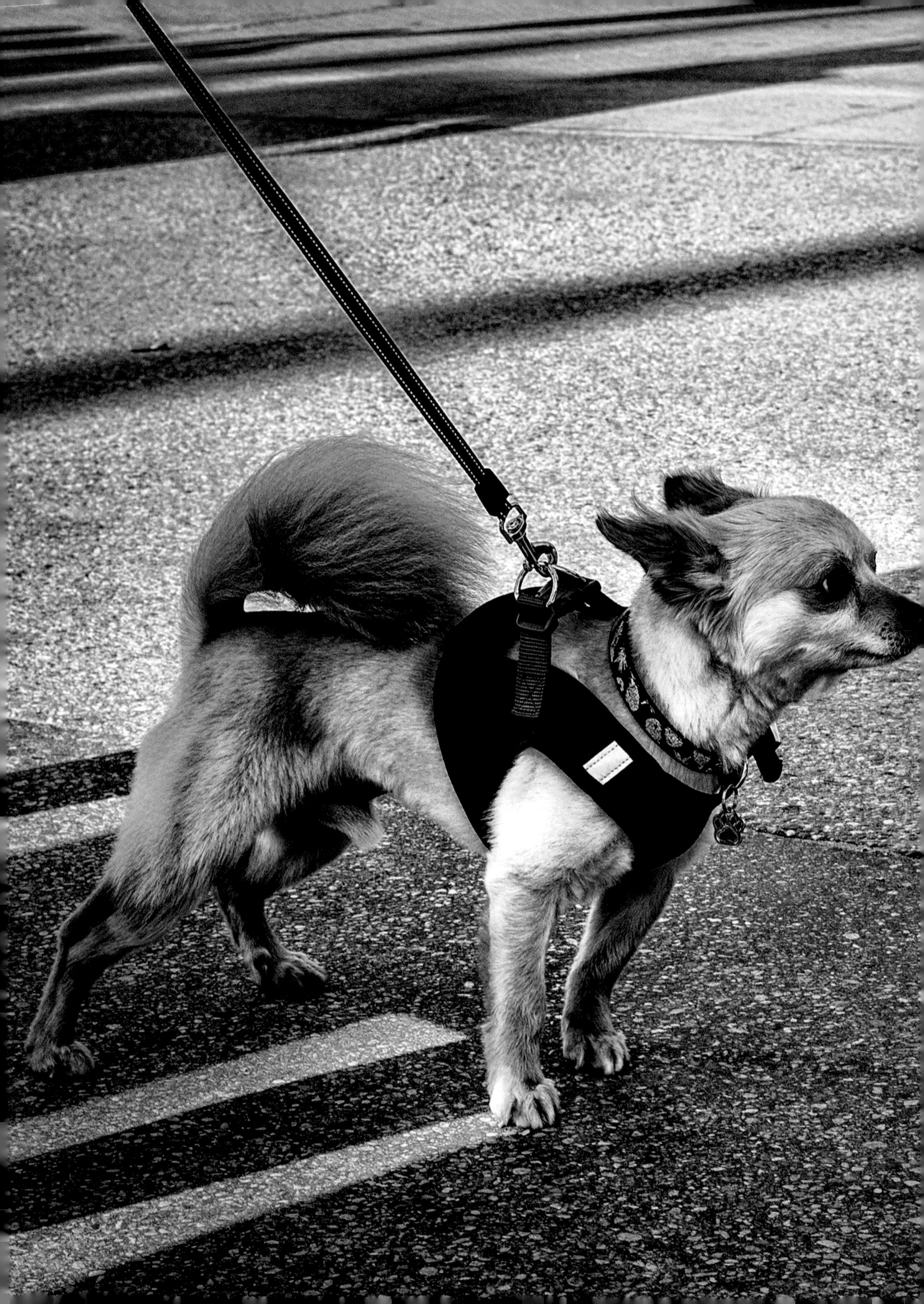

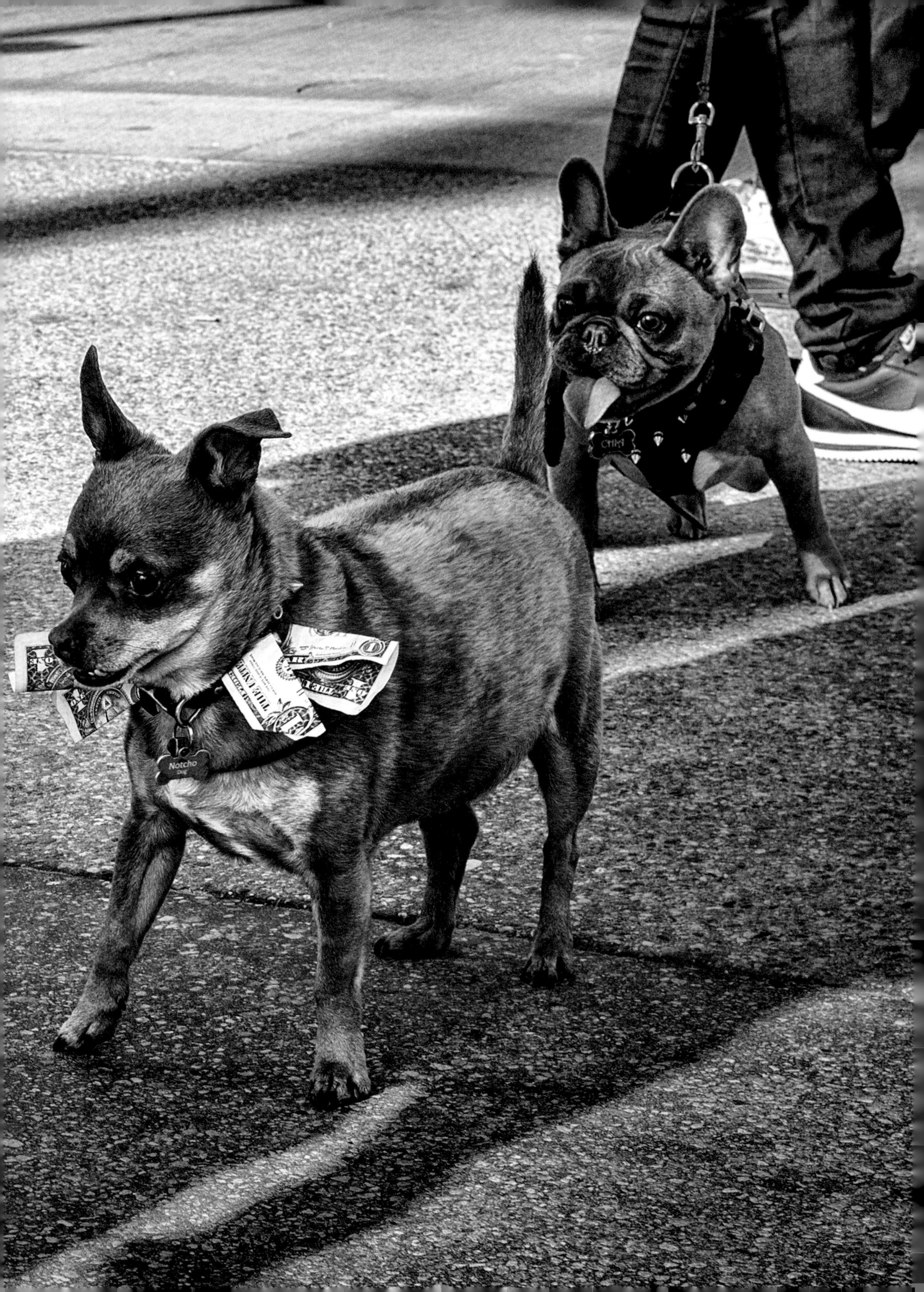

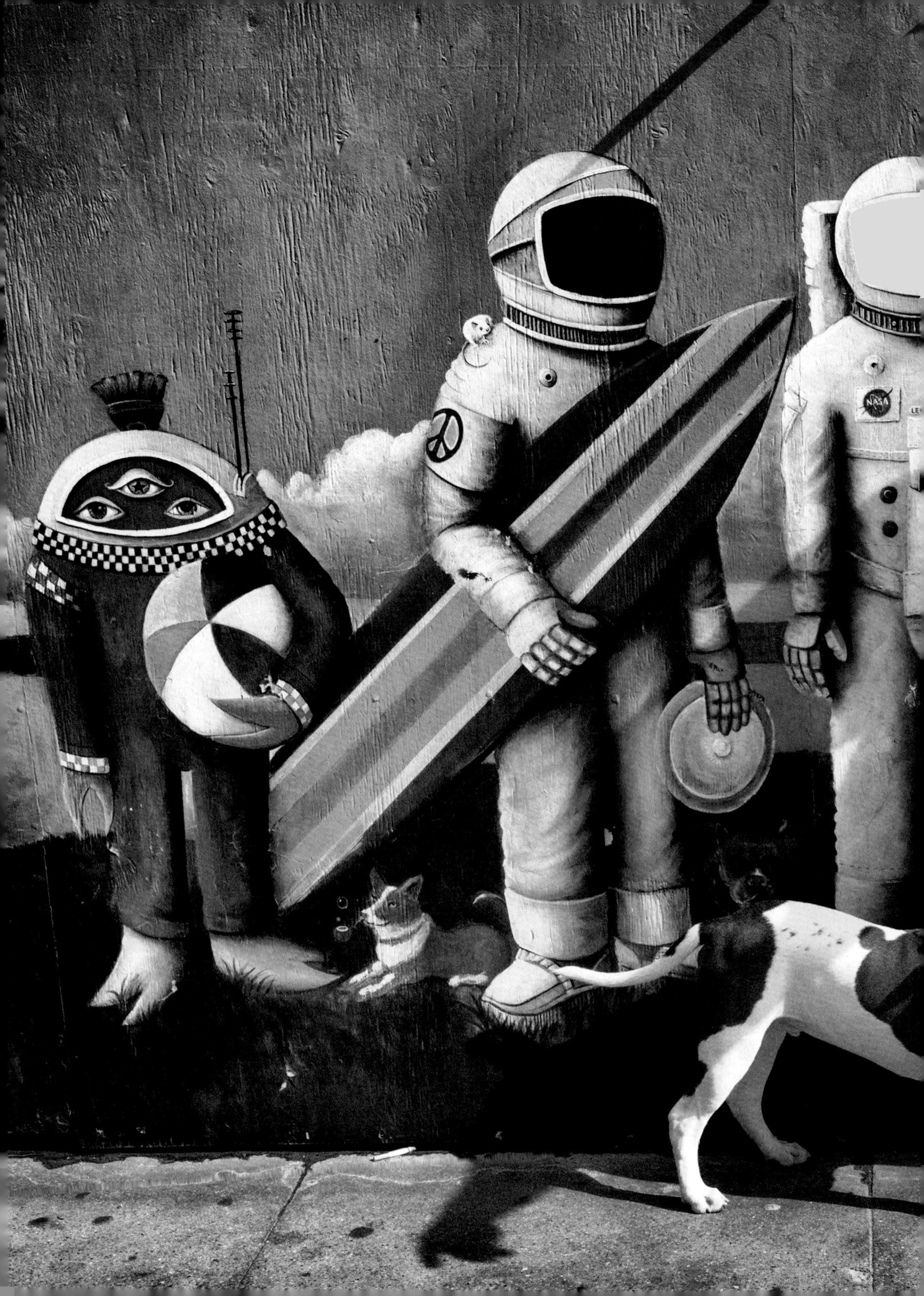
NASA

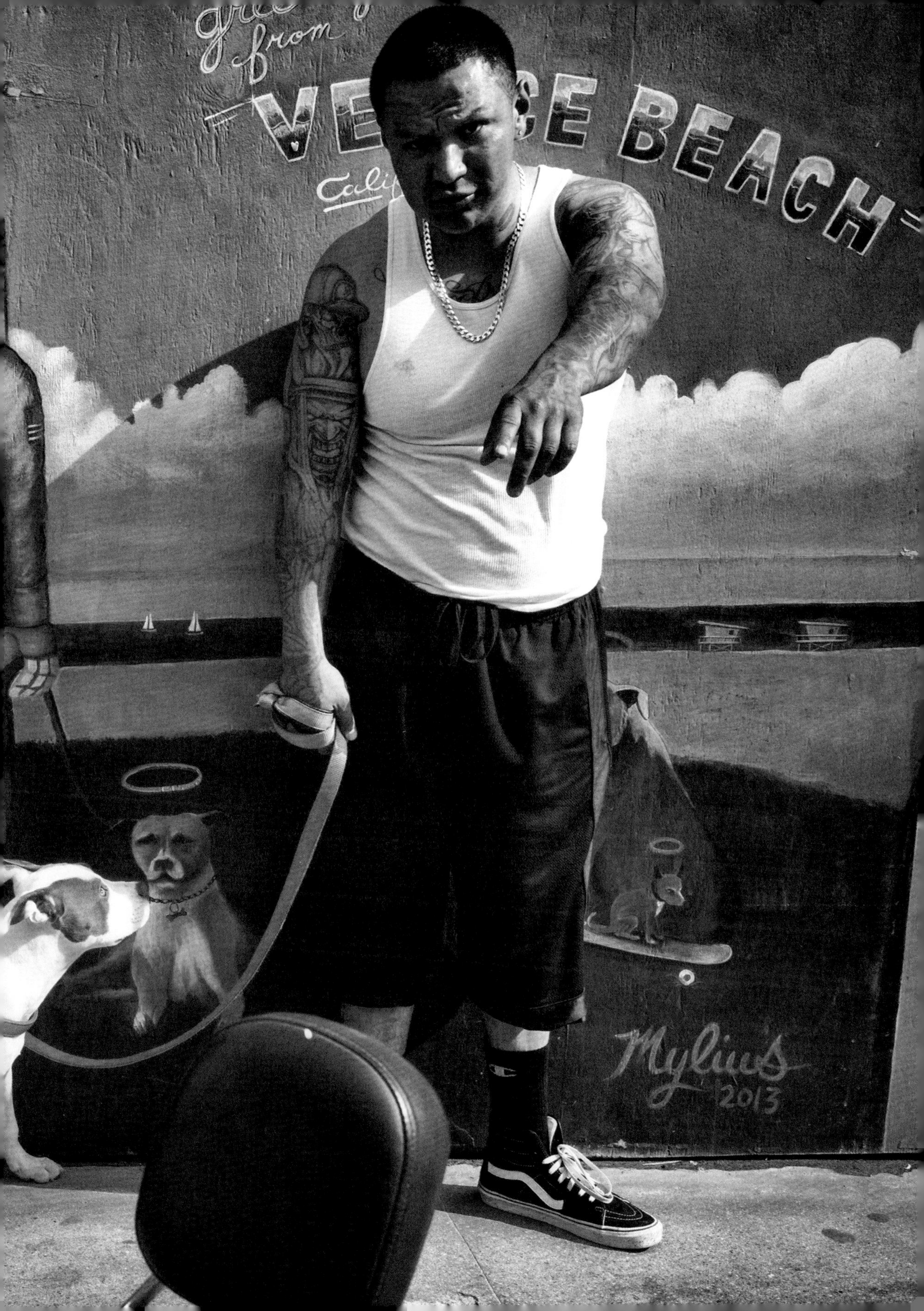
from
BEACH
Mylius
2013

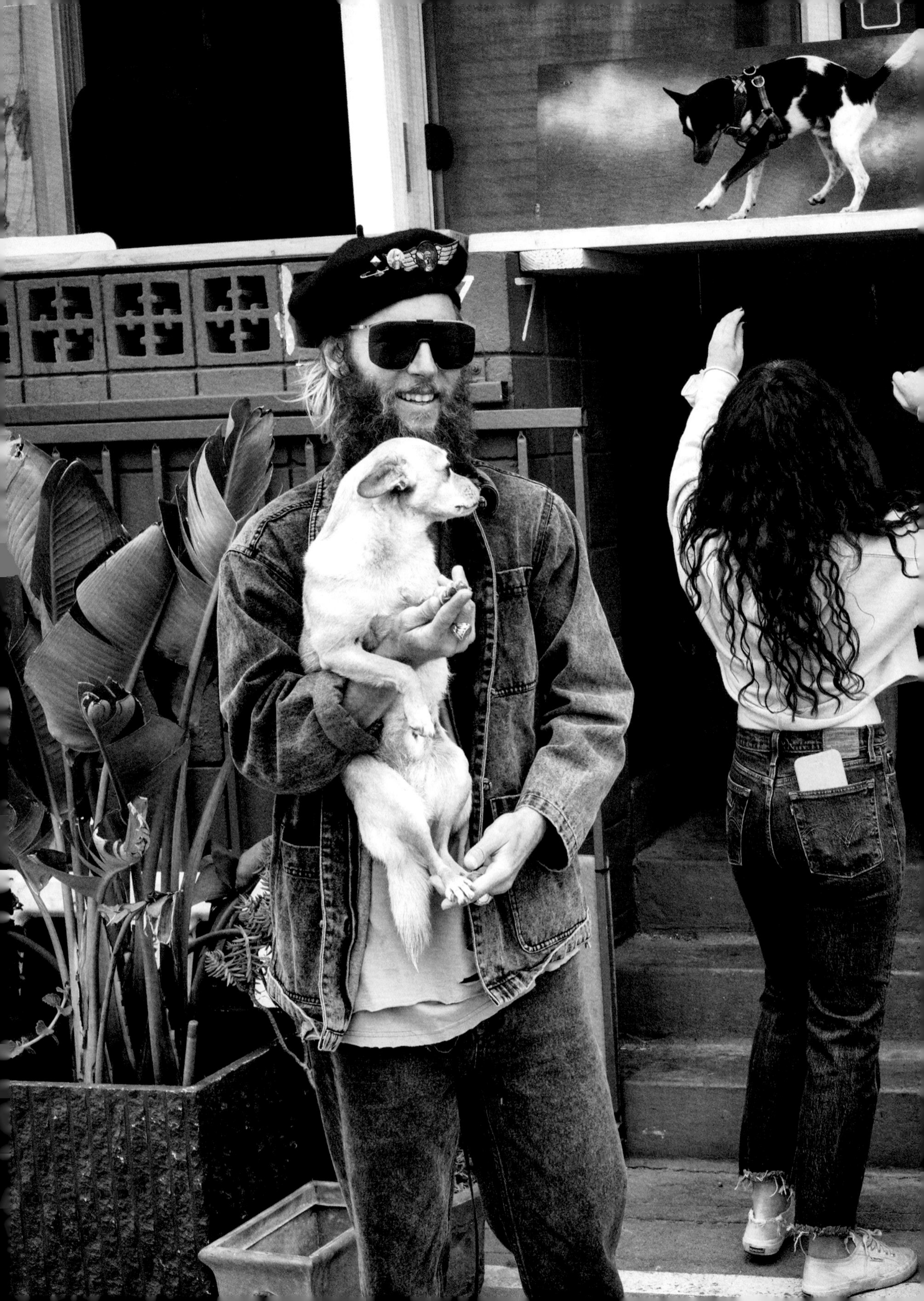

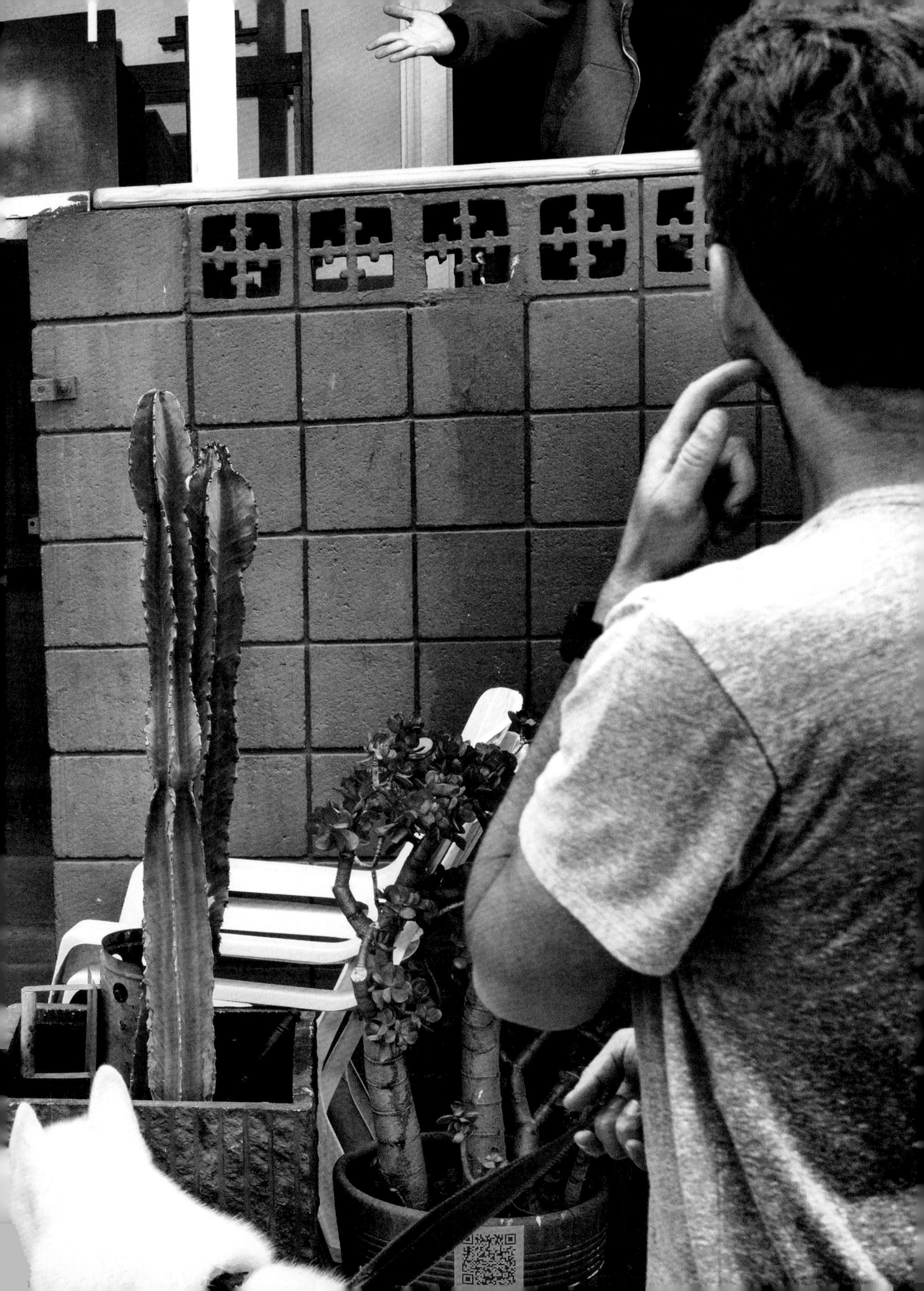

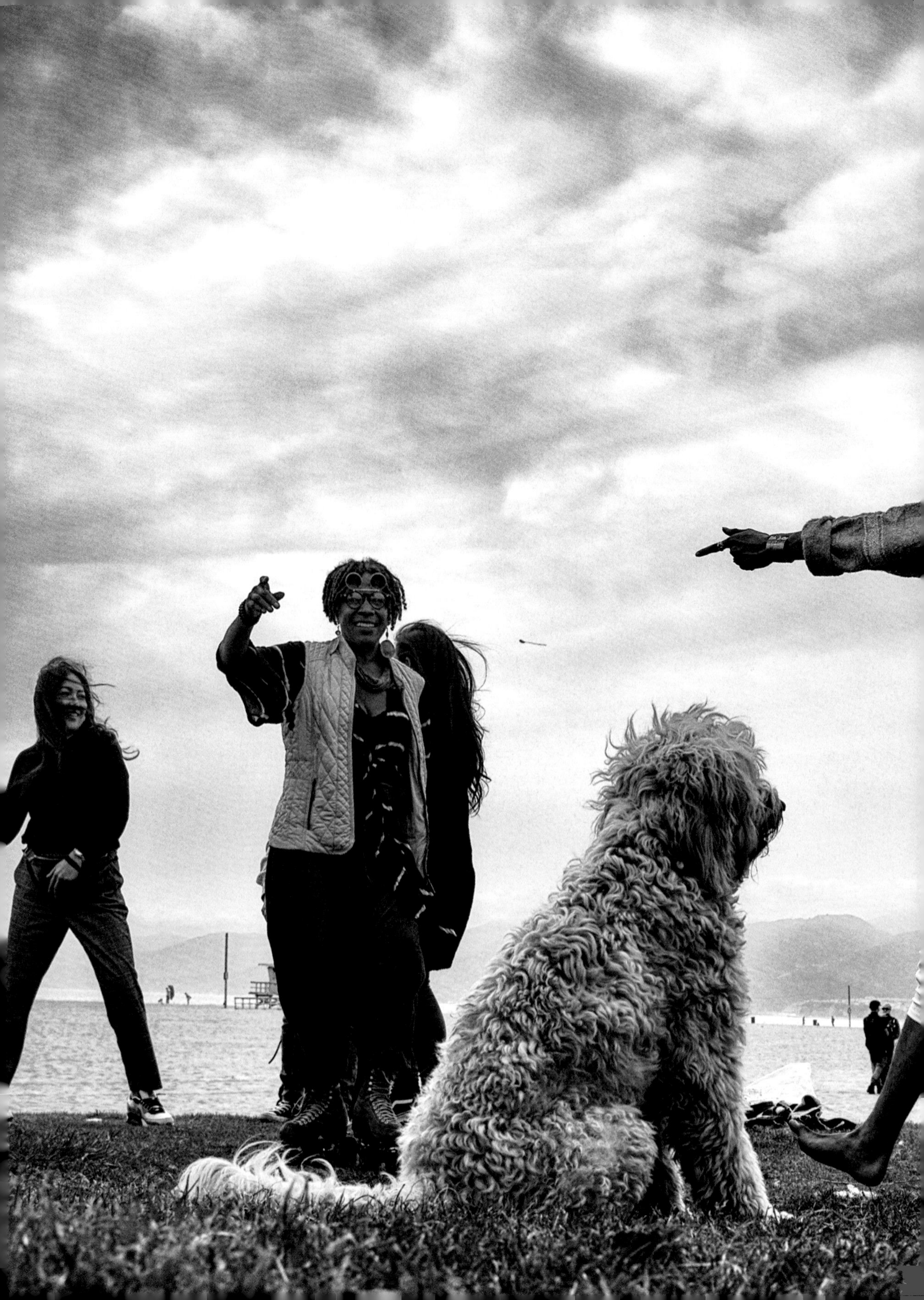

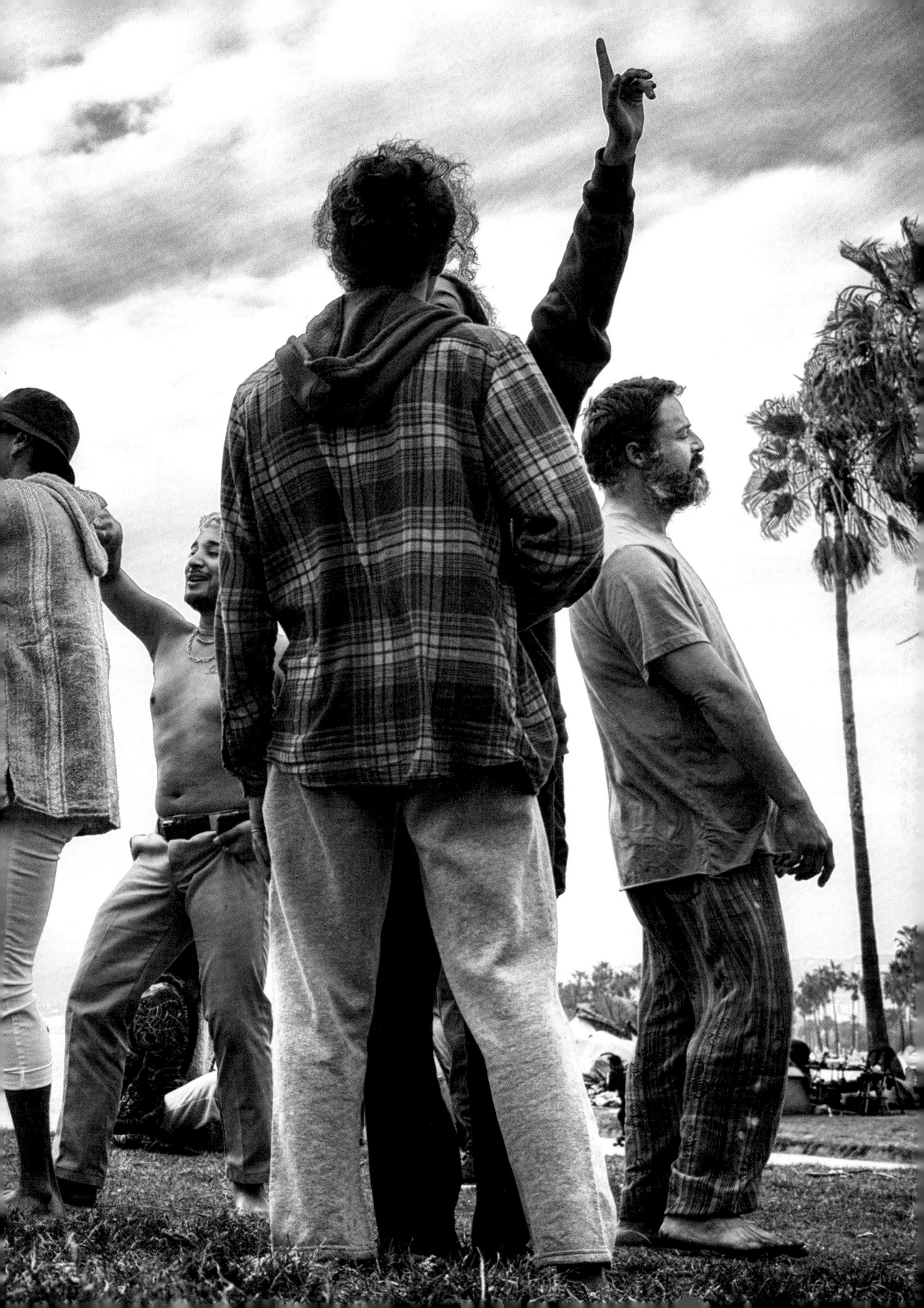

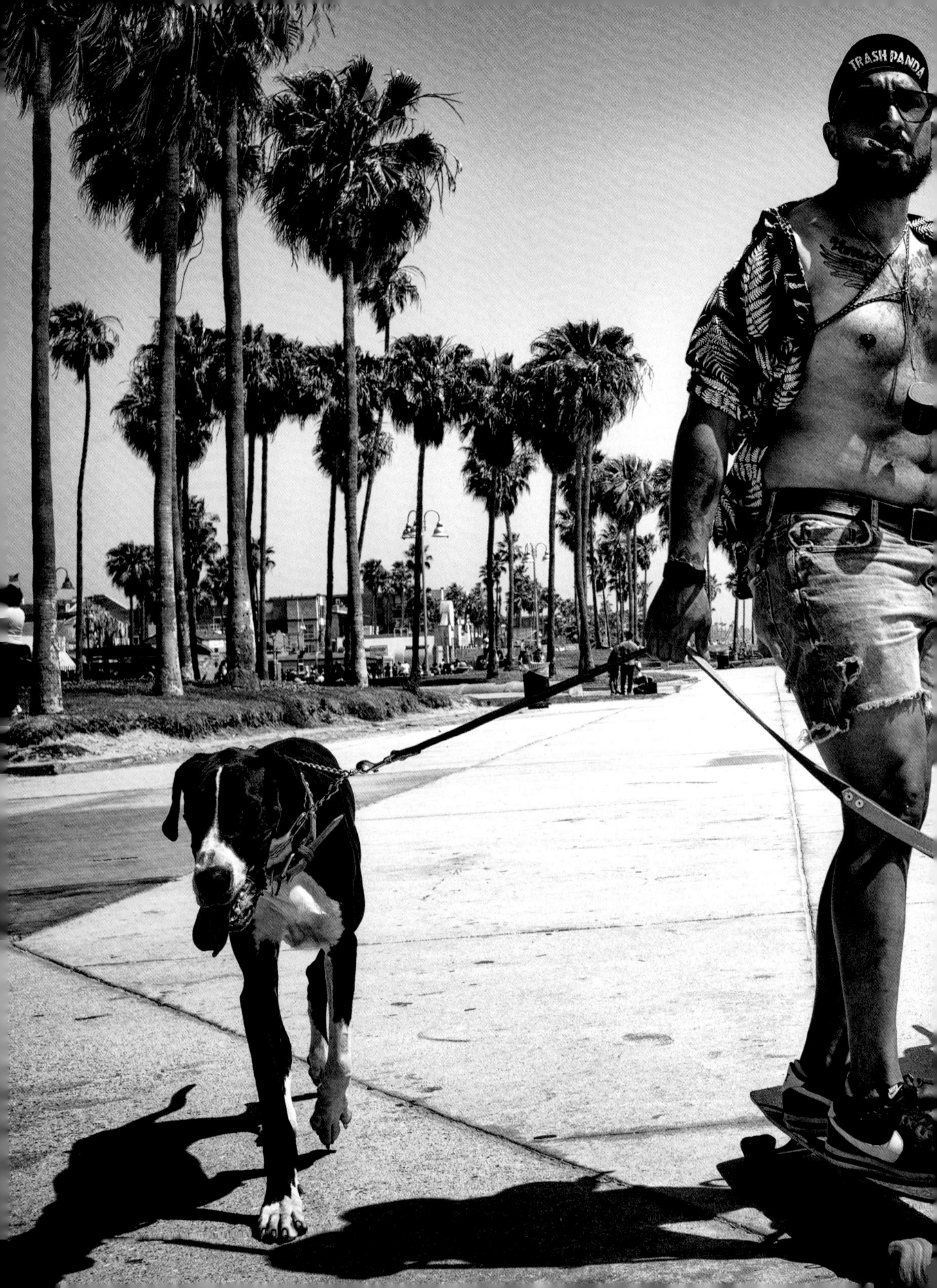
TRASH PANDA

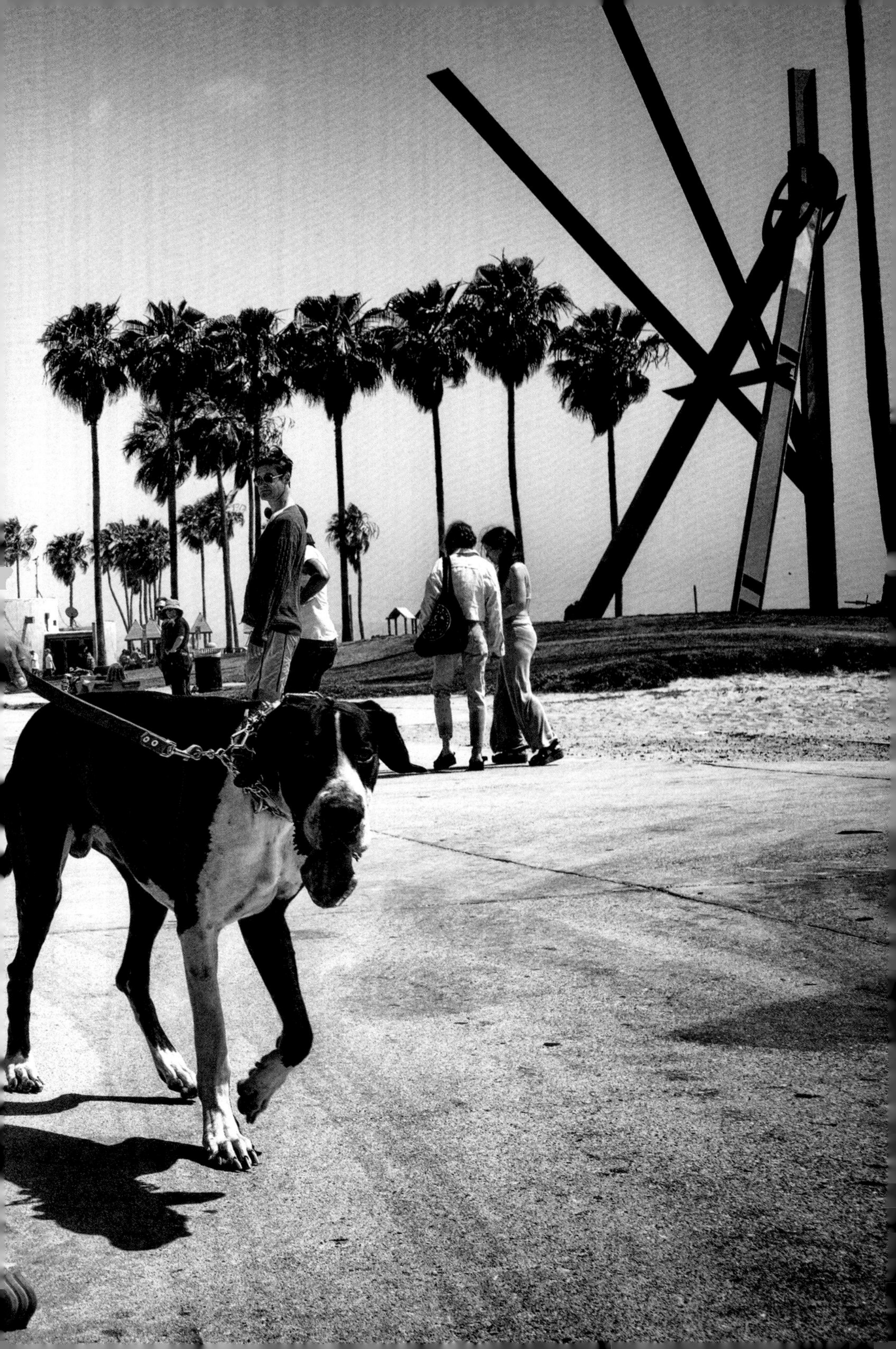

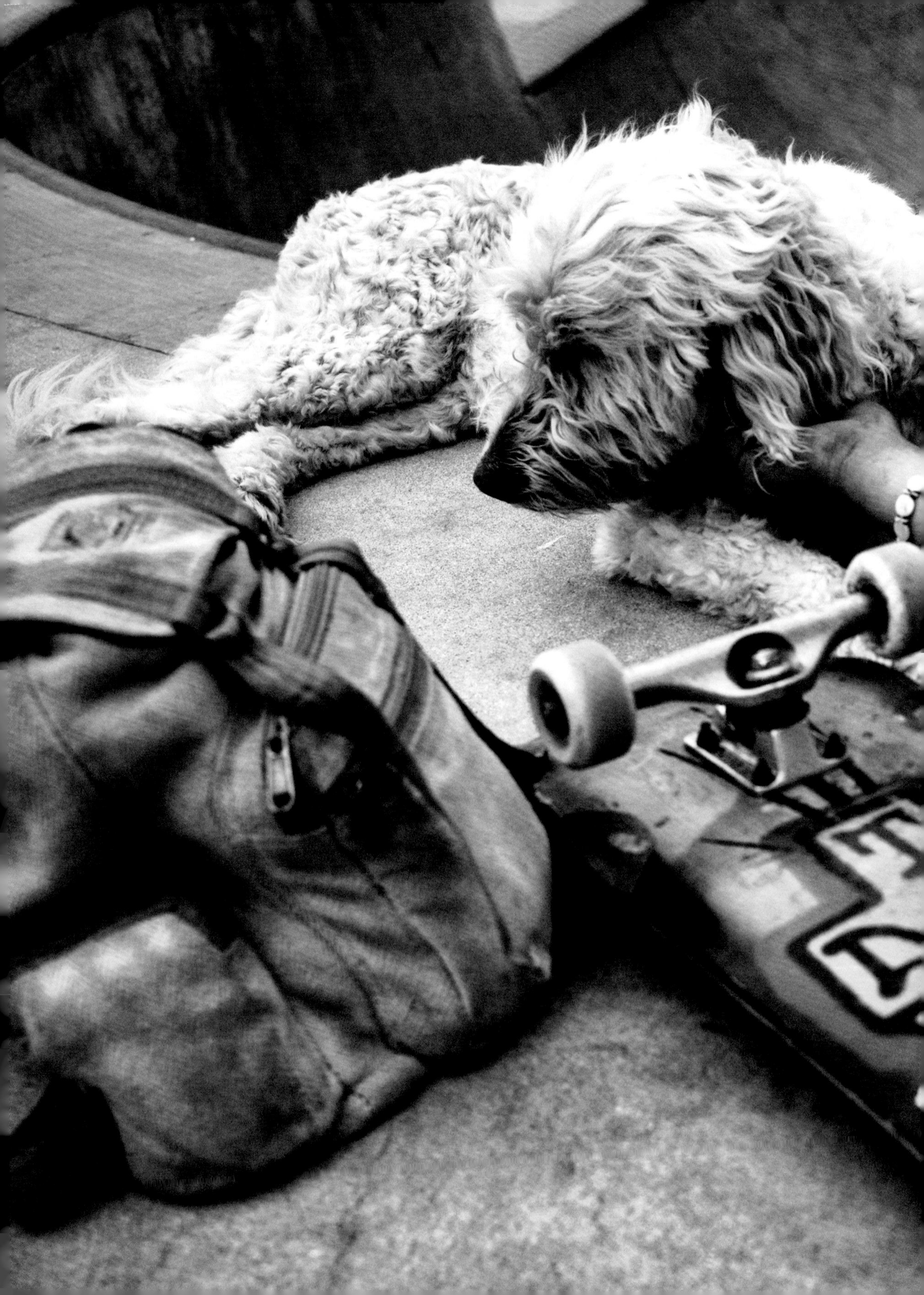

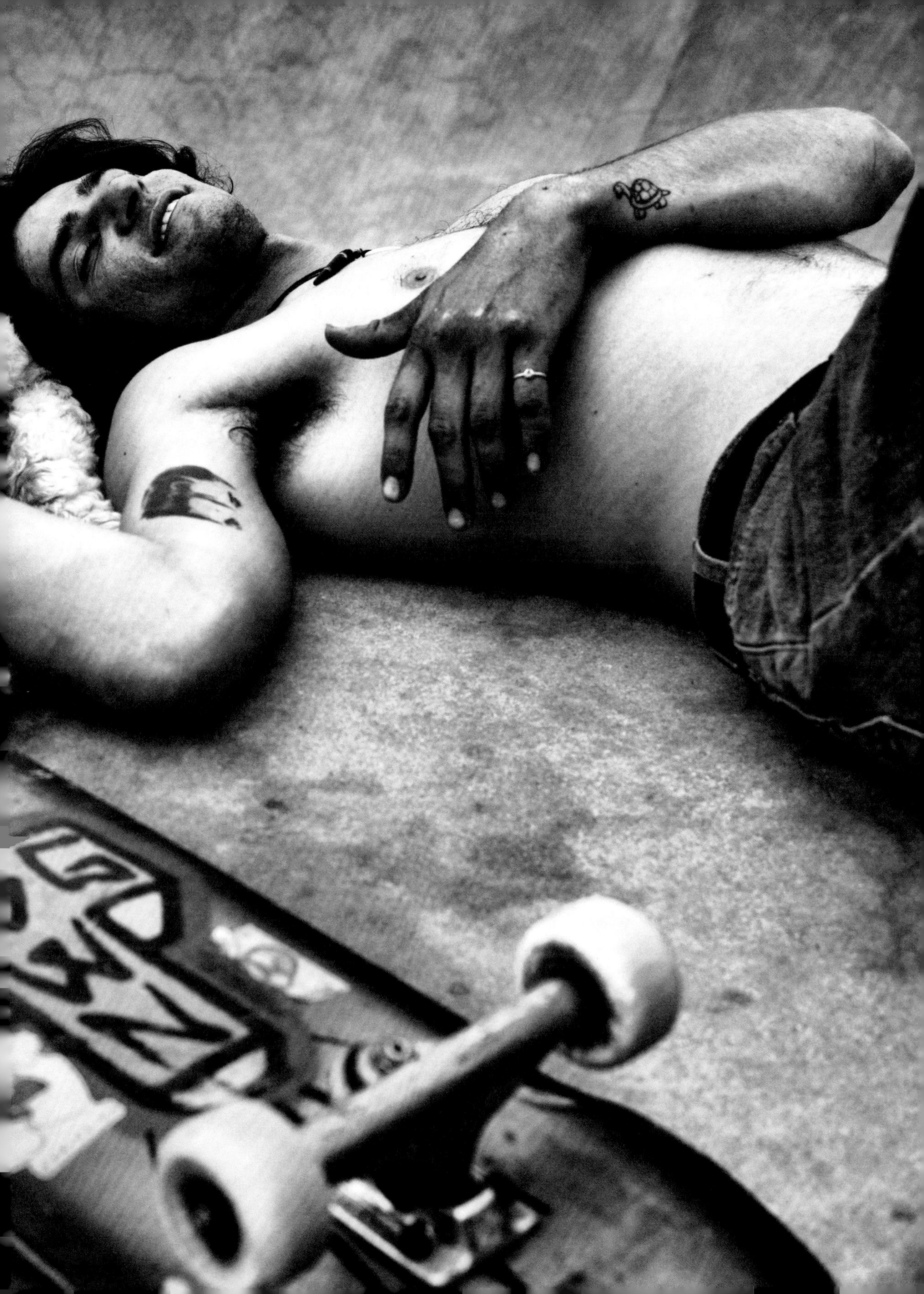

Locals
Only
No kooks

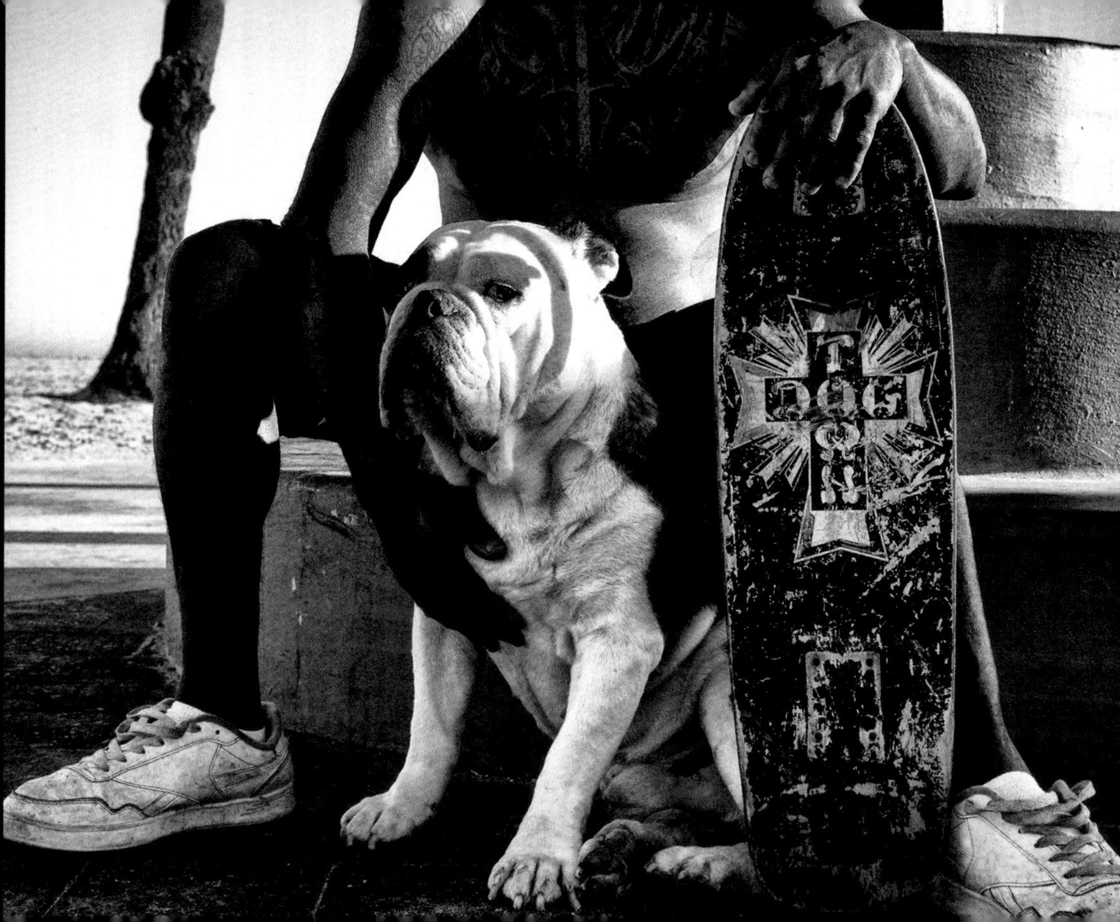
DOG

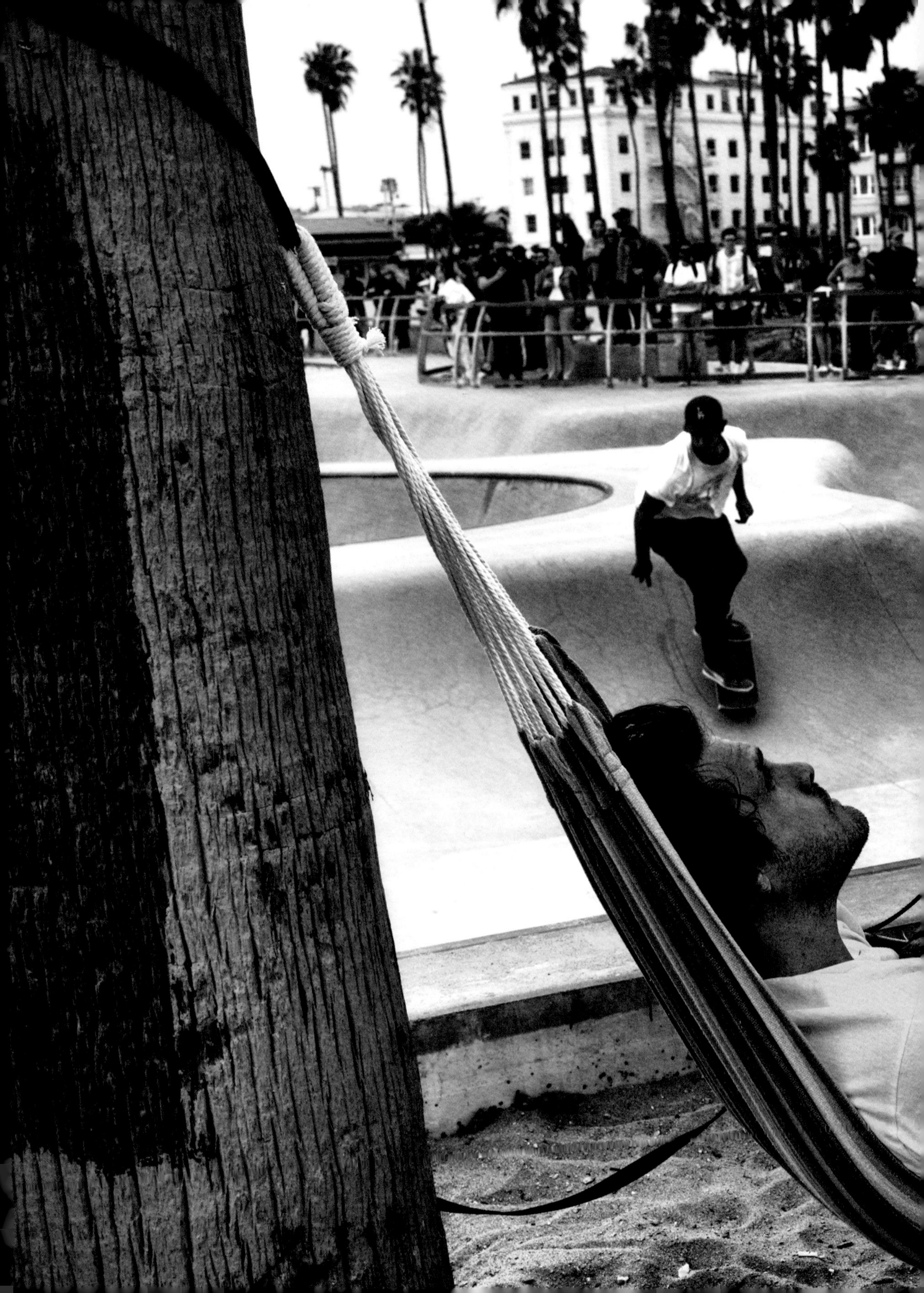

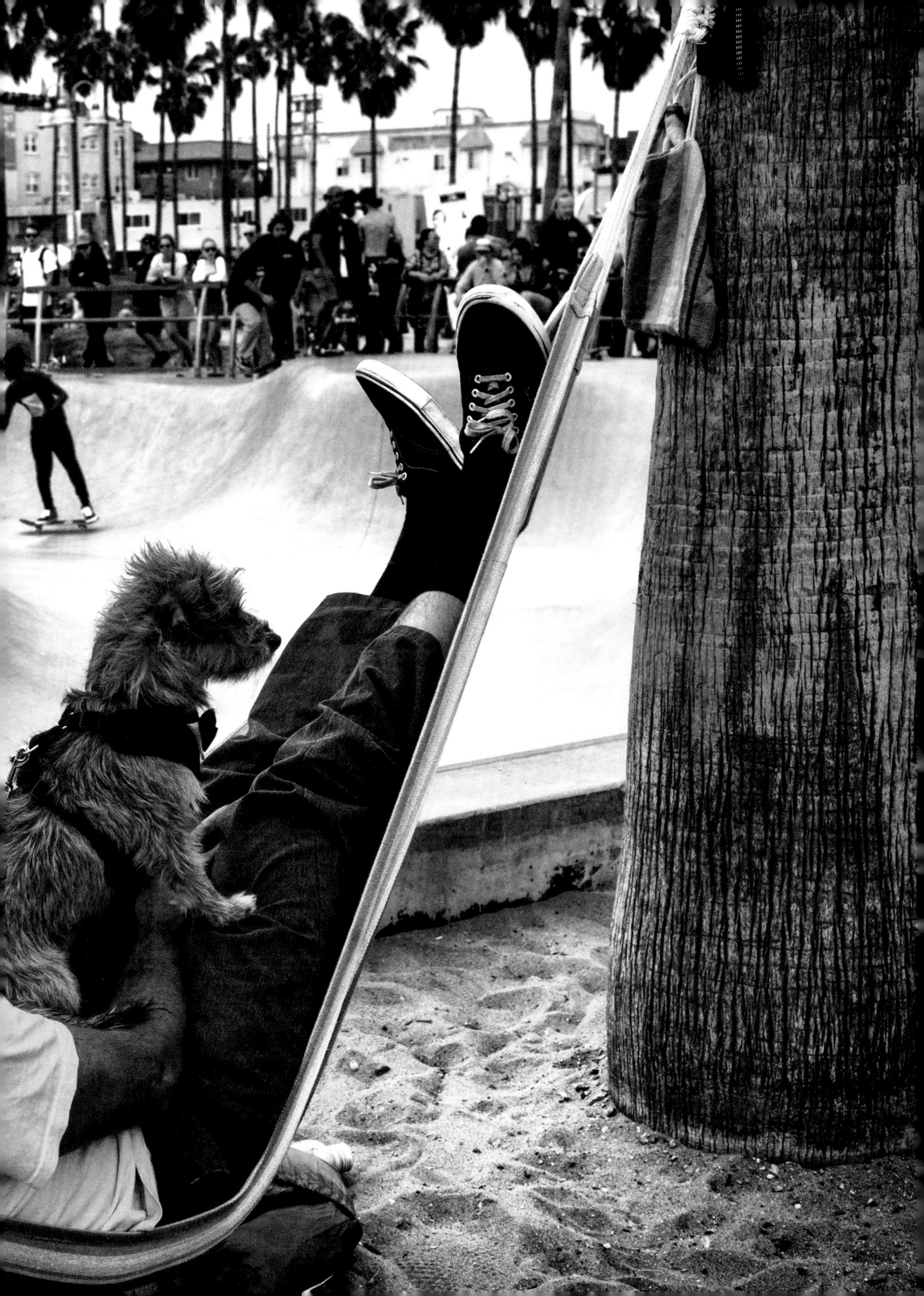

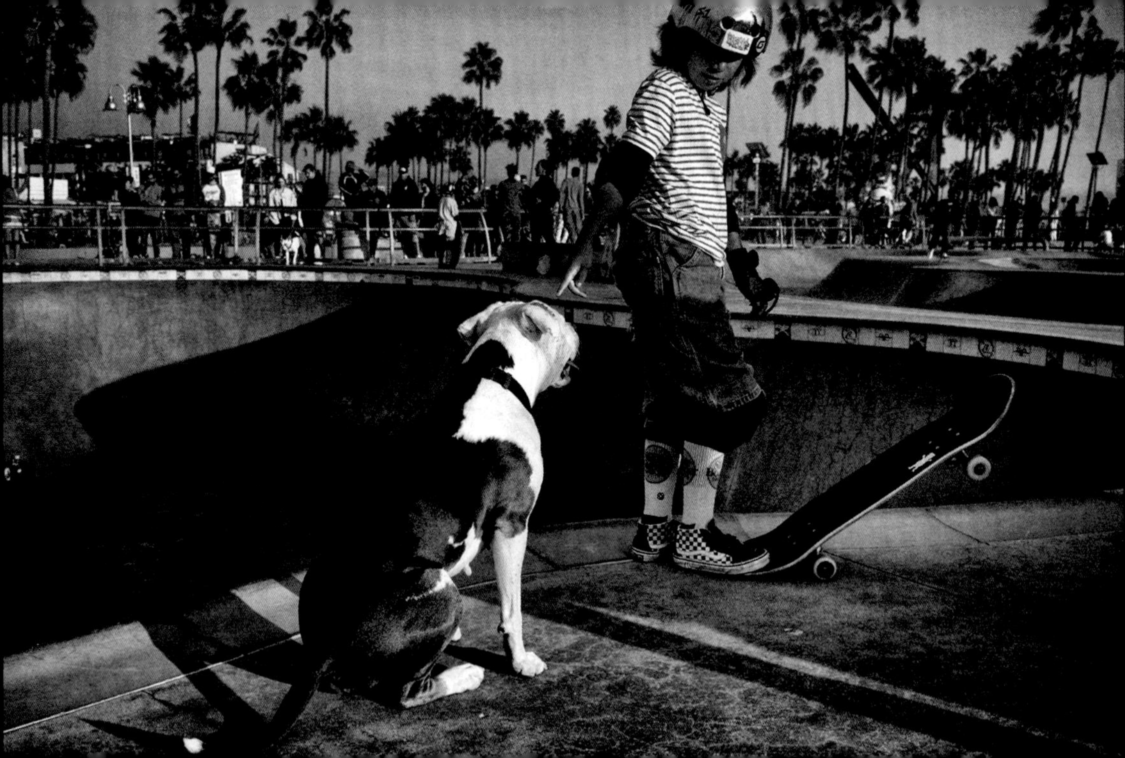

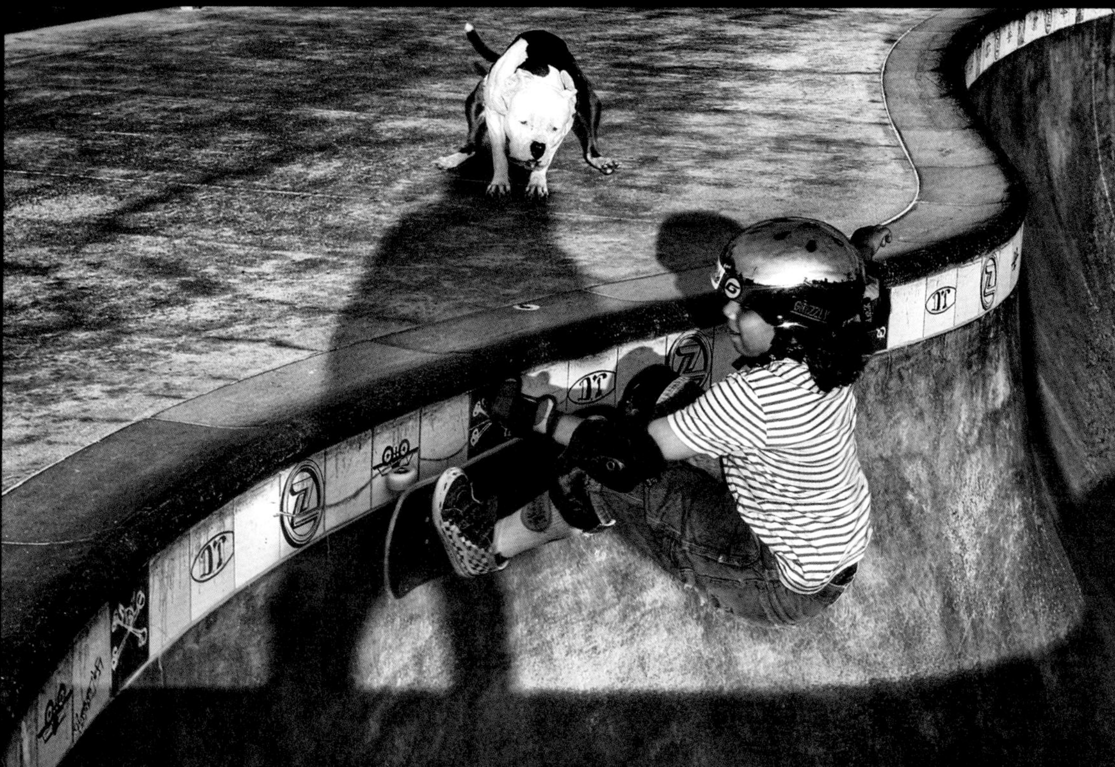

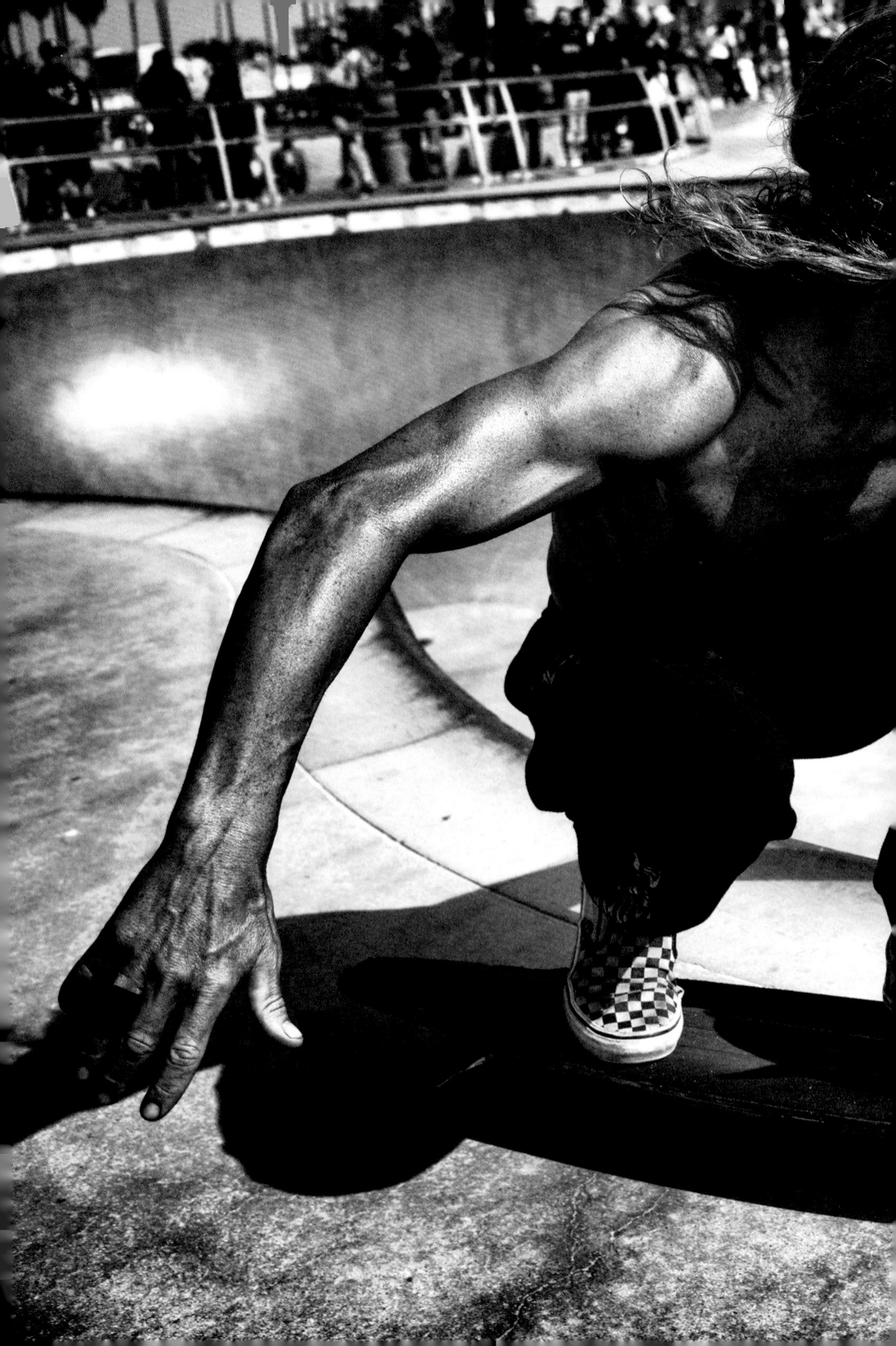

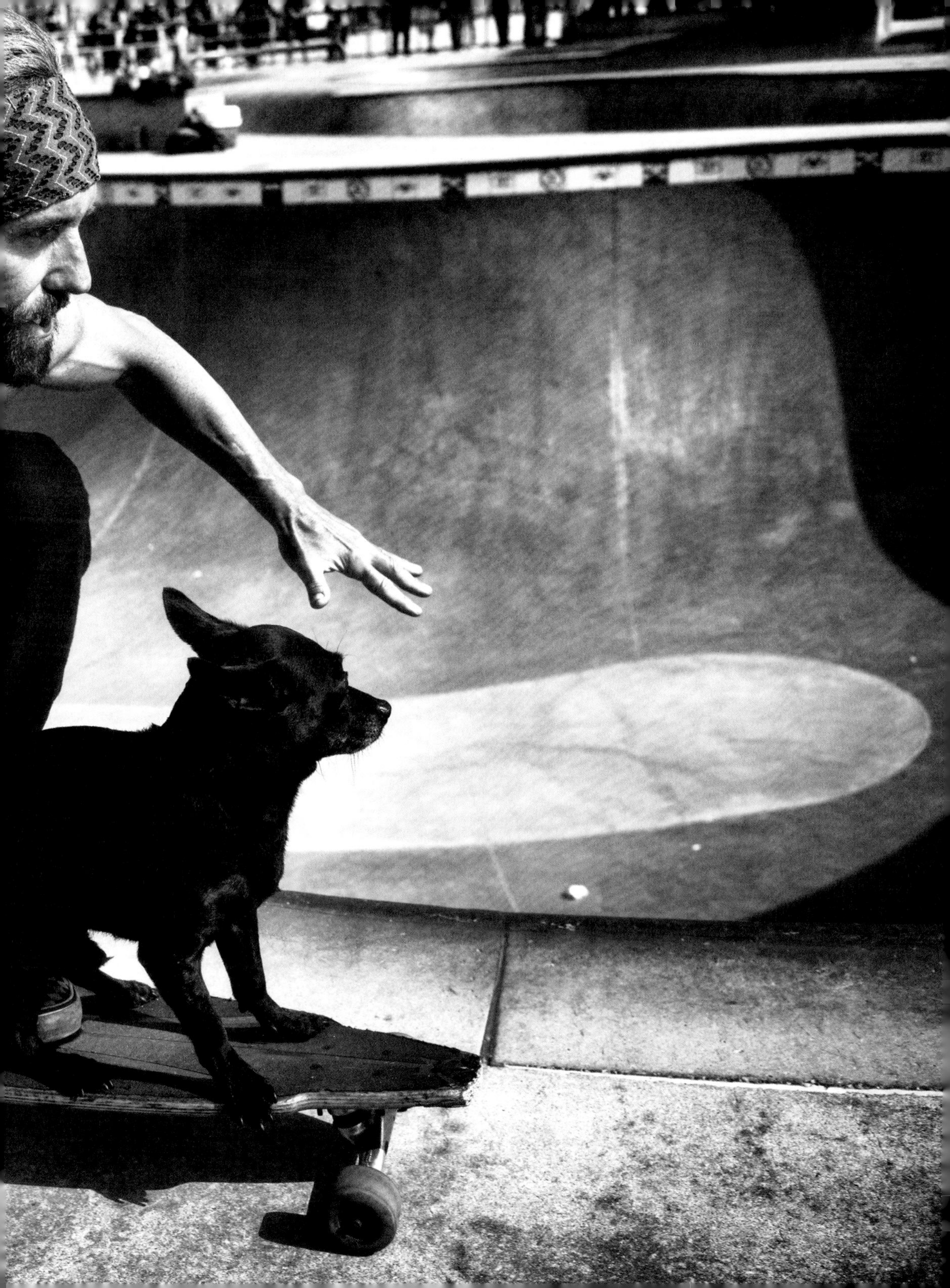

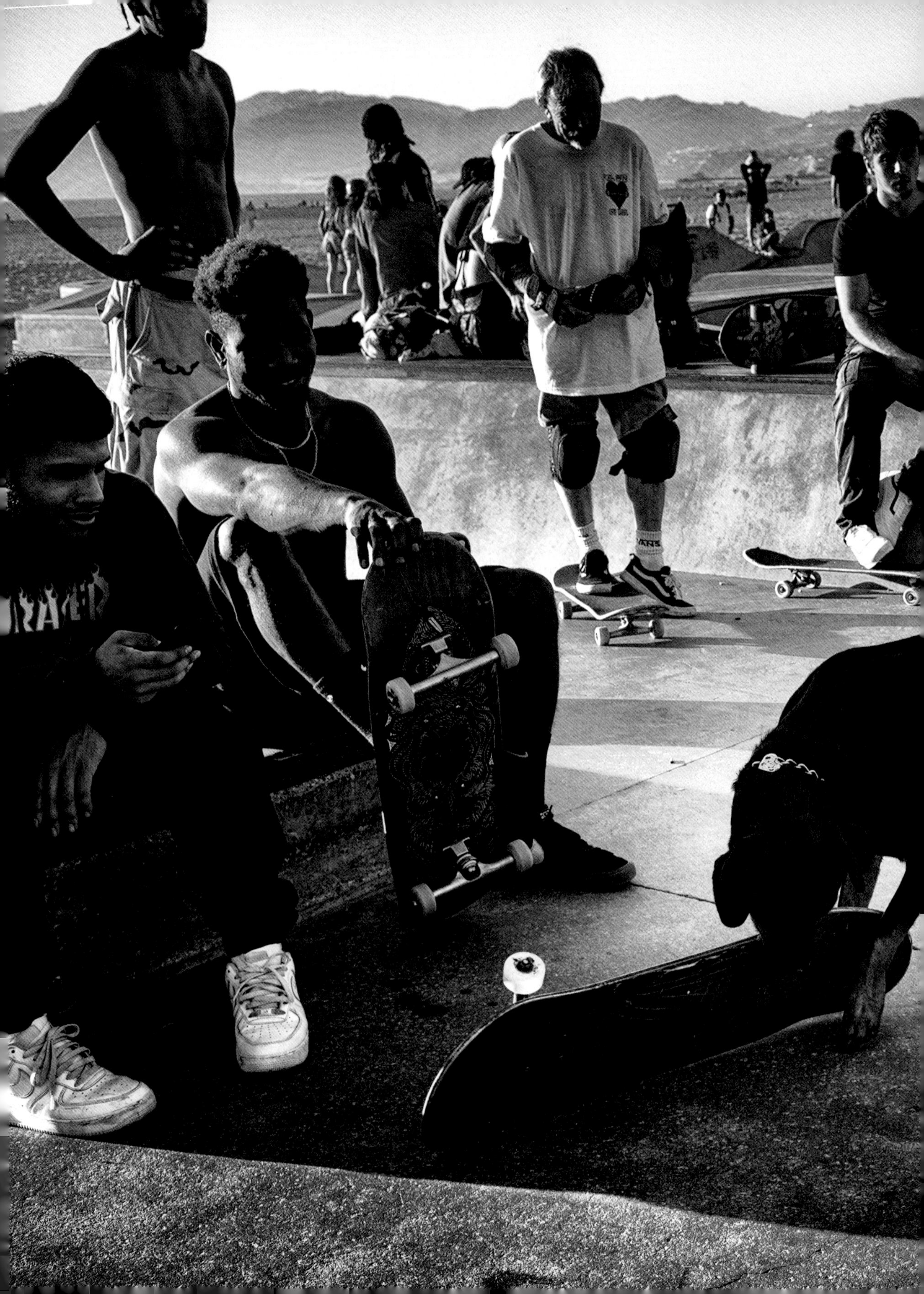

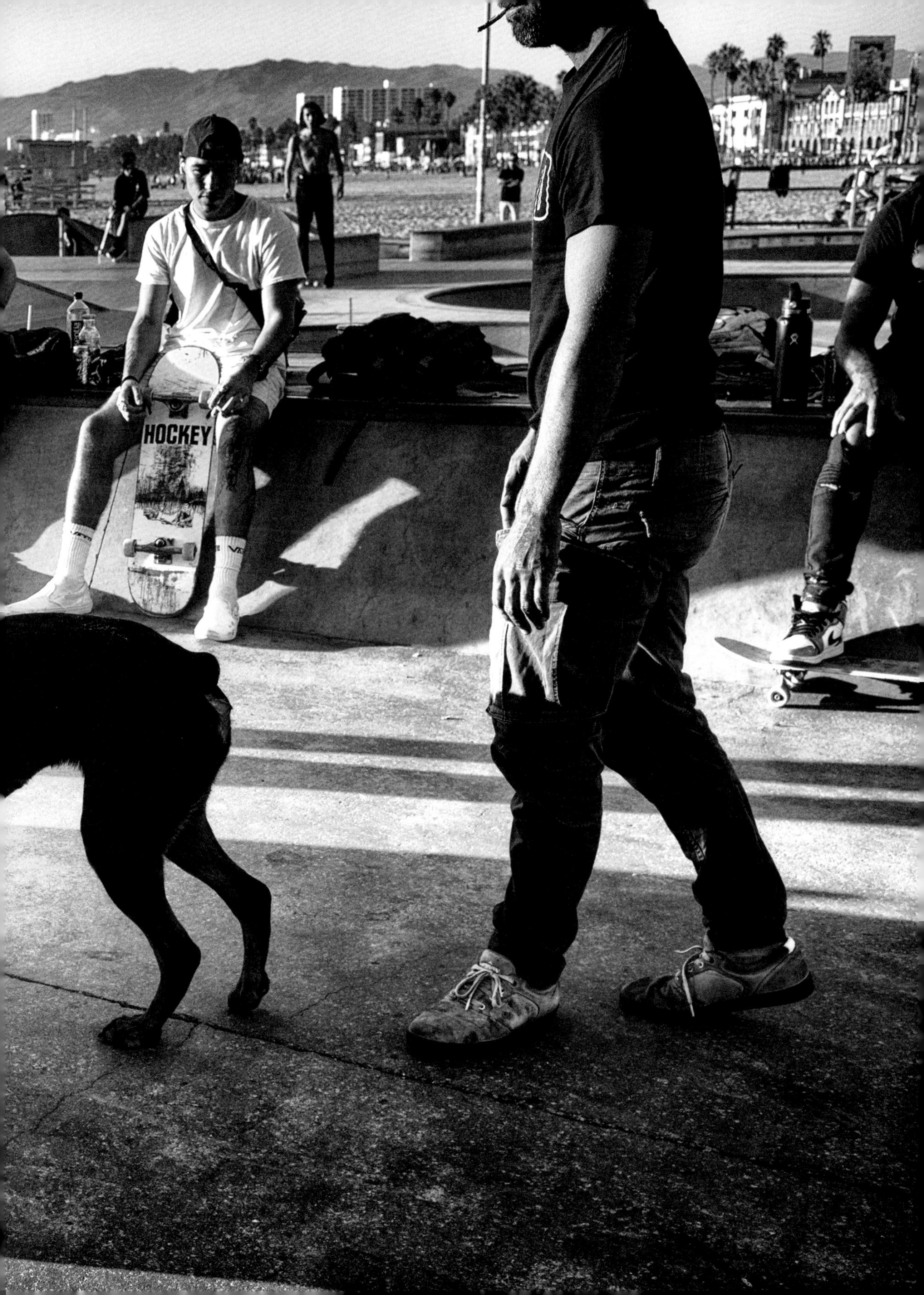
HOCKEY

tOO FASt
FOR SAtAN

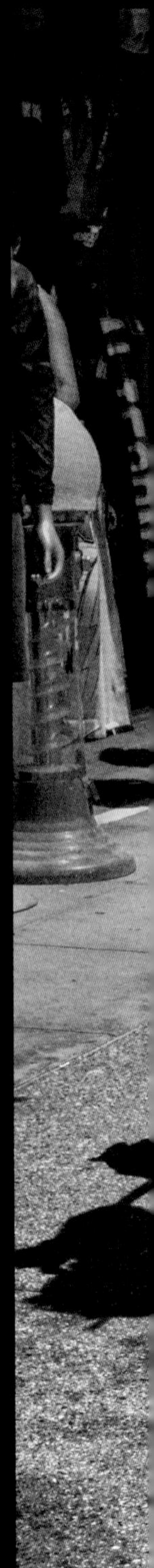

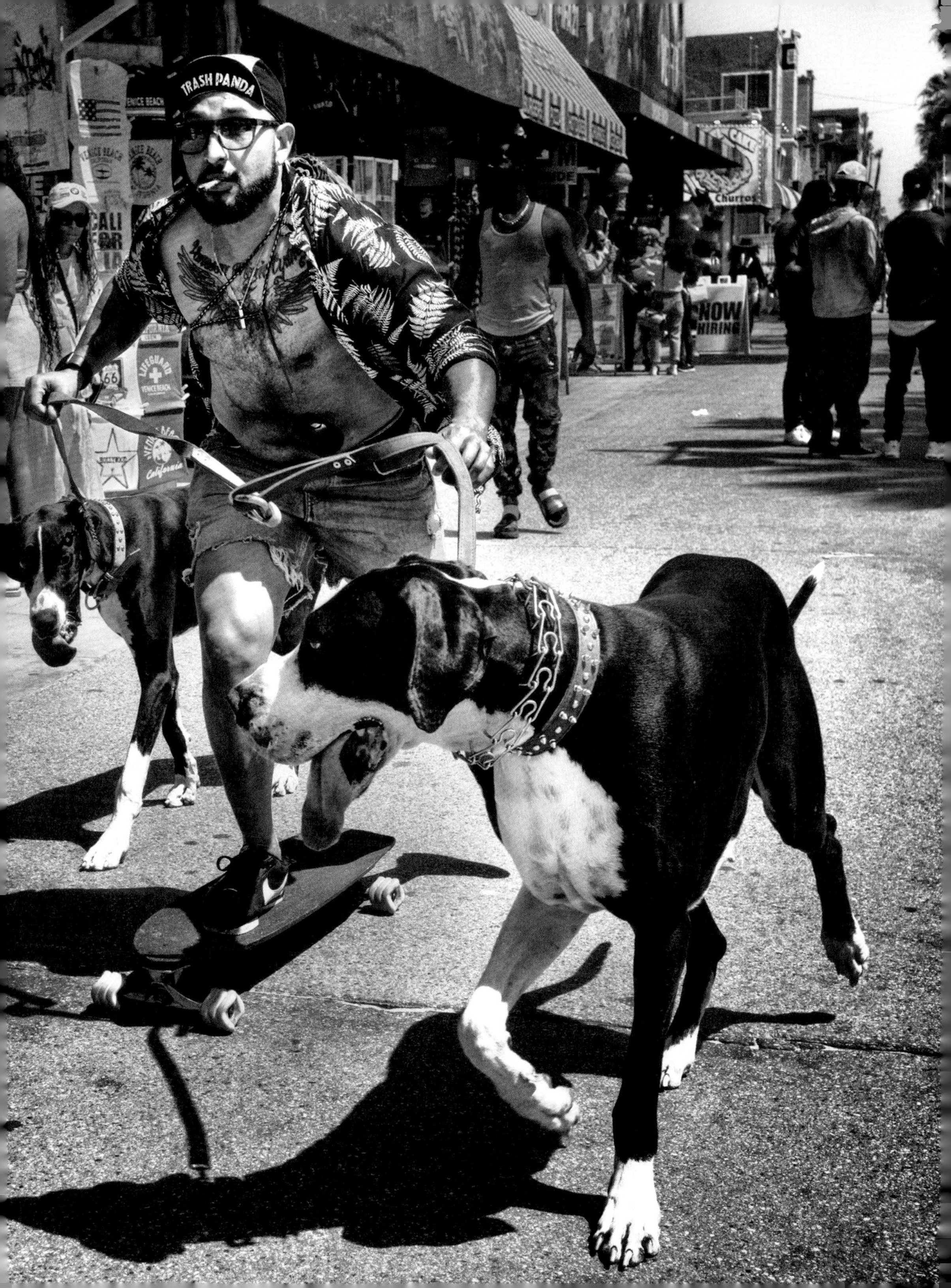
TRASH PANDA
NOW HIRING
Churros

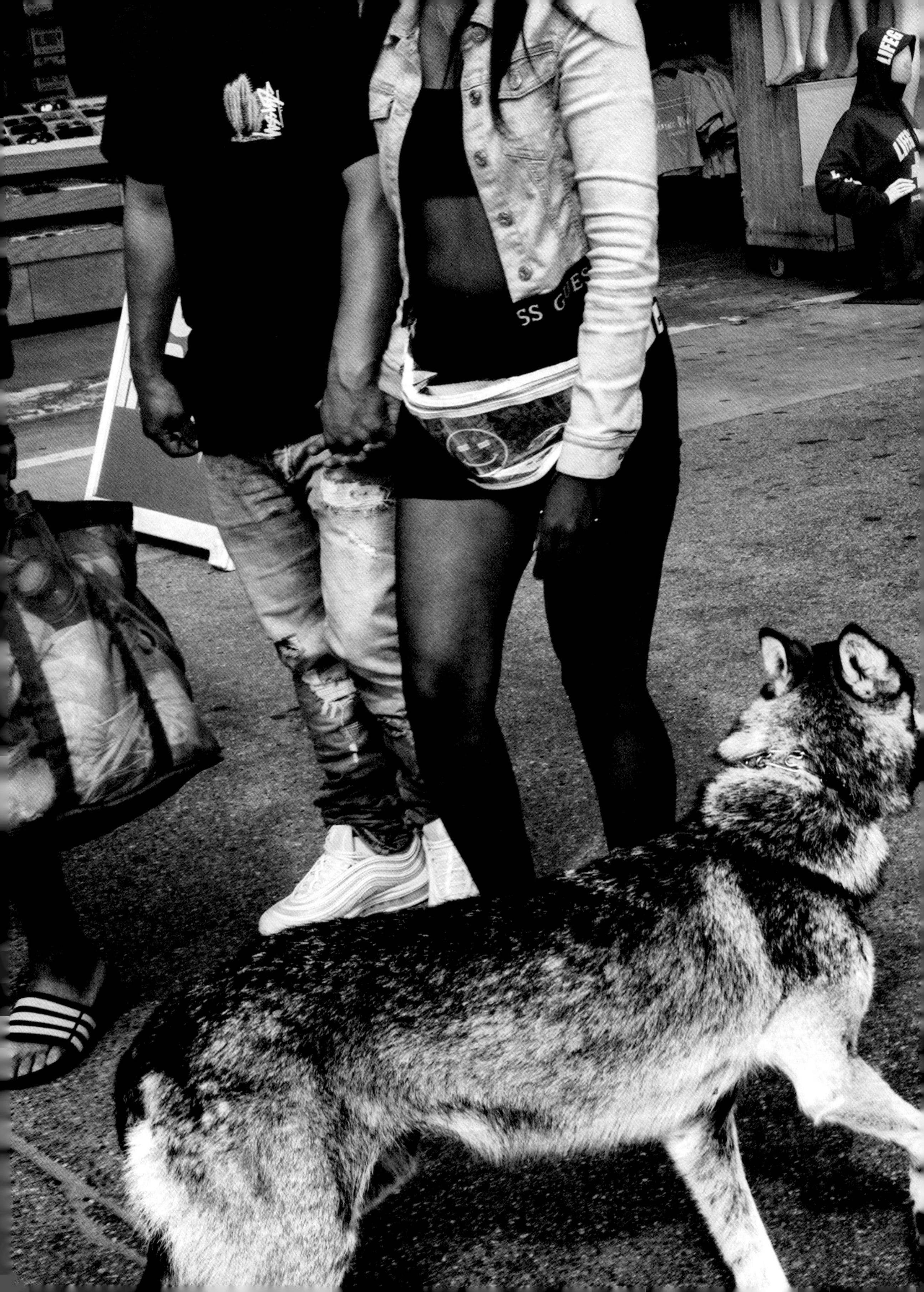
SS GUES

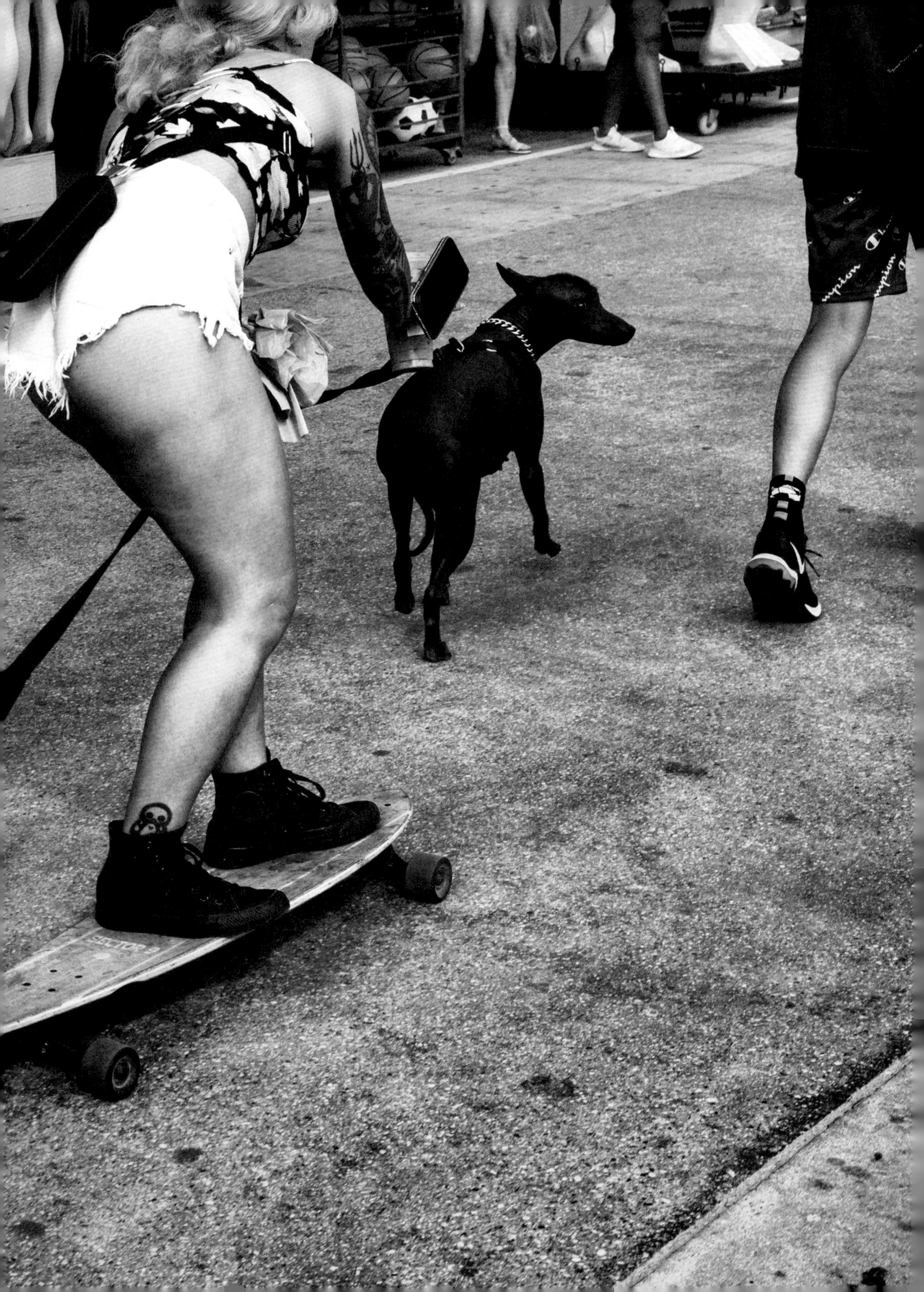

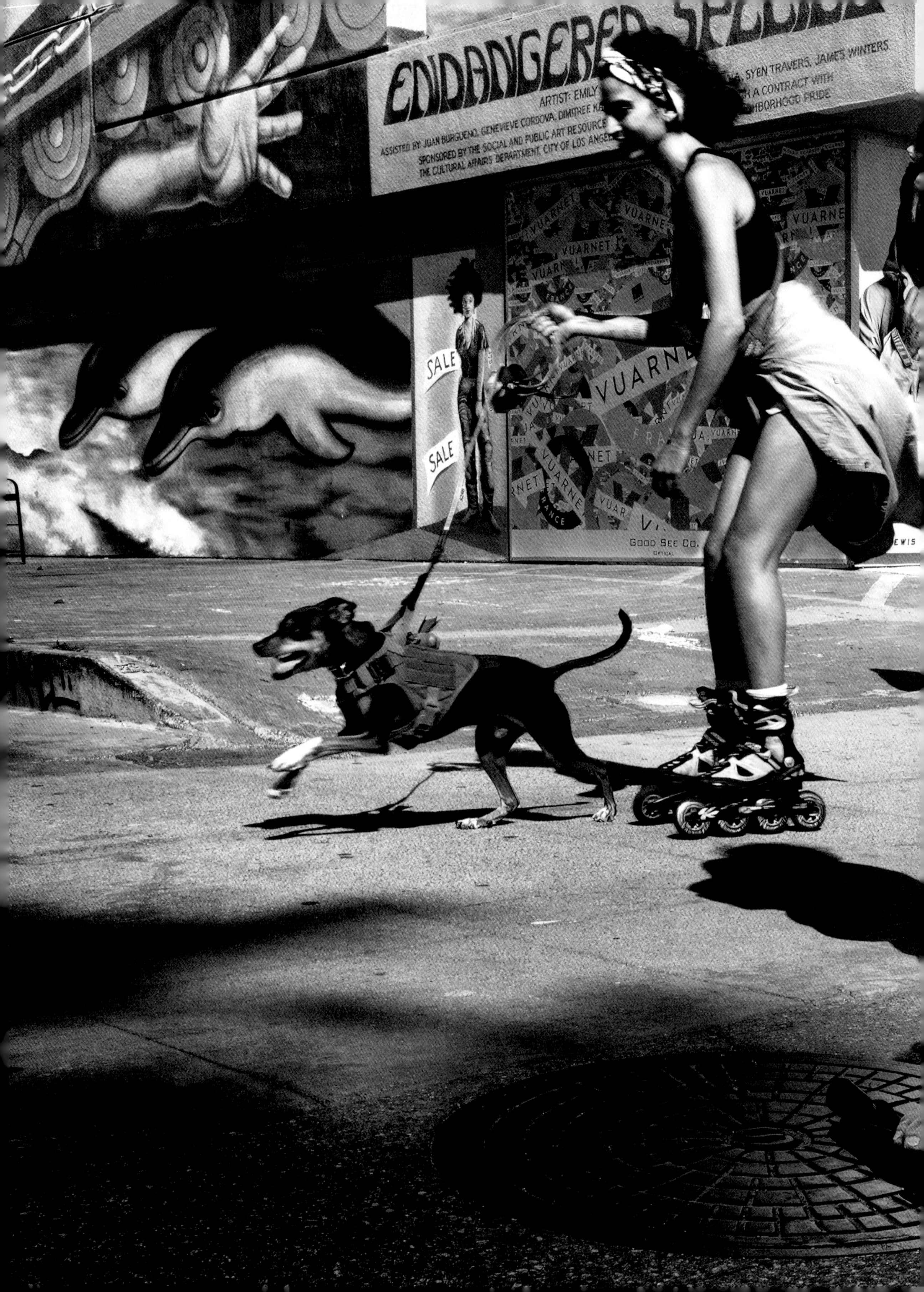
ENDANGERED
ARTIST: EMILY
ASSISTED BY: JUAN BURGUENO, GENEVIEVE CORDOVA, DIMITREE KA
SPONSORED BY THE SOCIAL AND PUBLIC ART RESOURCE
THE CULTURAL AFFAIRS DEPARTMENT, CITY OF LOS ANGE
SYEN TRAVERS, JAMES WINTERS
SALE
SALE
VUARNET
VUARNET
GOOD SEE CO.

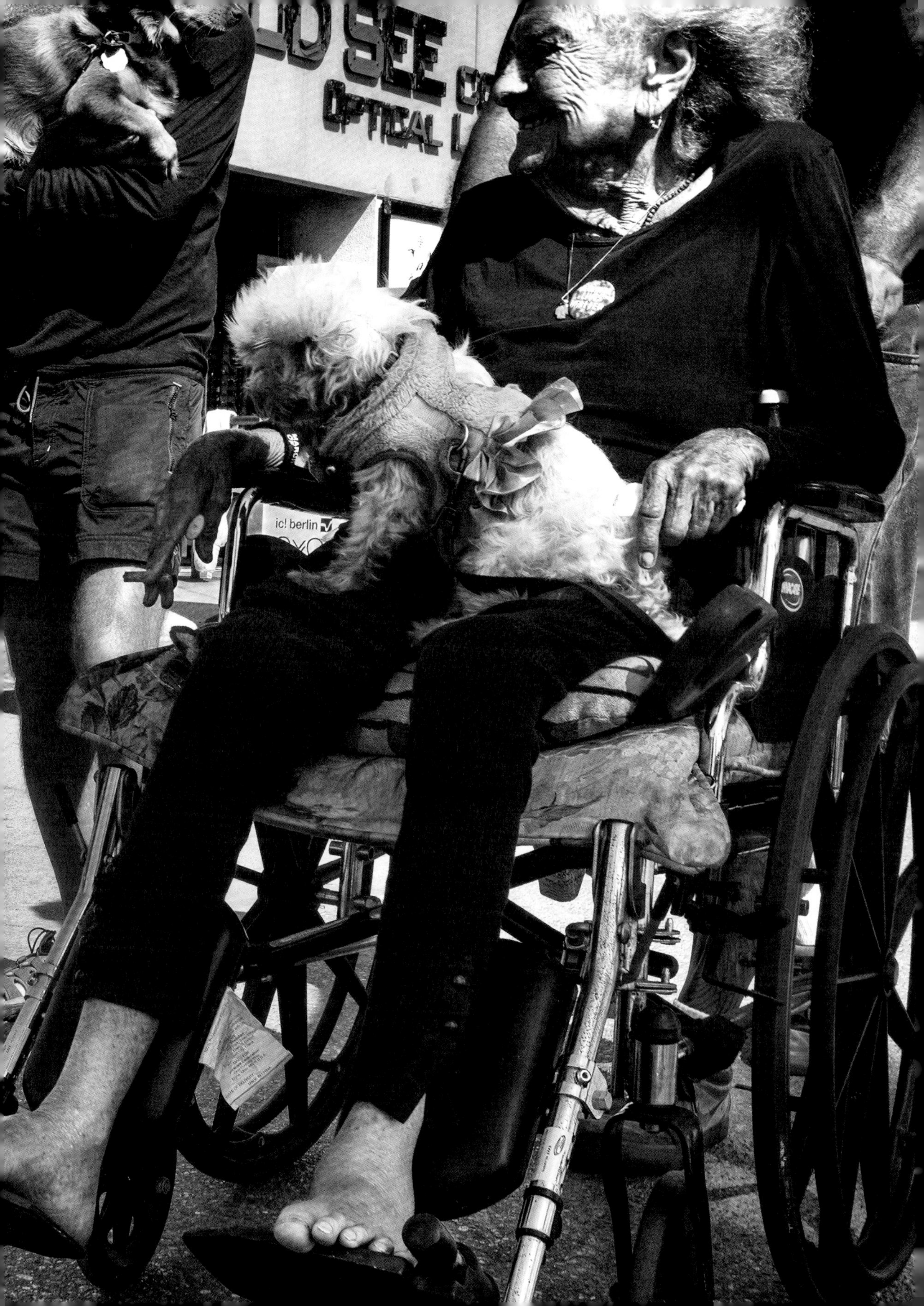
OPTICAL
ic! berlin

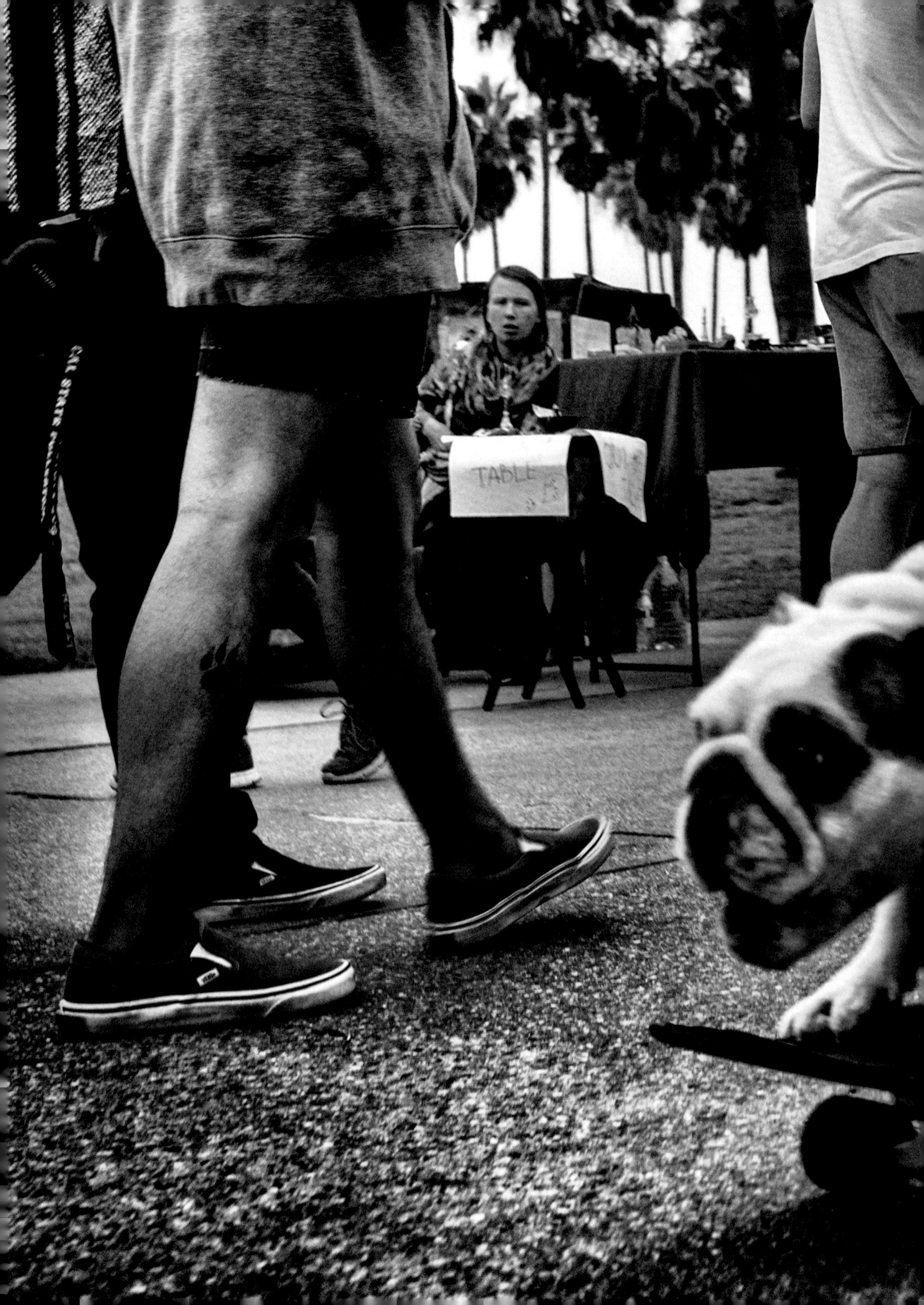
TABLE

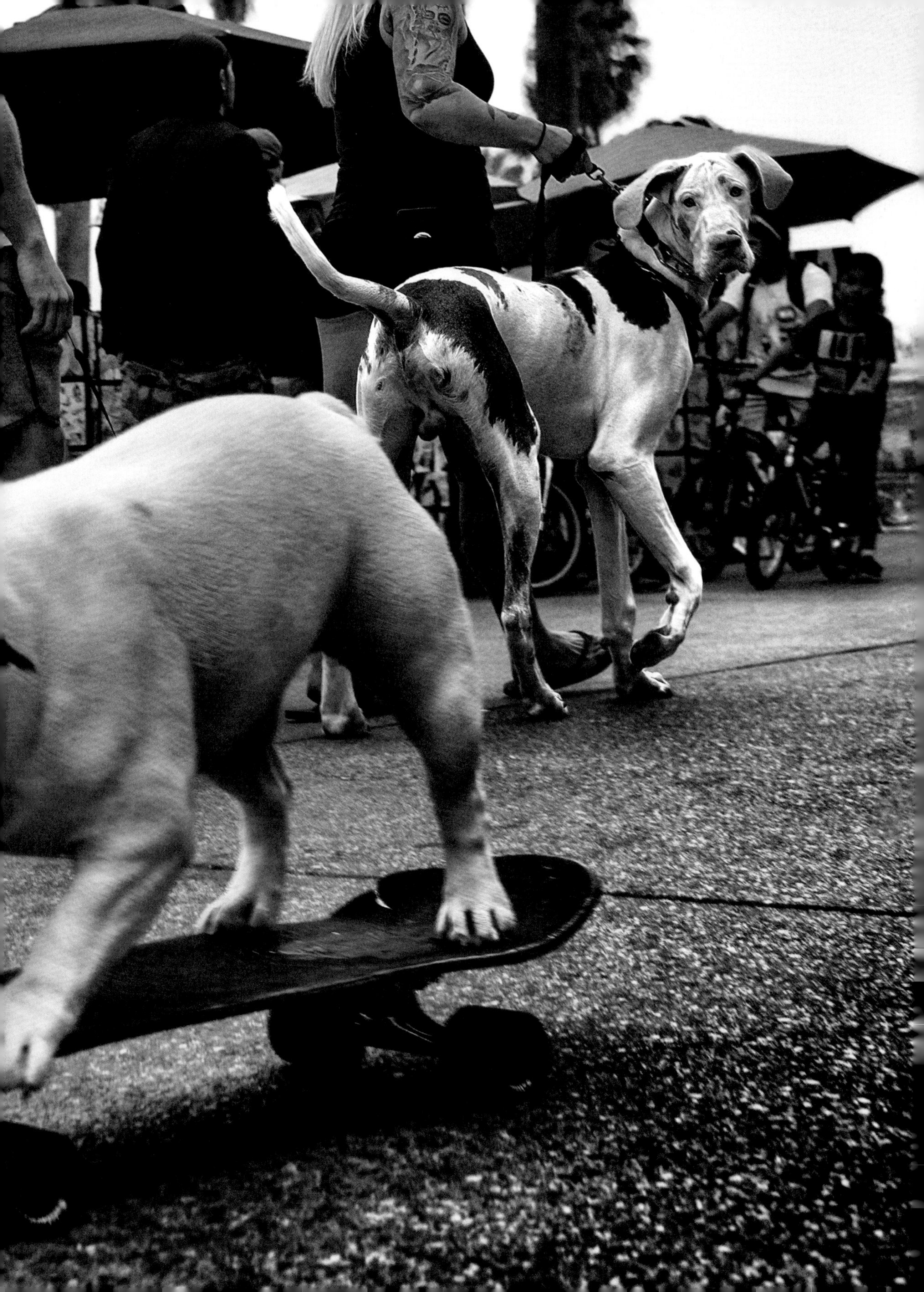

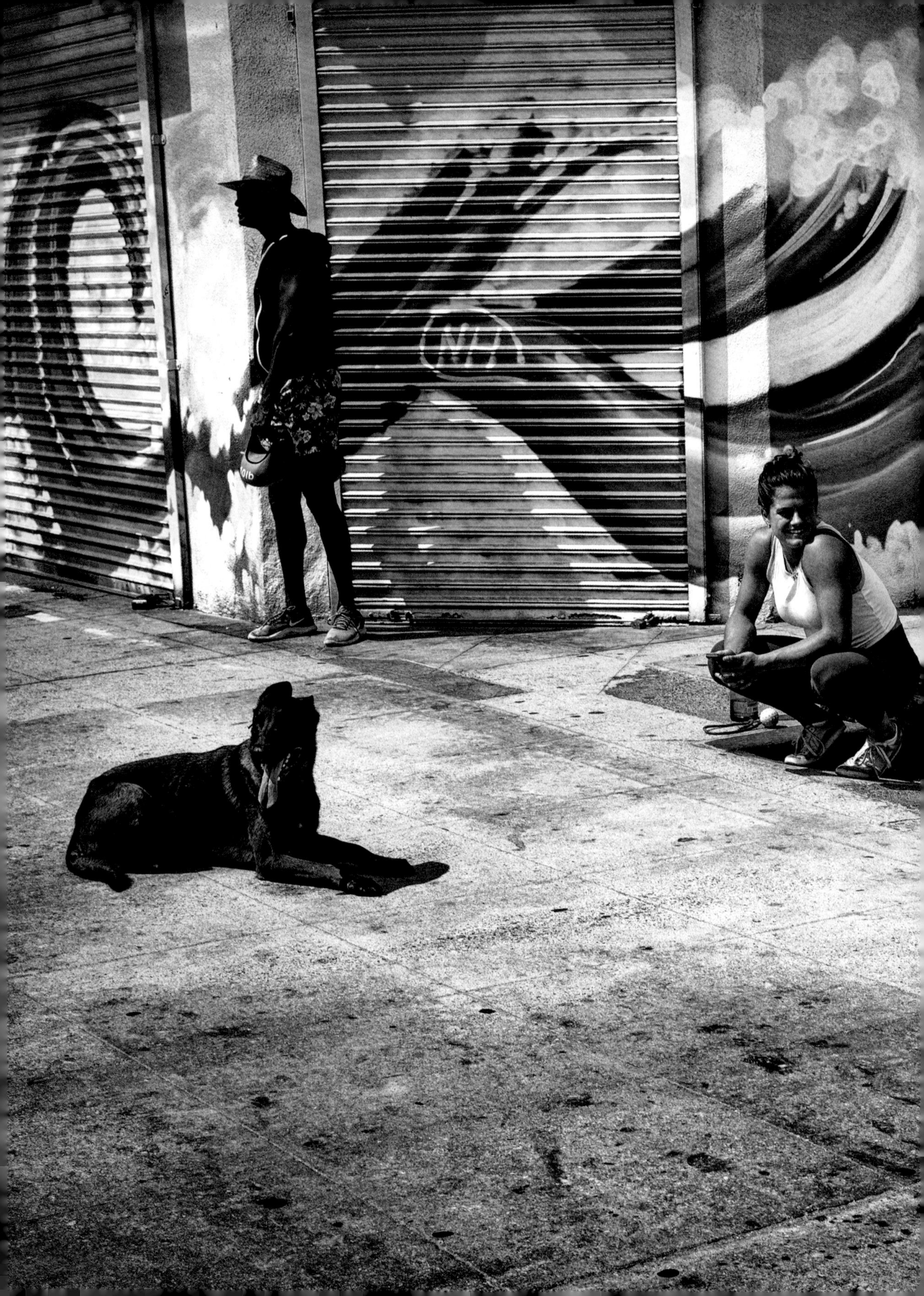
NH

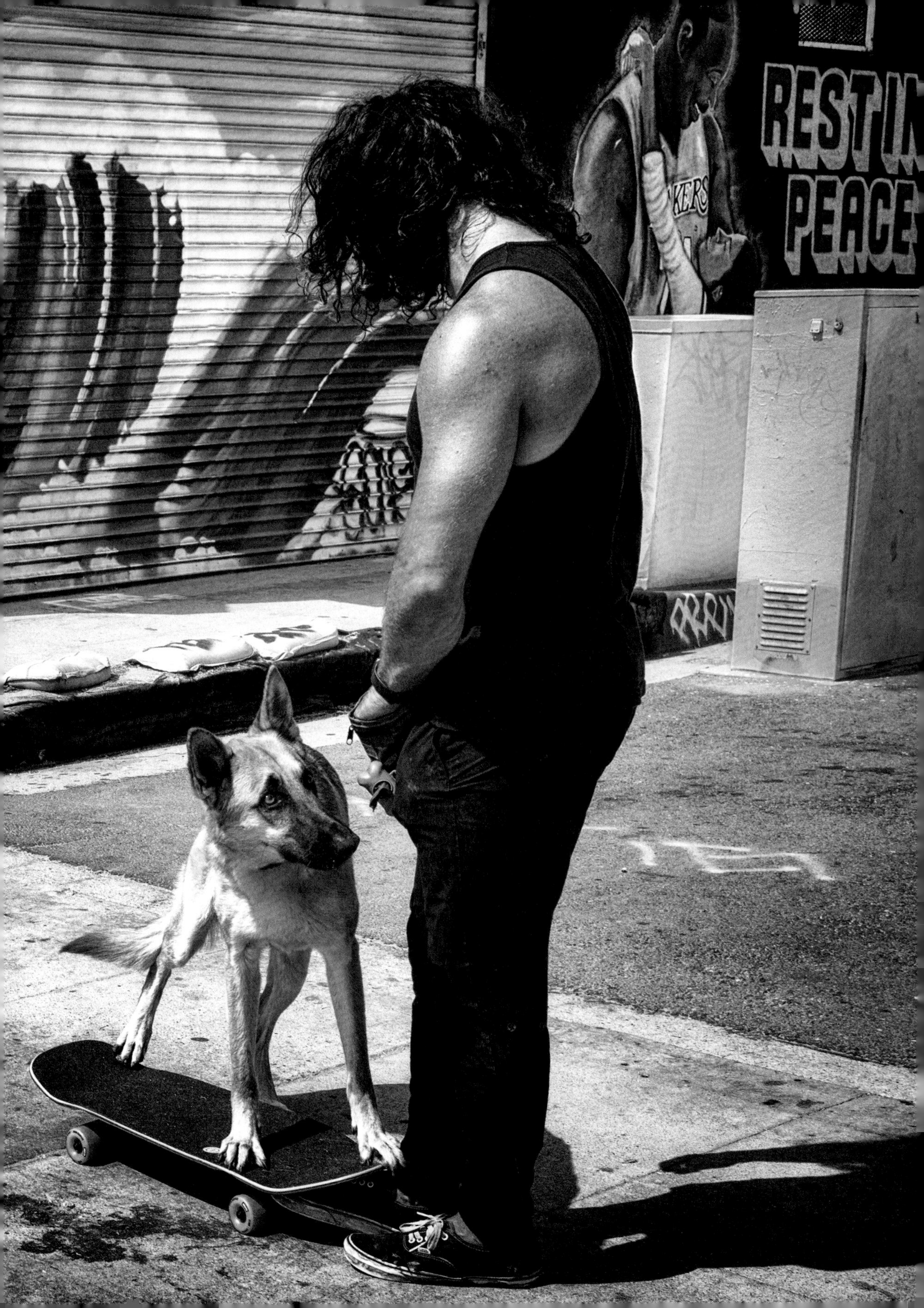
REST IN
PEACE

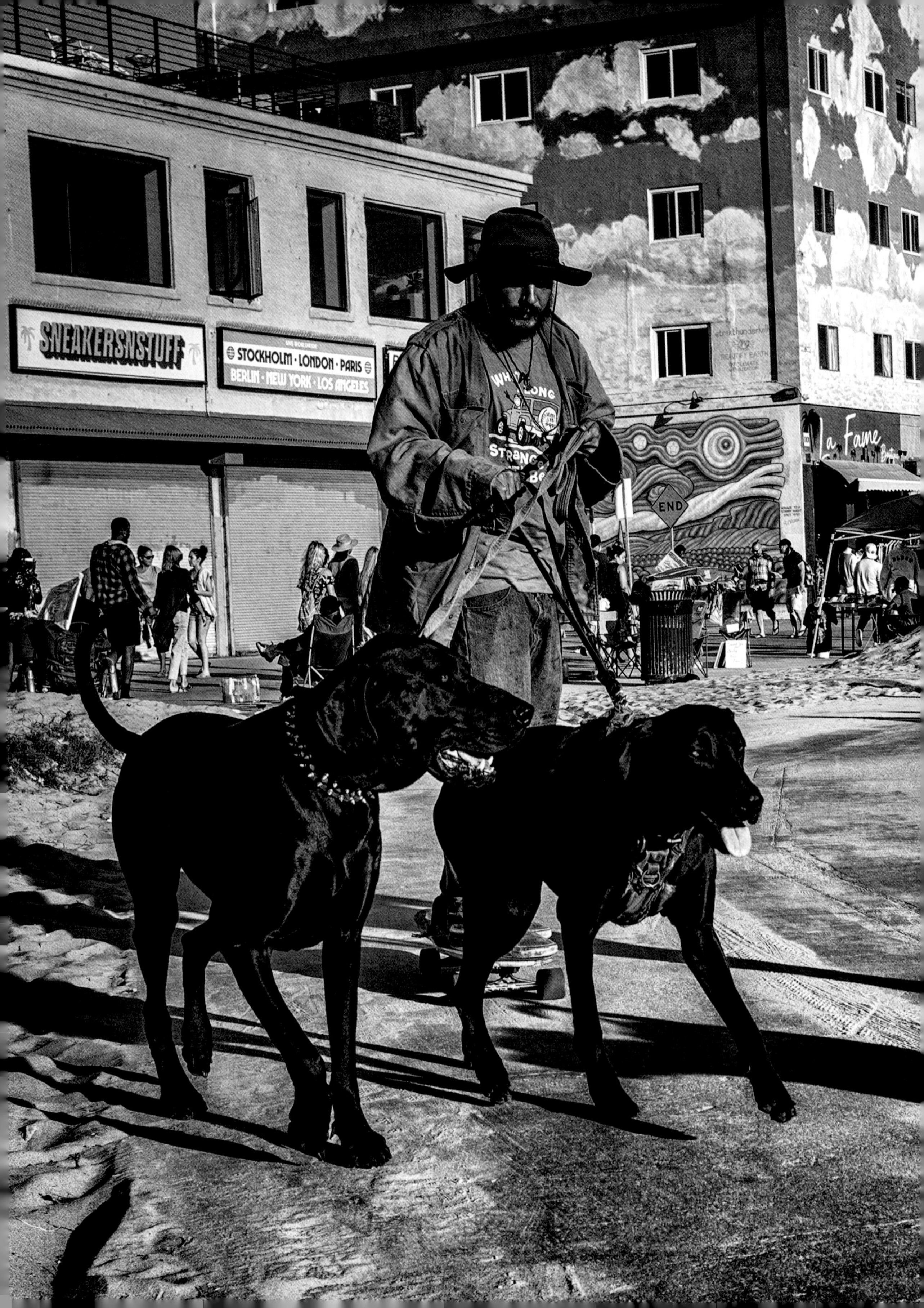
SNEAKERSNSTUFF
STOCKHOLM · LONDON · PARIS
BERLIN · NEW YORK · LOS ANGELES
END

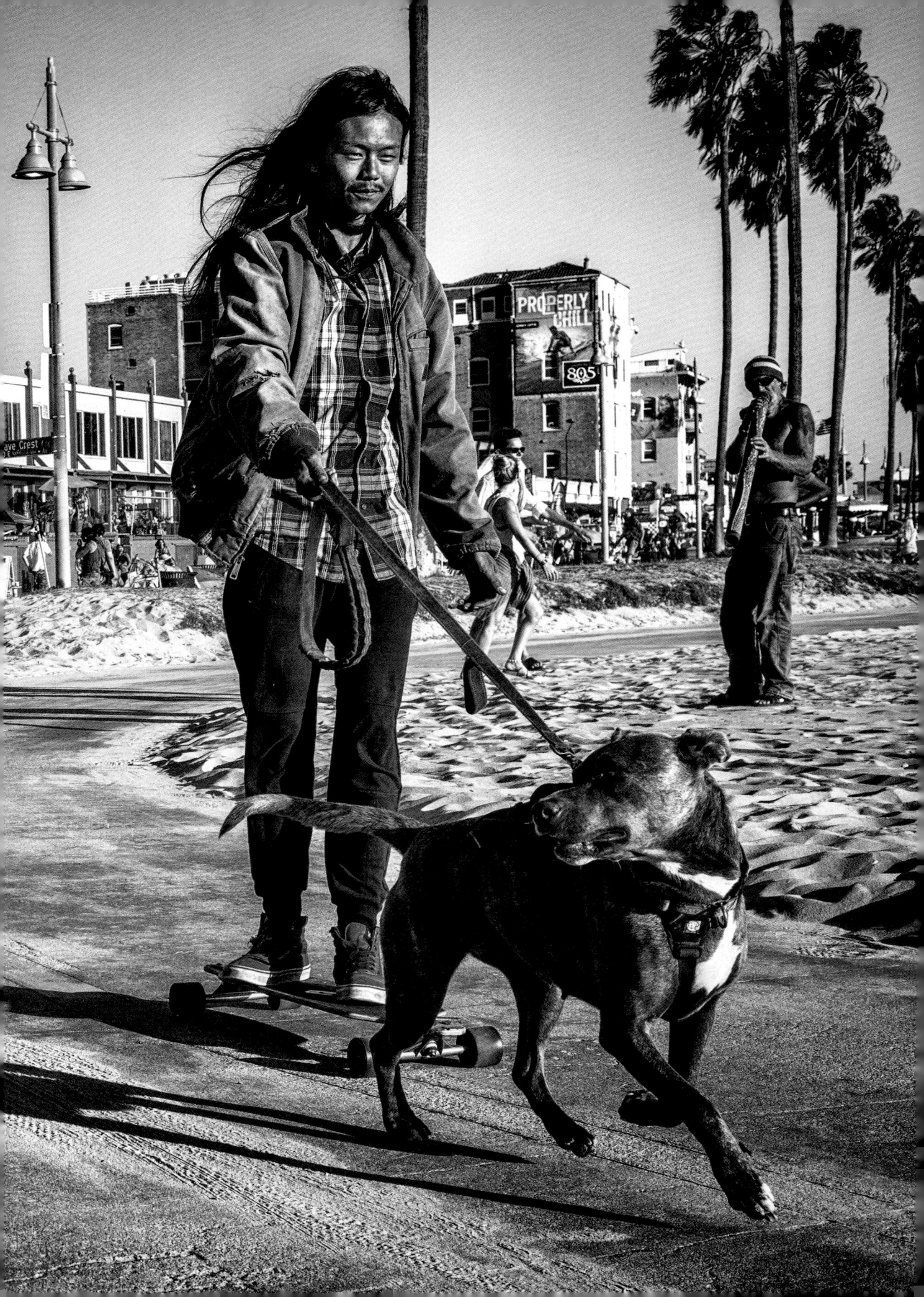
PROPERLY CHILL
805

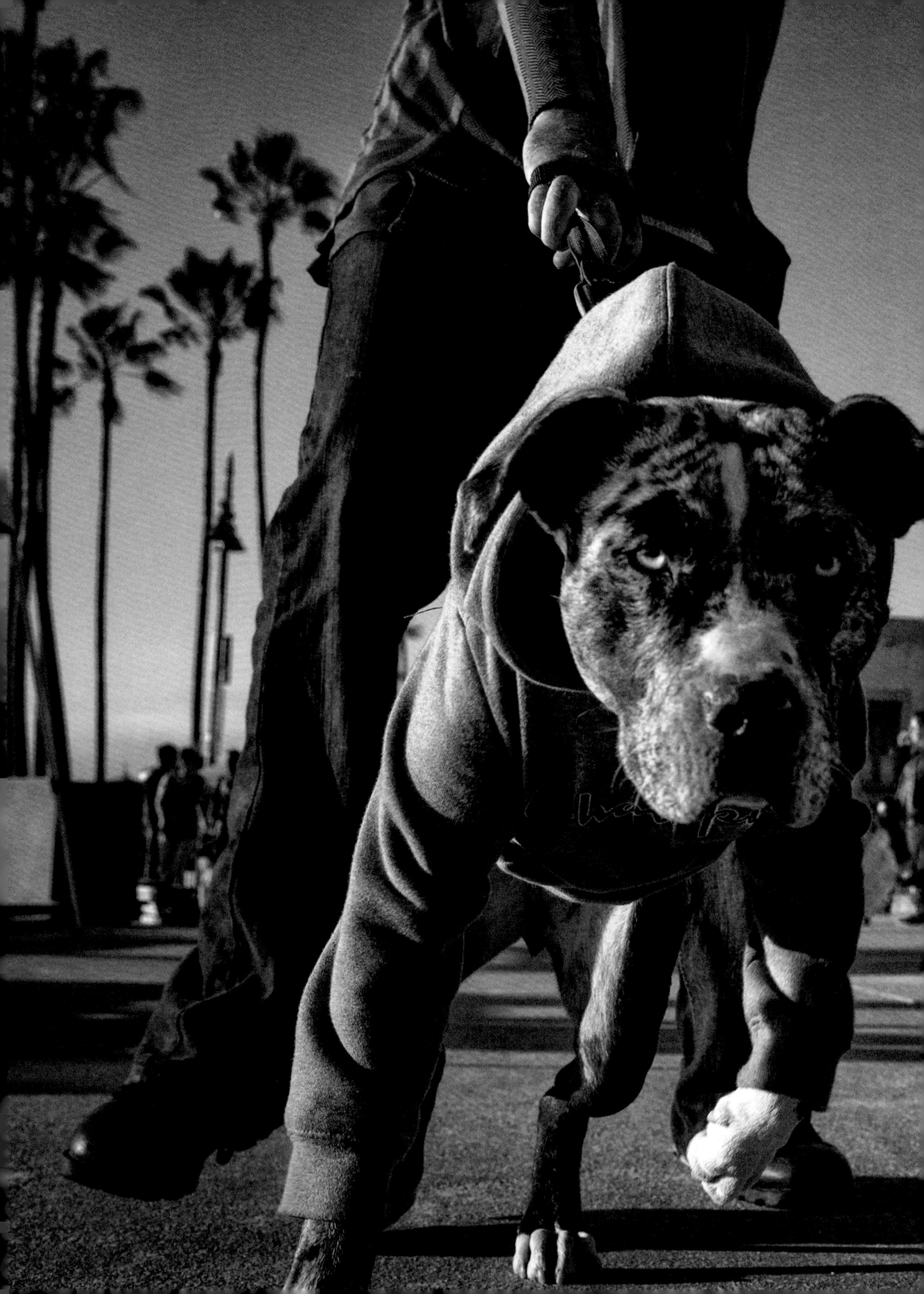

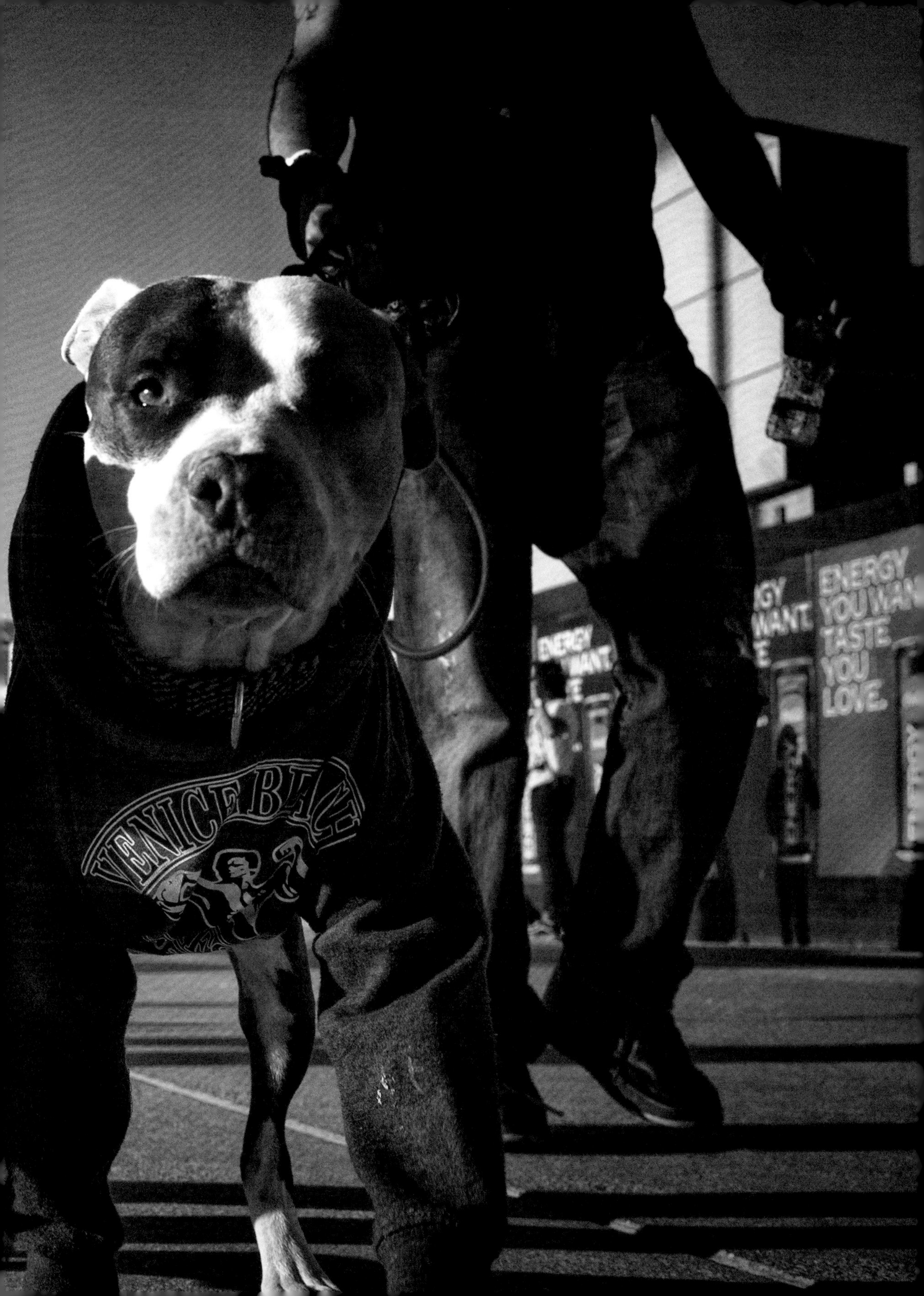
ENERGY
YOU WAN
TASTE
YOU
LOVE.
VENICE

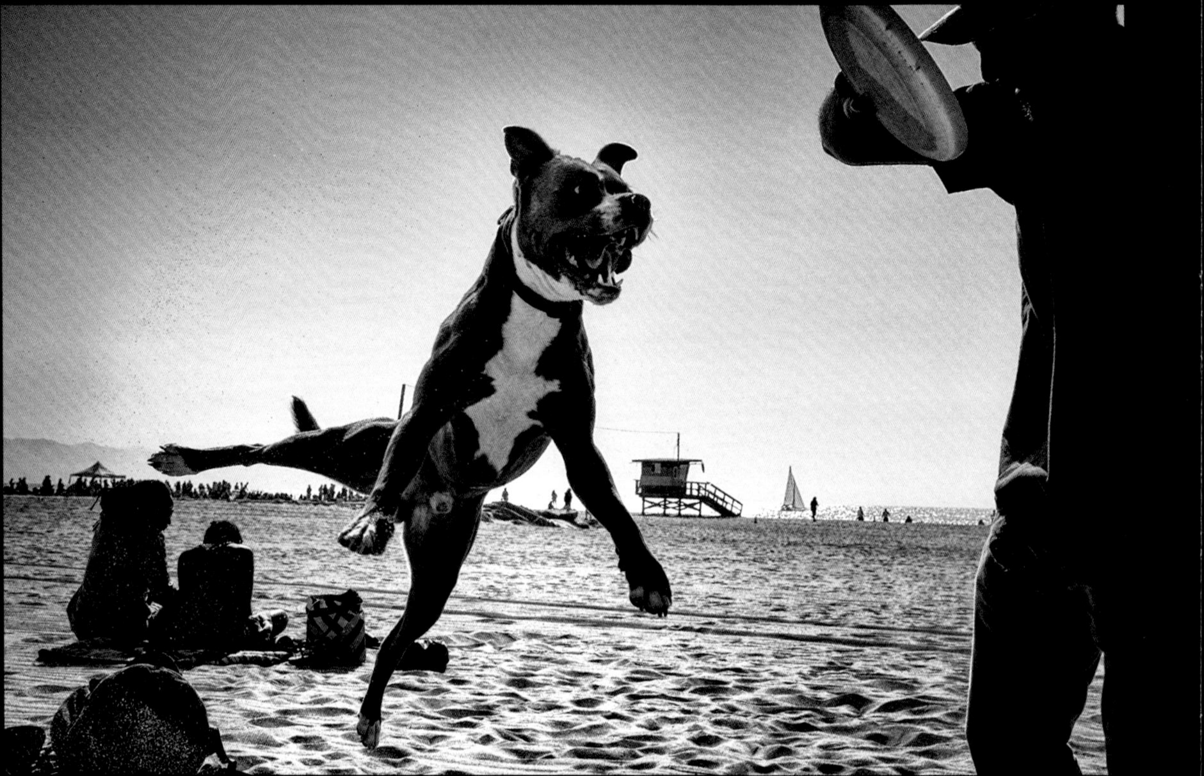

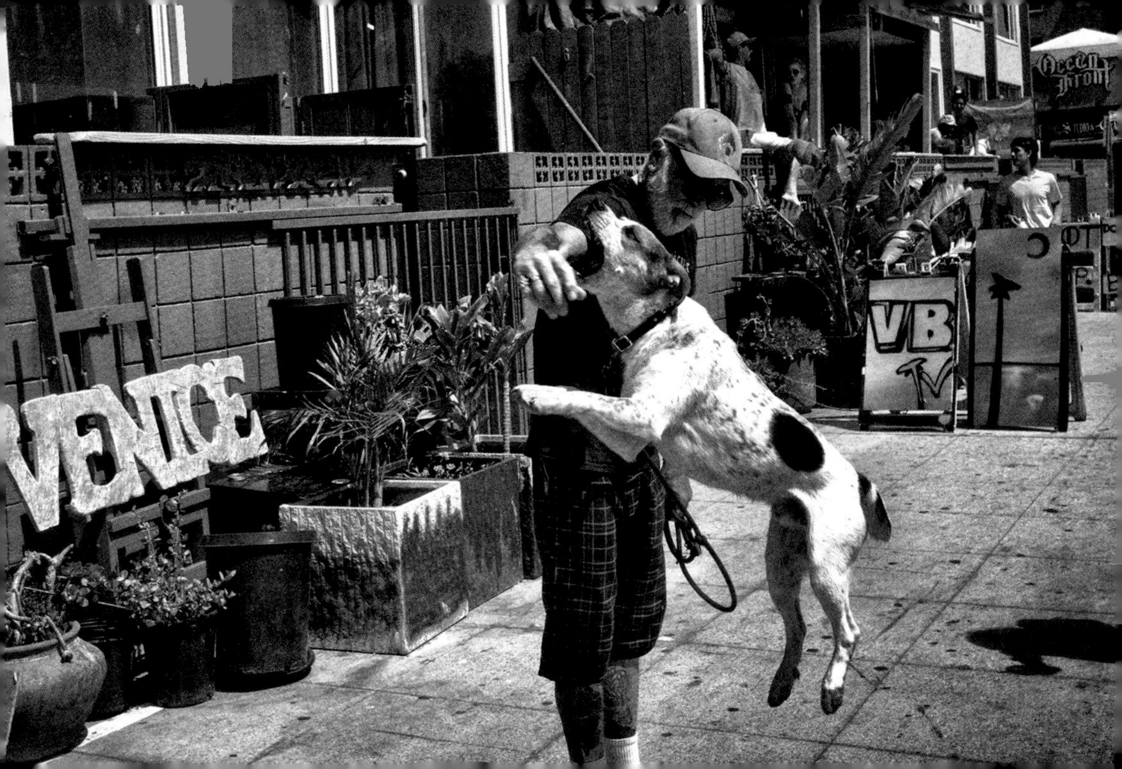
VENICE
VB

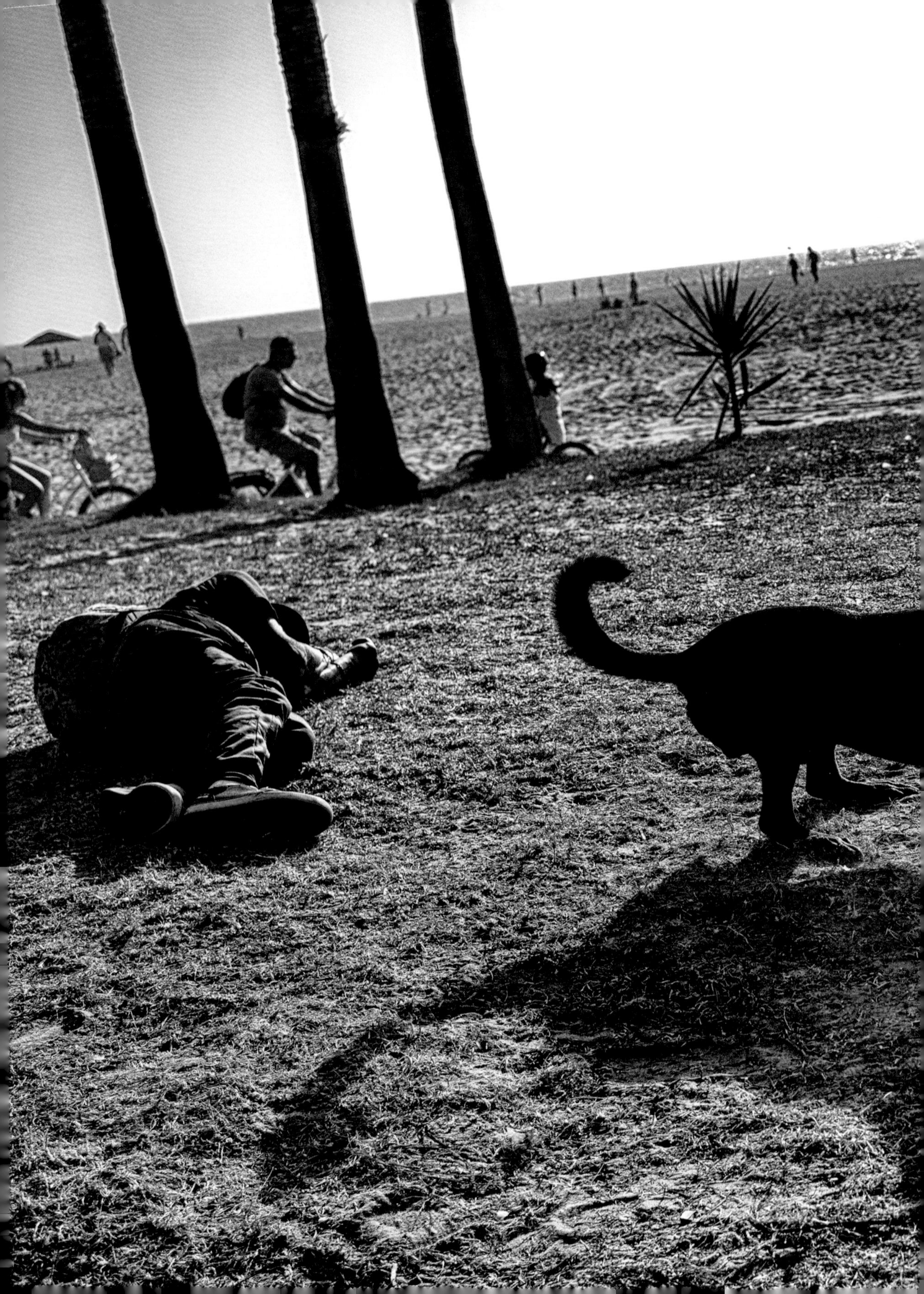

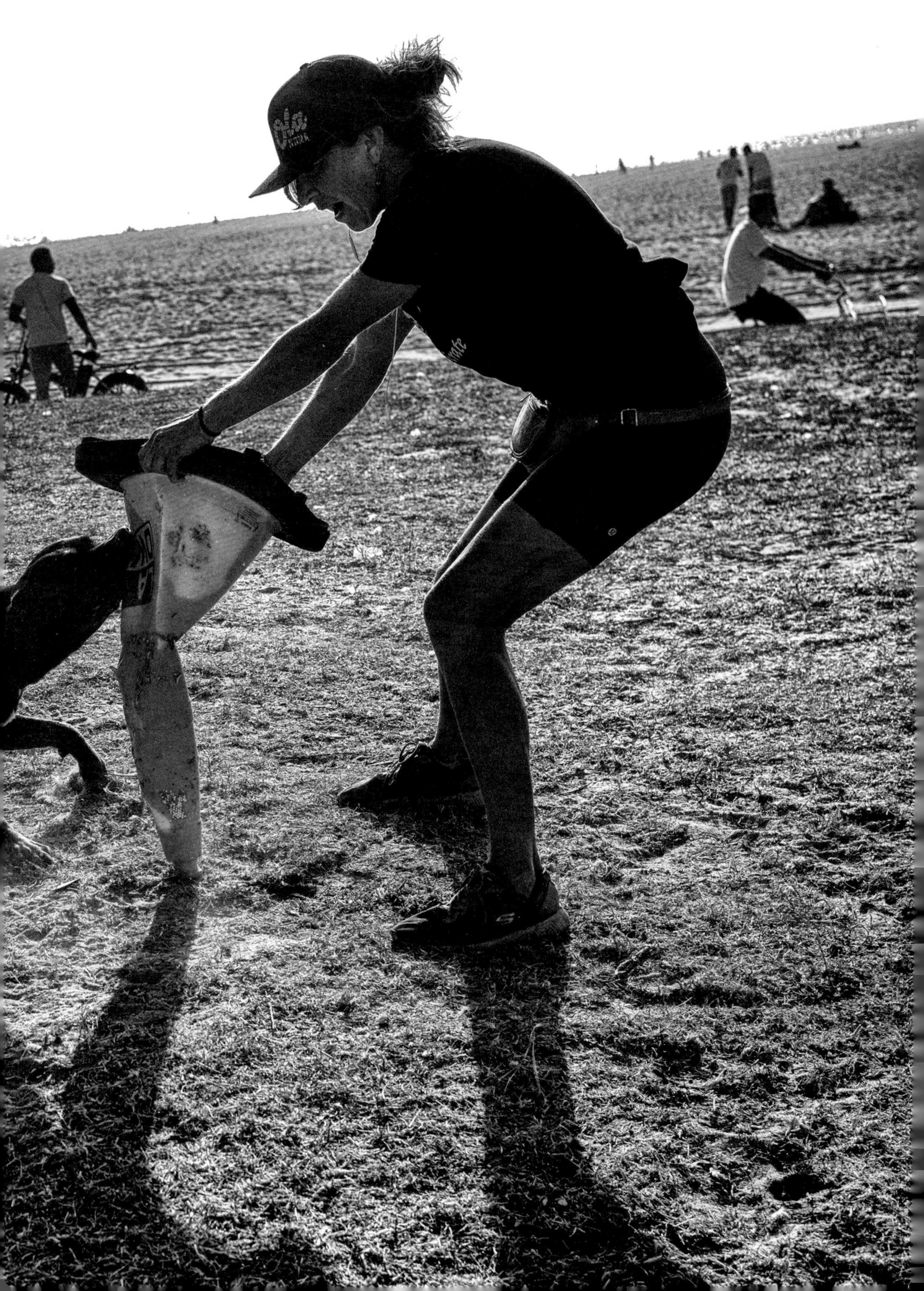

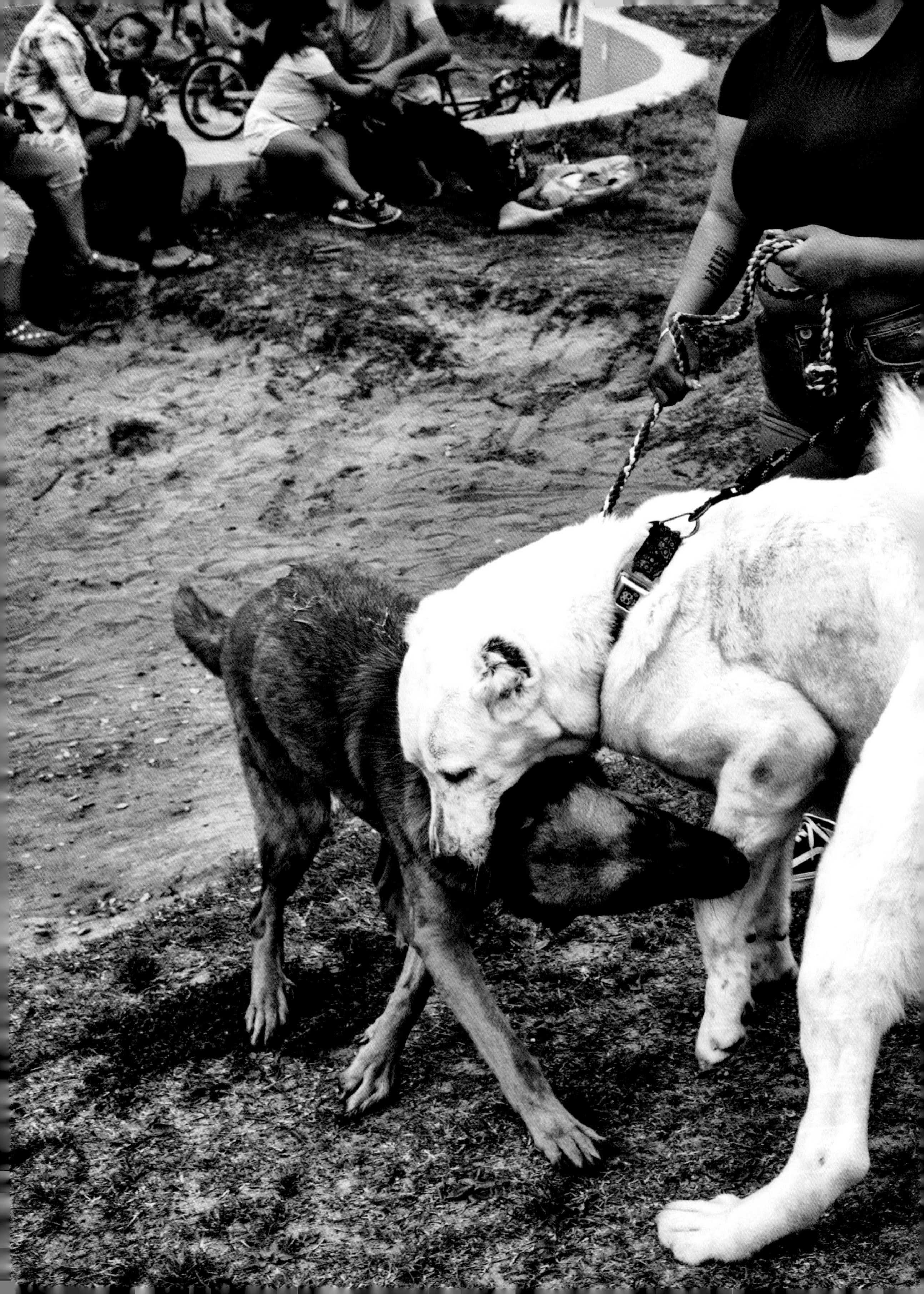

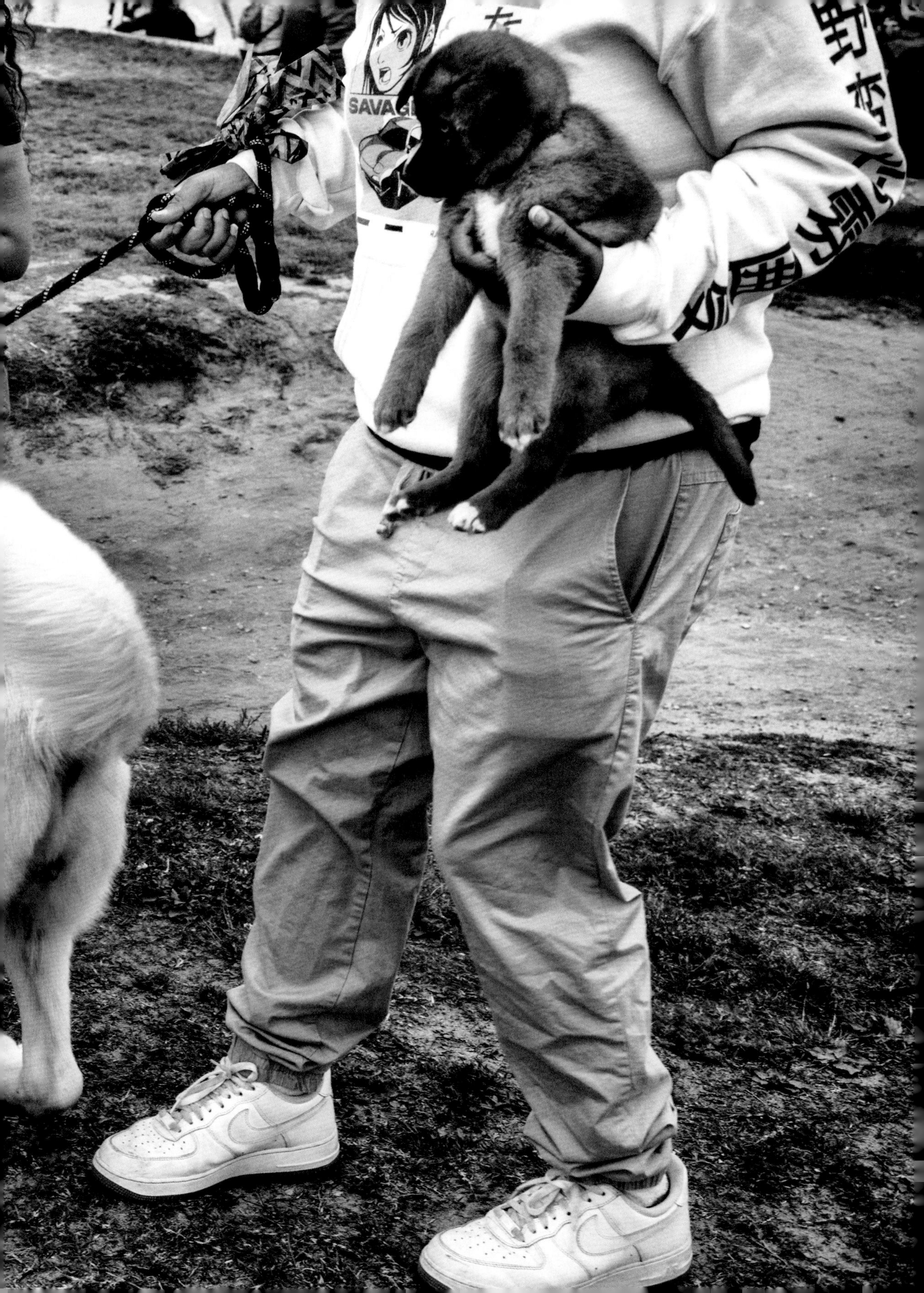

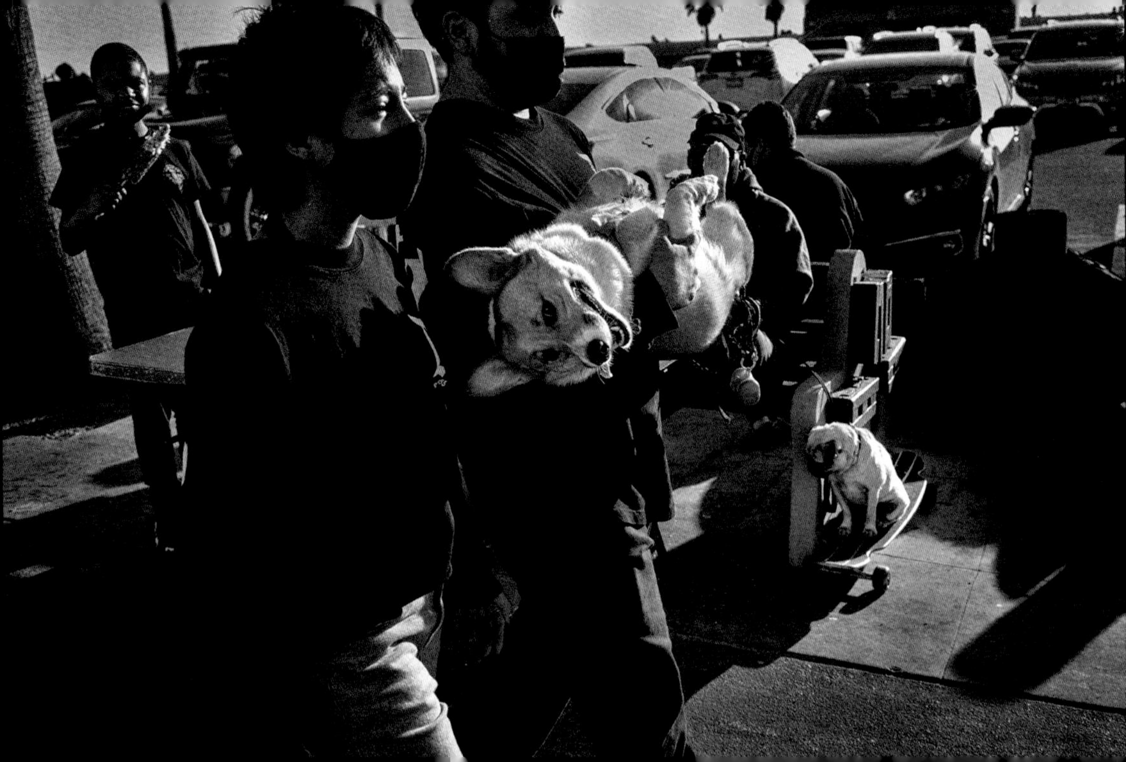

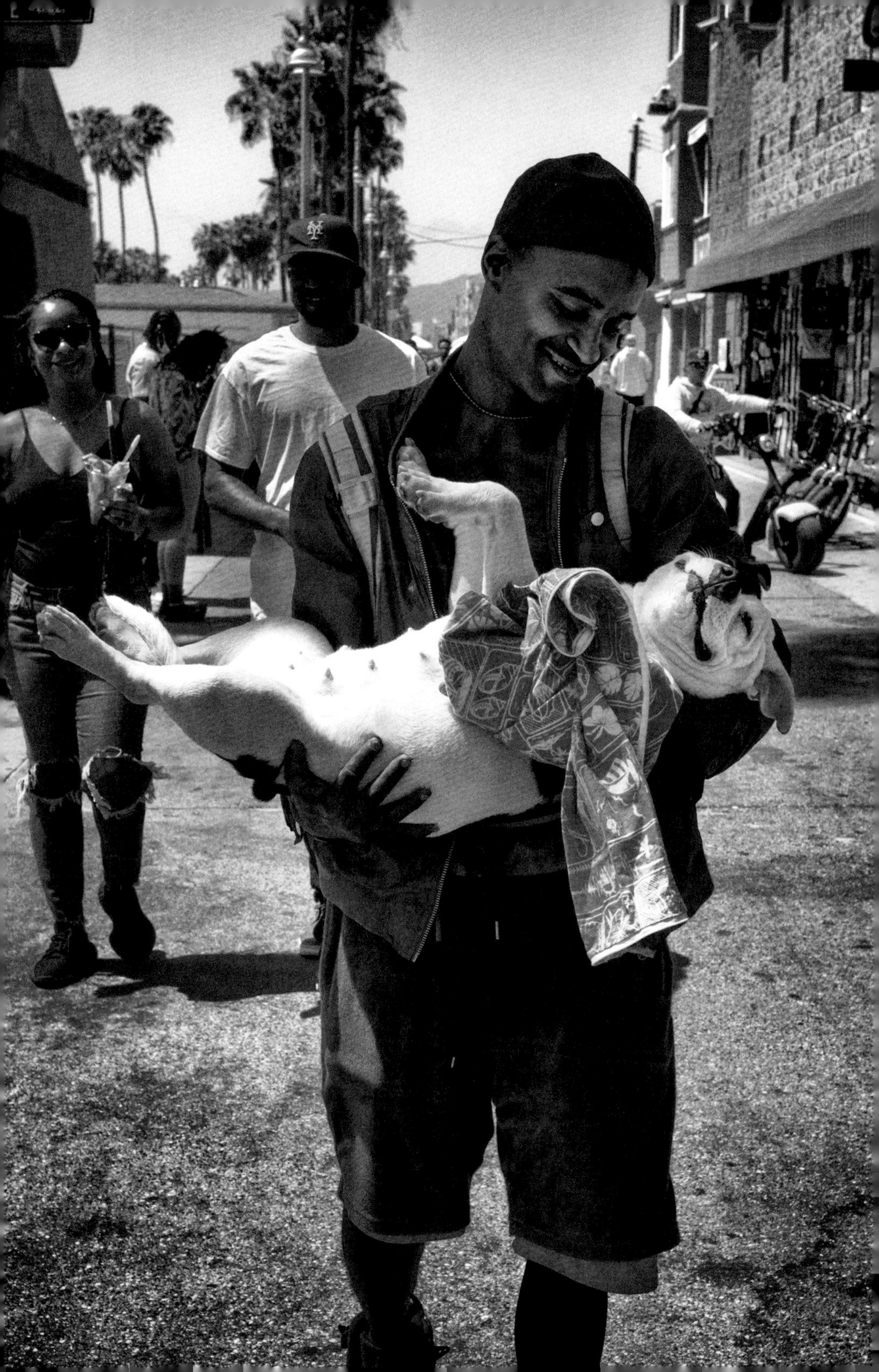

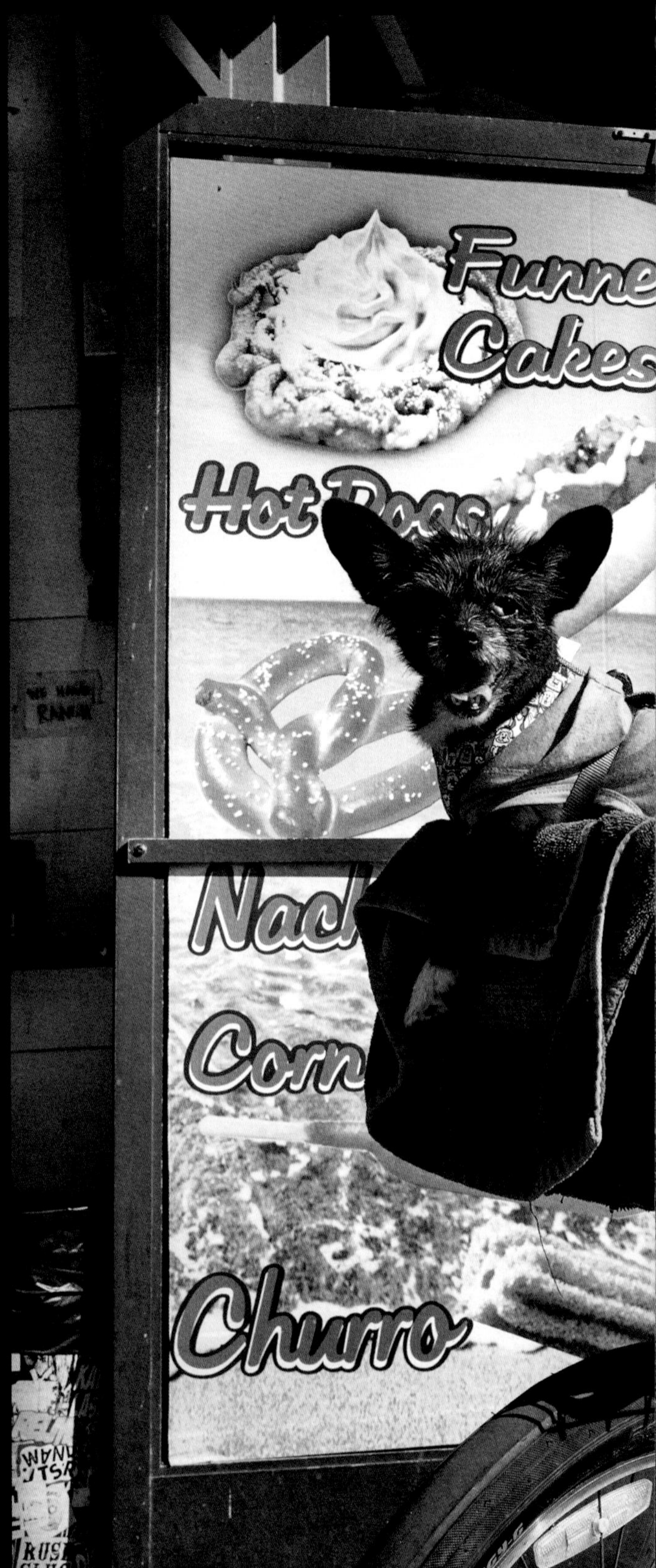

Funne
Cakes
Hot
Nach
Corn
Churro

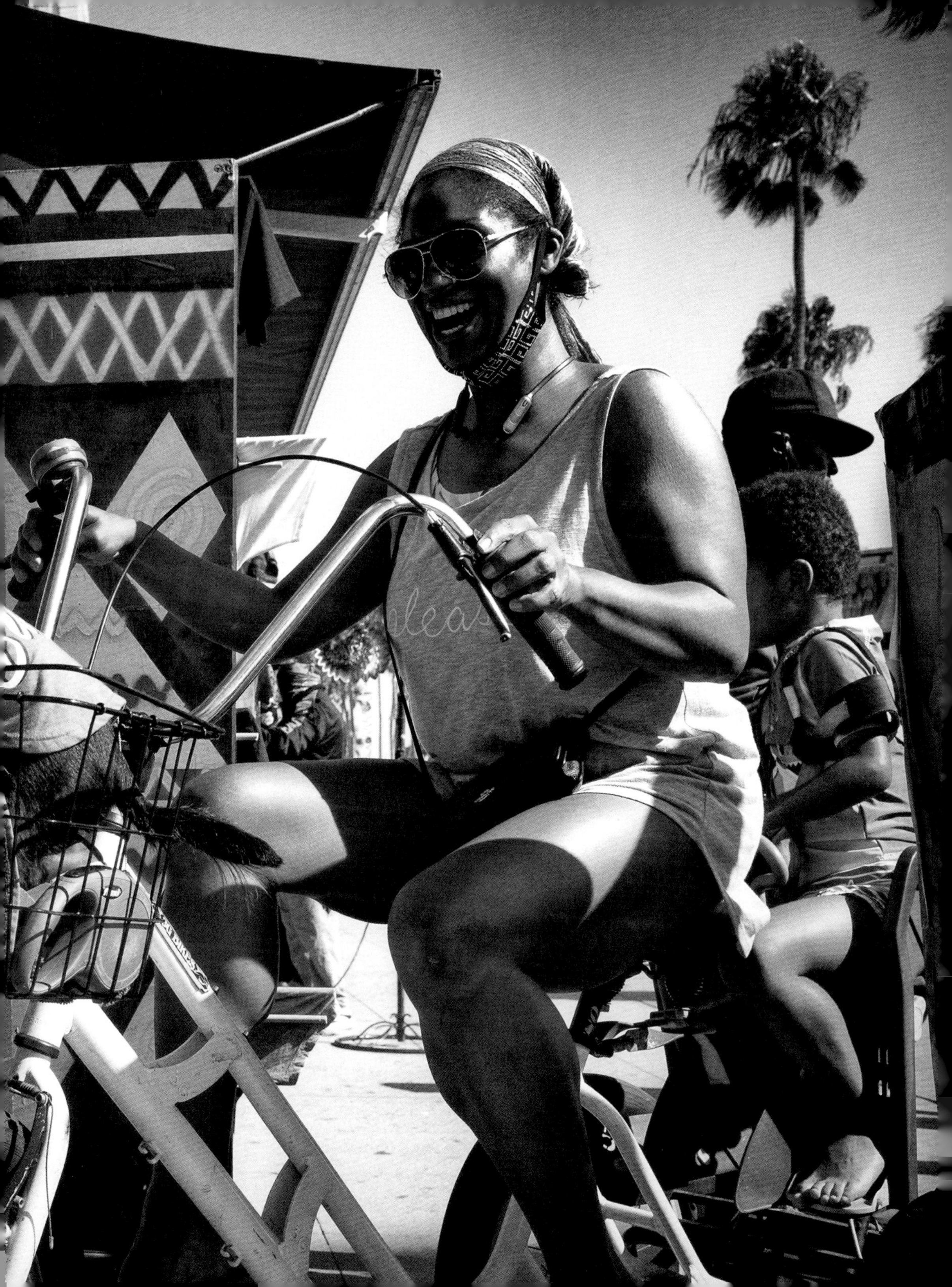

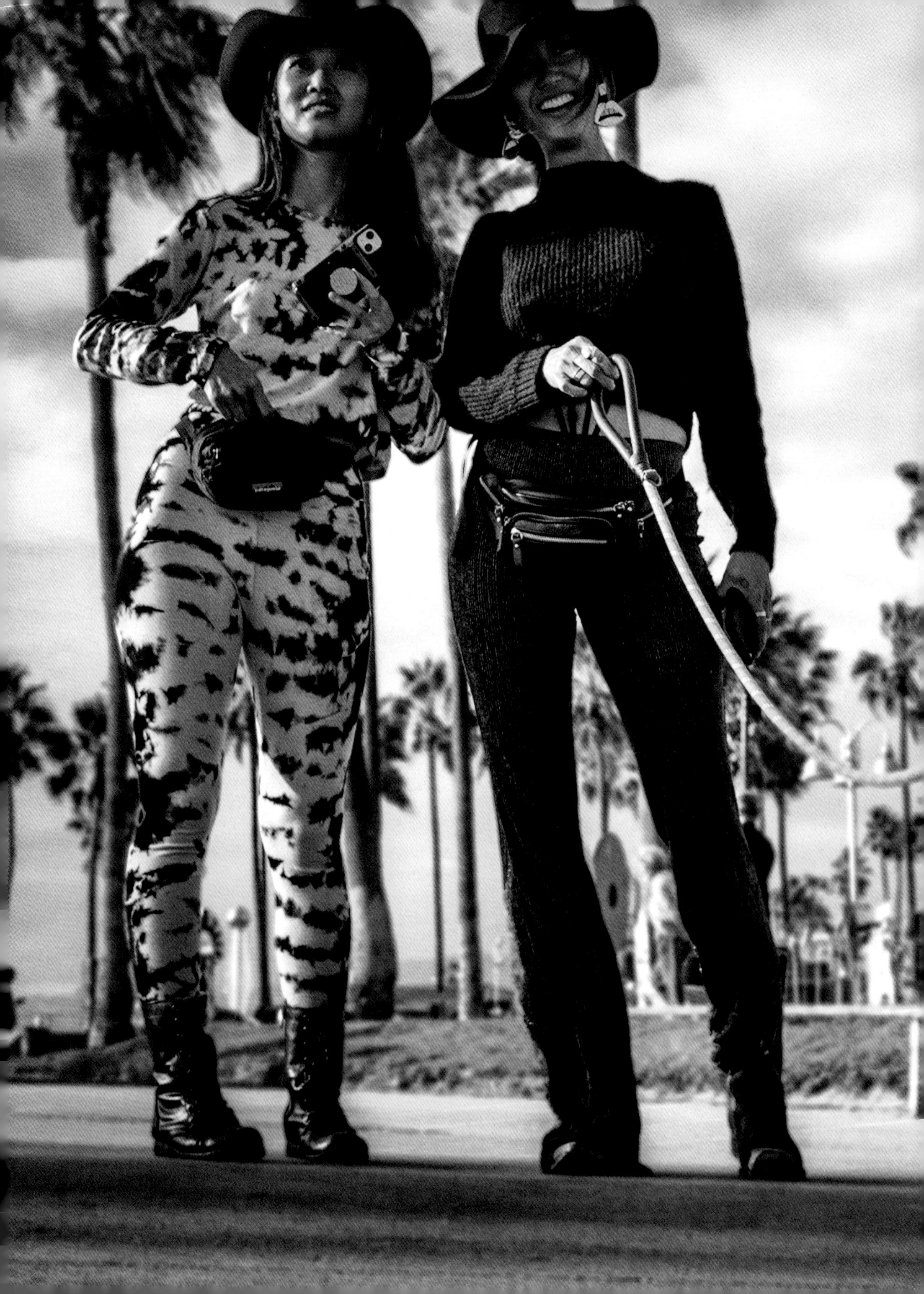

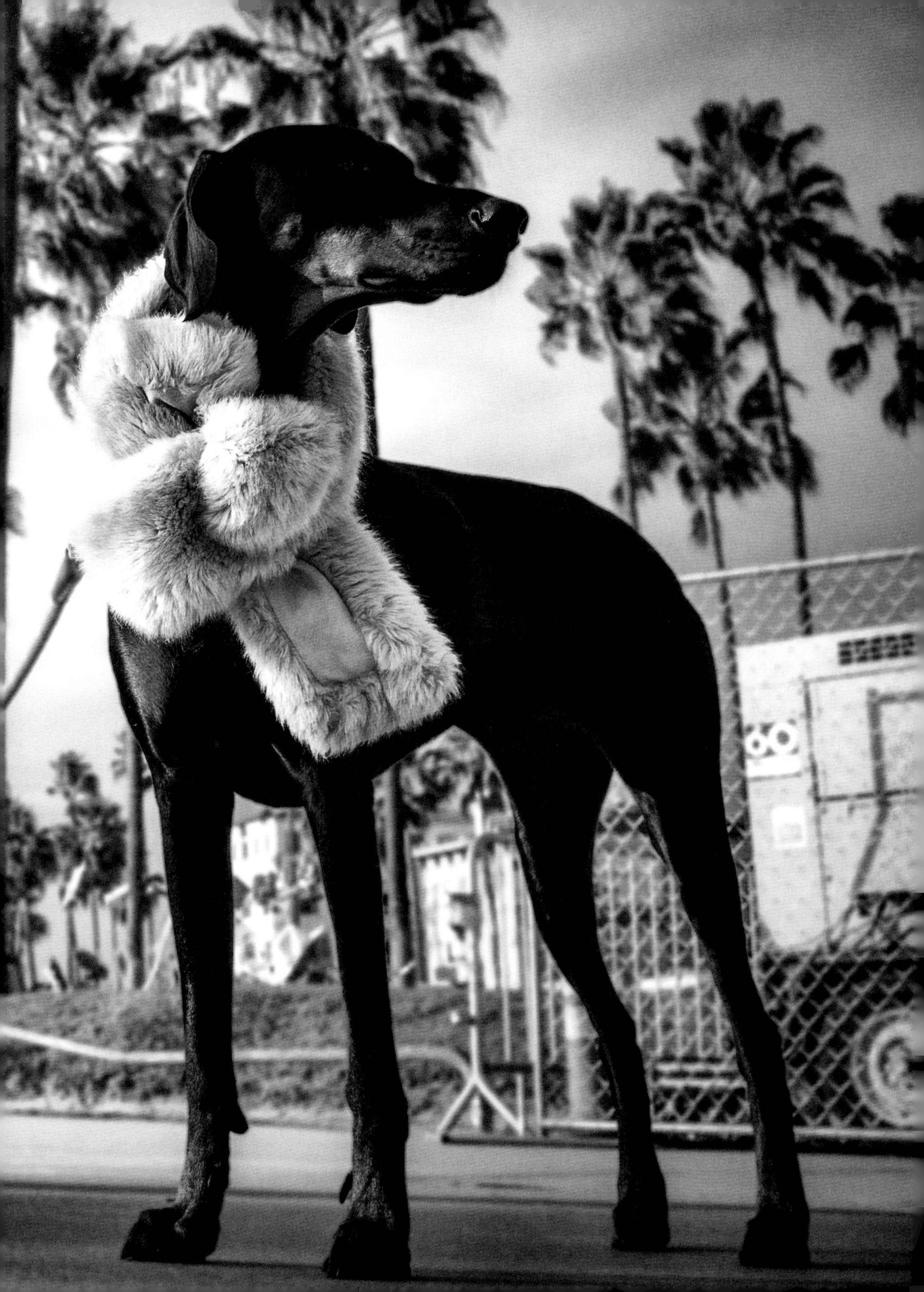

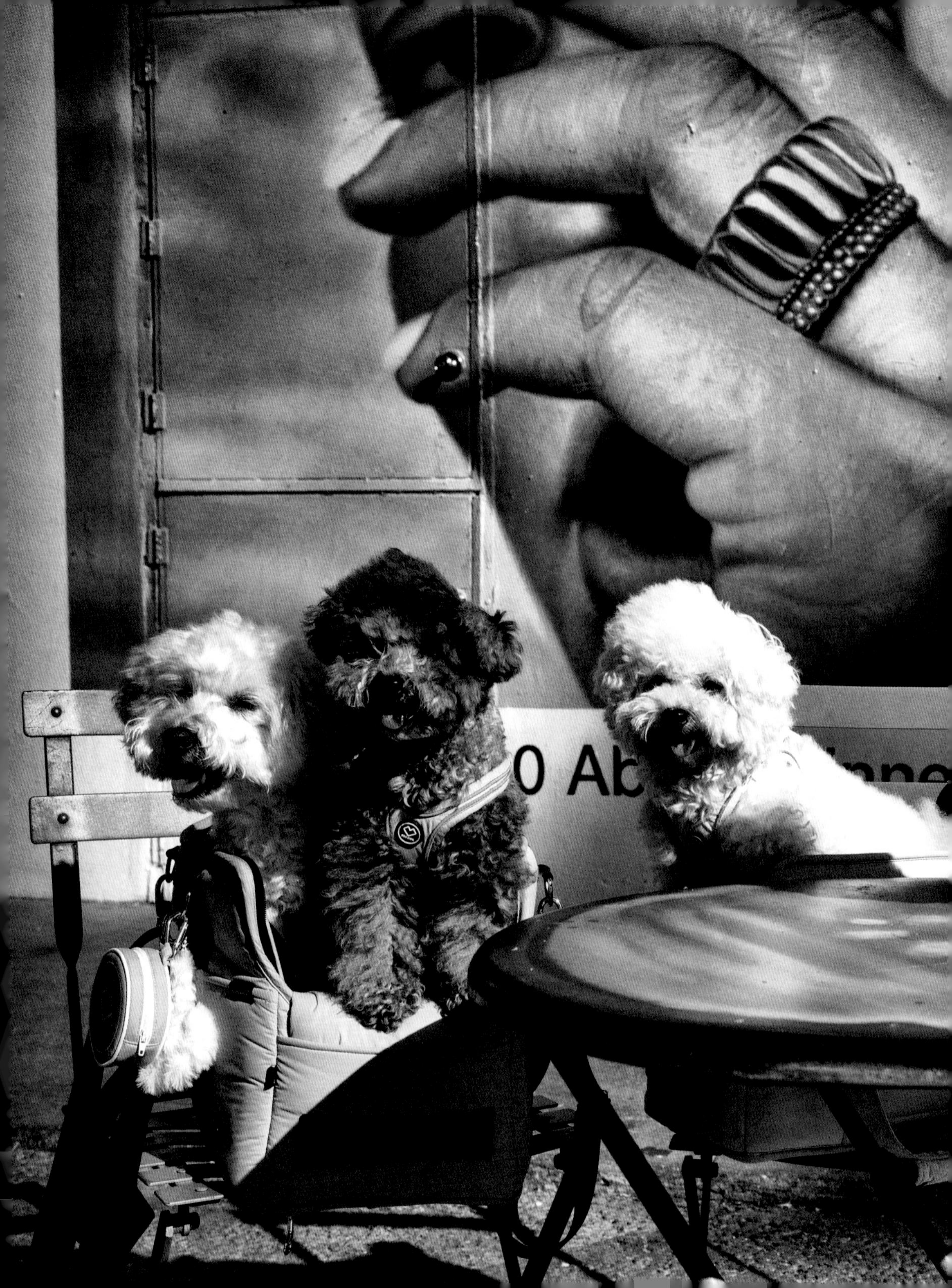

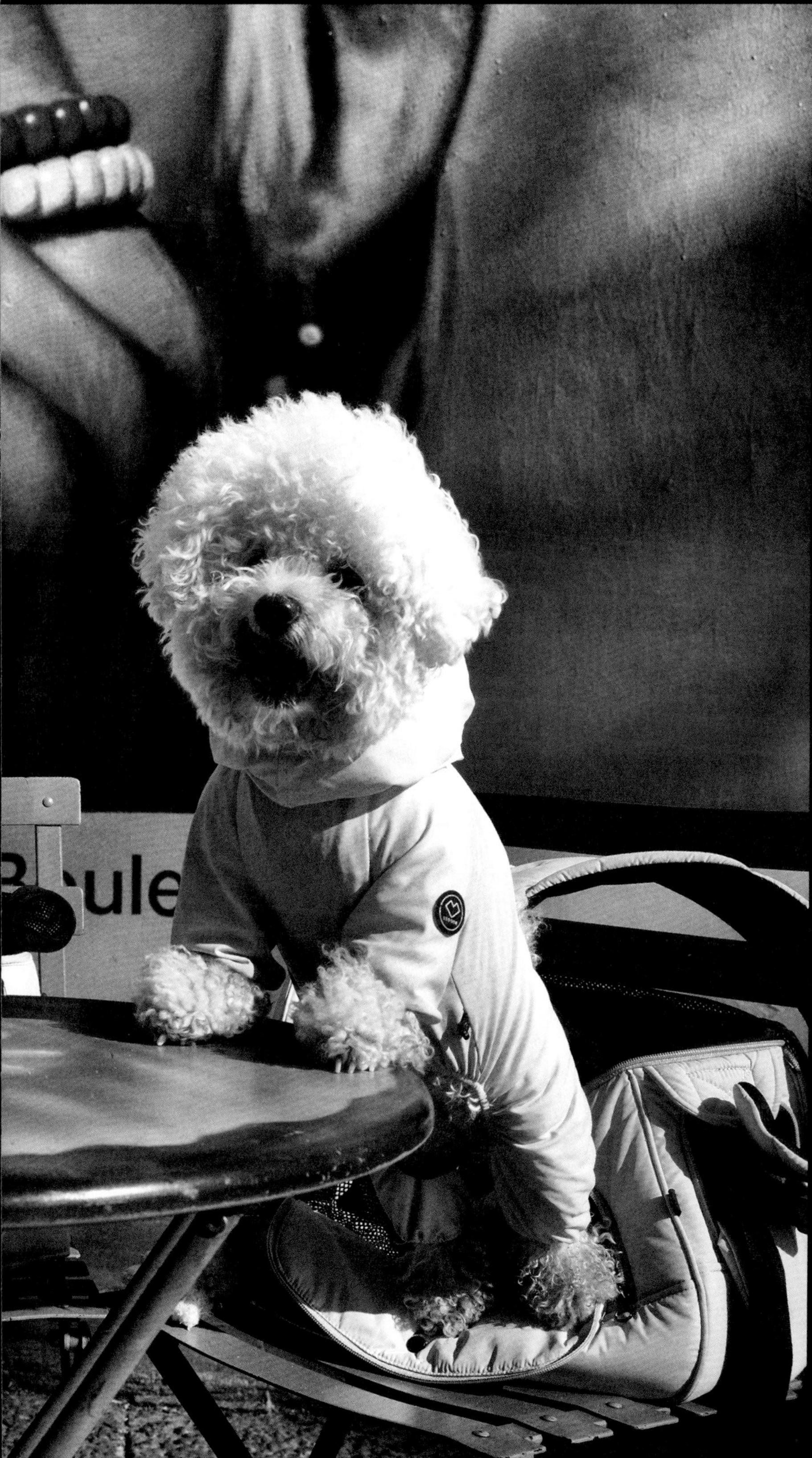

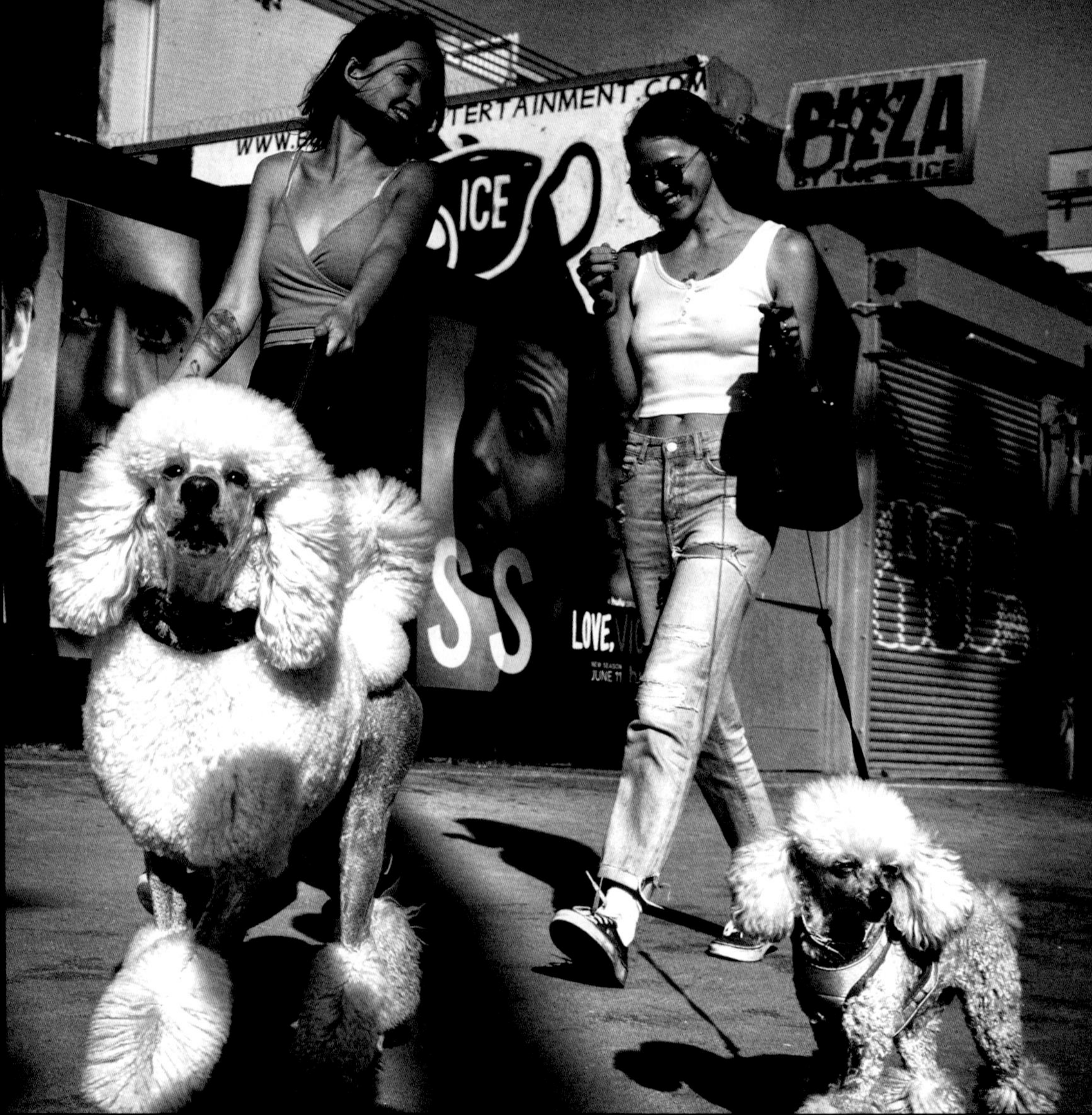
TERTAINMENT.COM
ICE
SS
LOVE,
NEW SEASON
JUNE 11

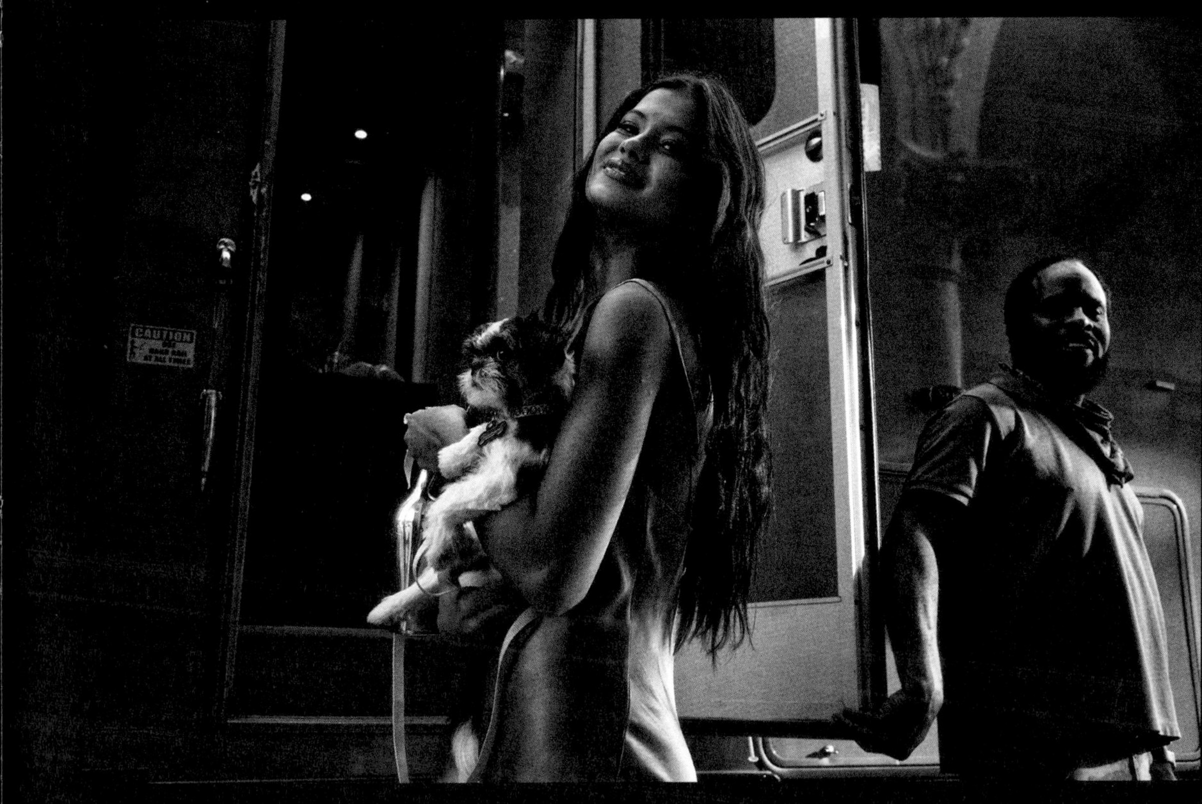
CAUTION

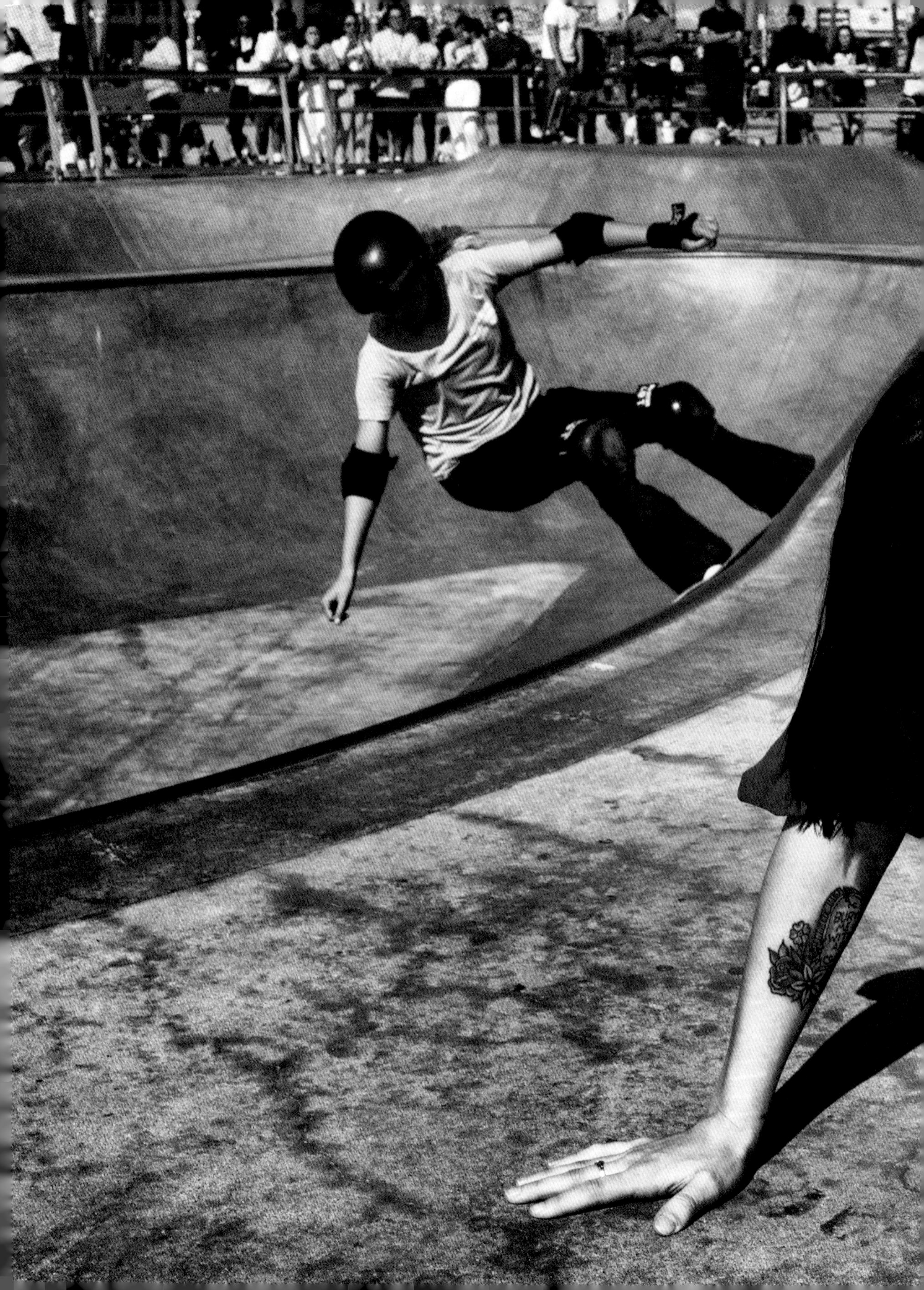

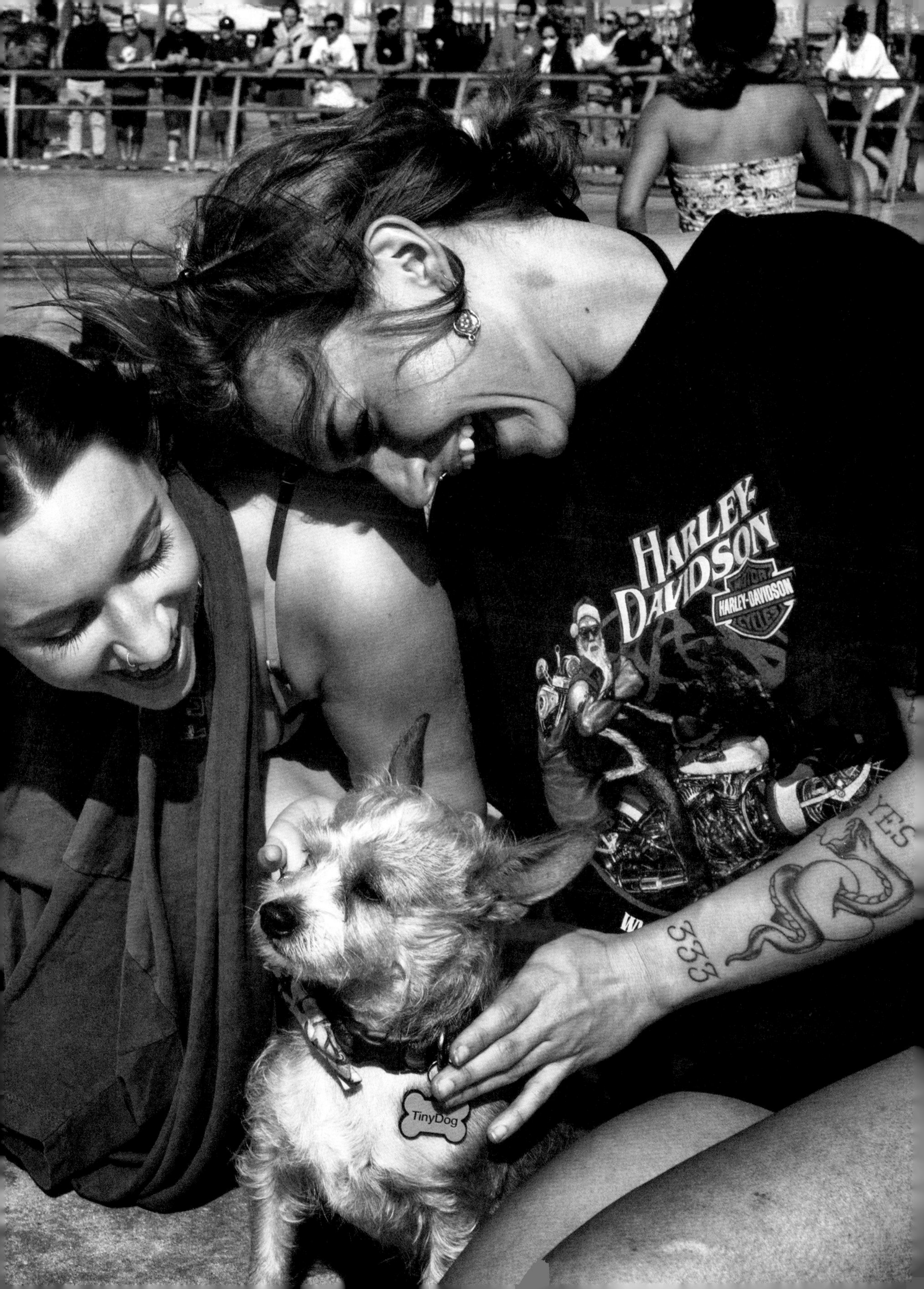
HARLEY-DAVIDSON
HARLEY-DAVIDSON
TinyDog
YES
333

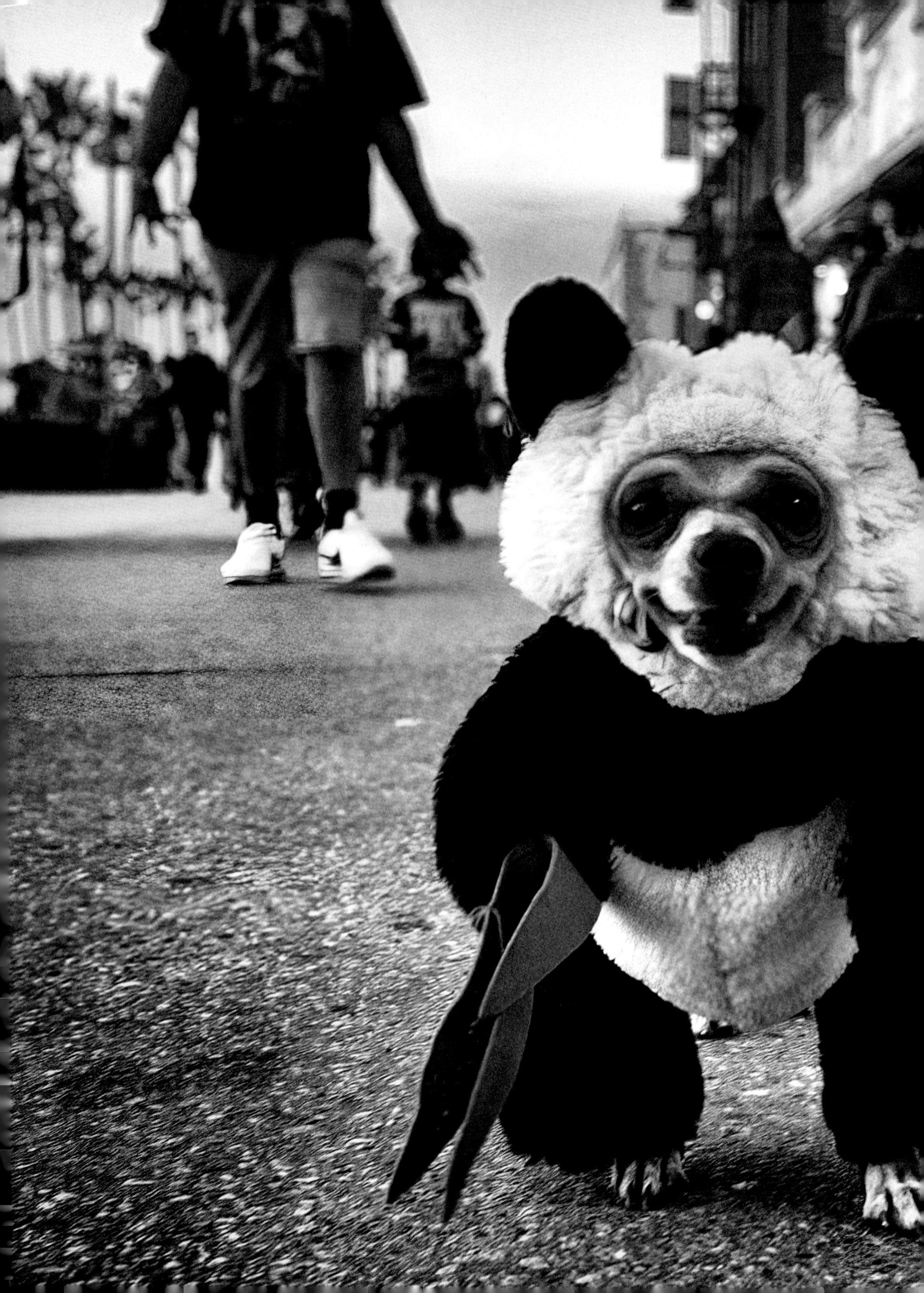

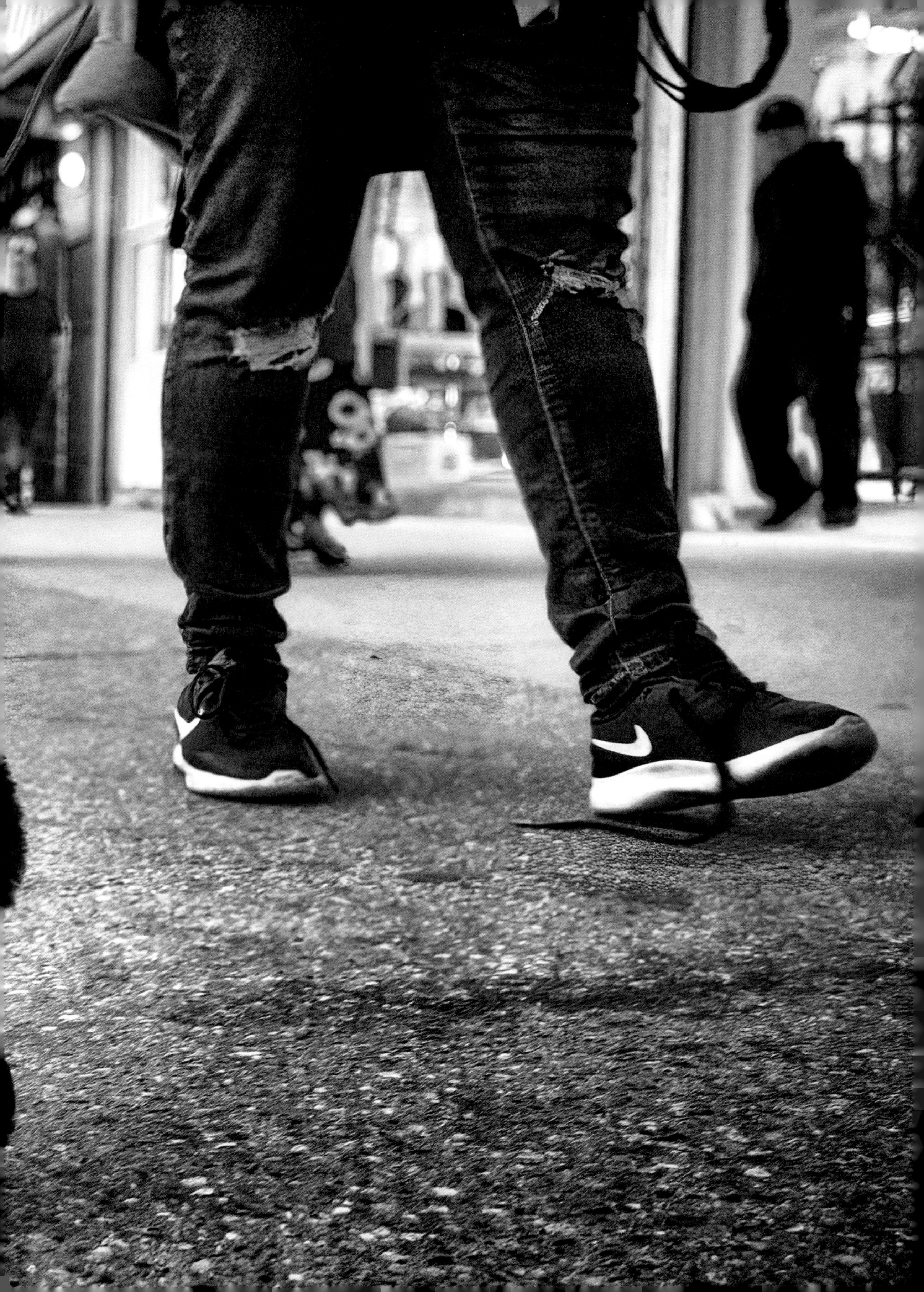

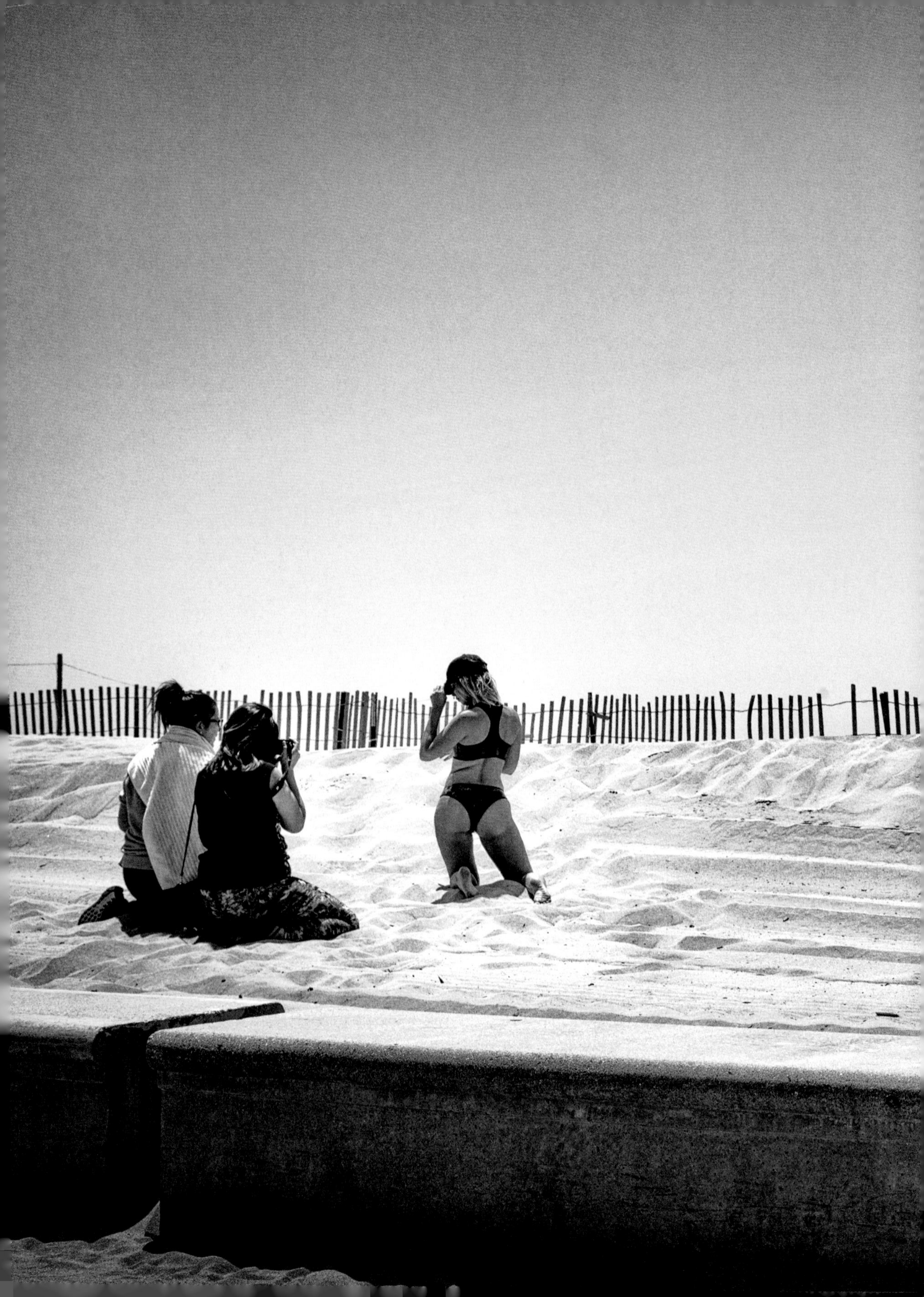

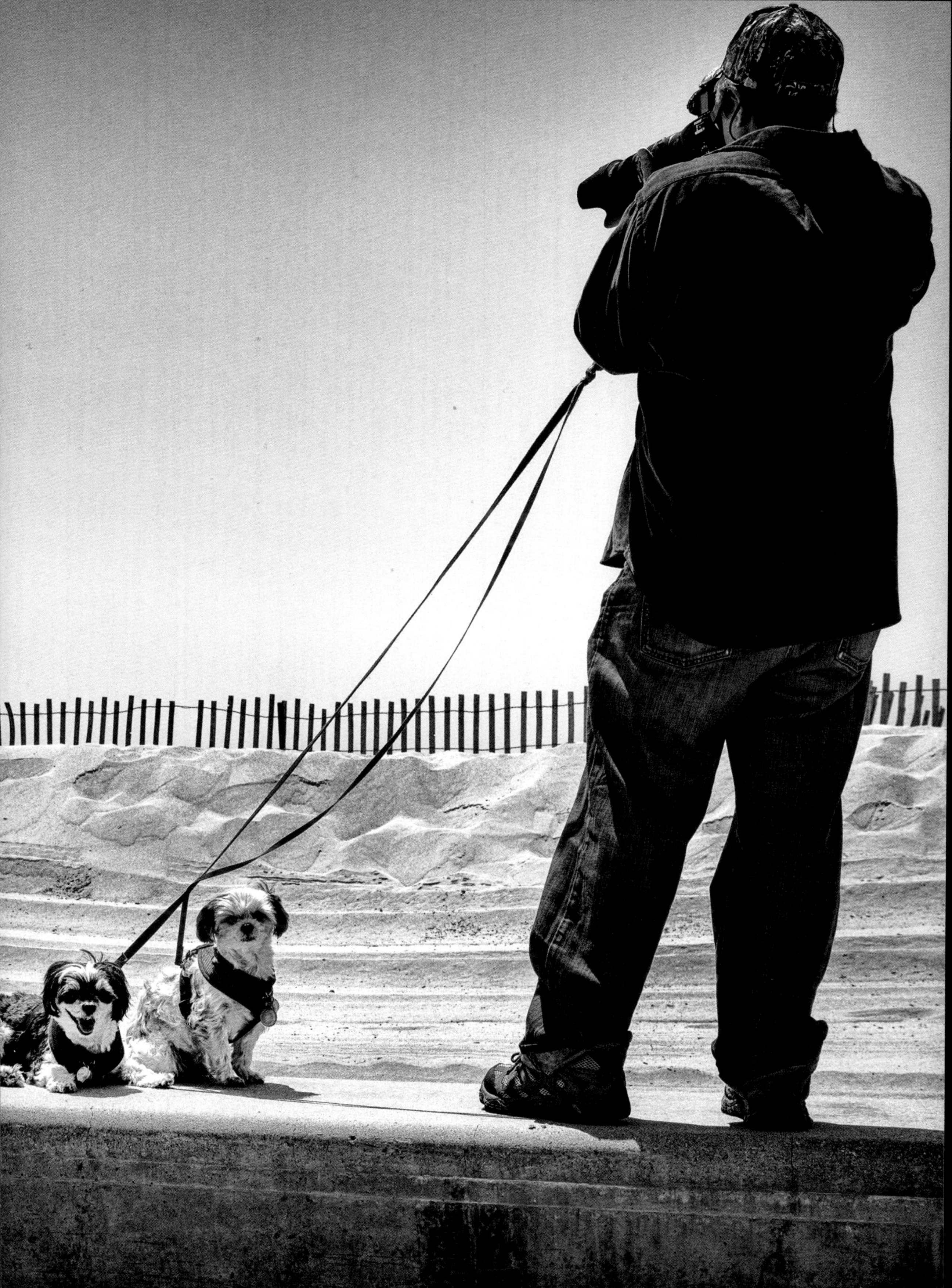

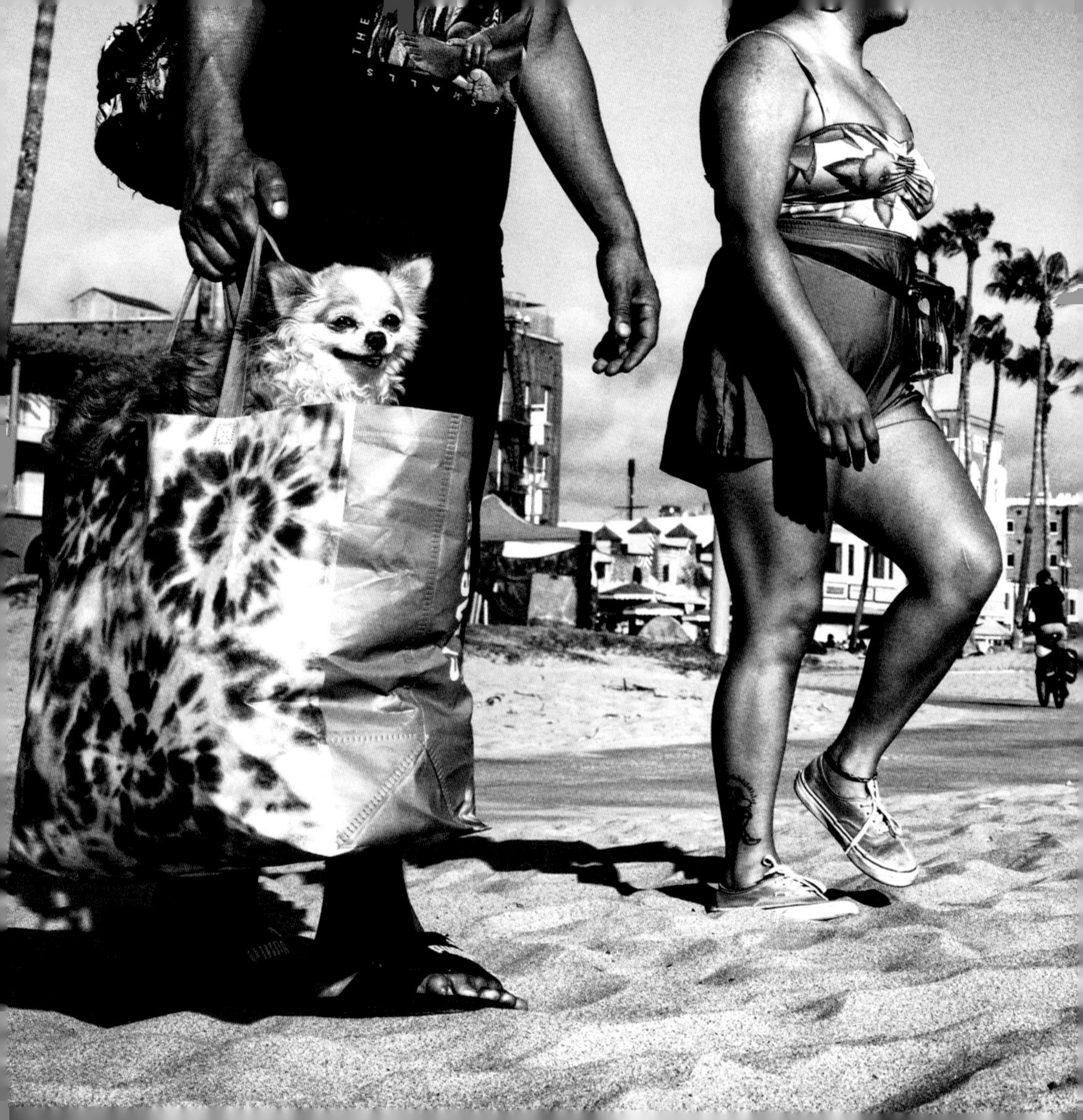

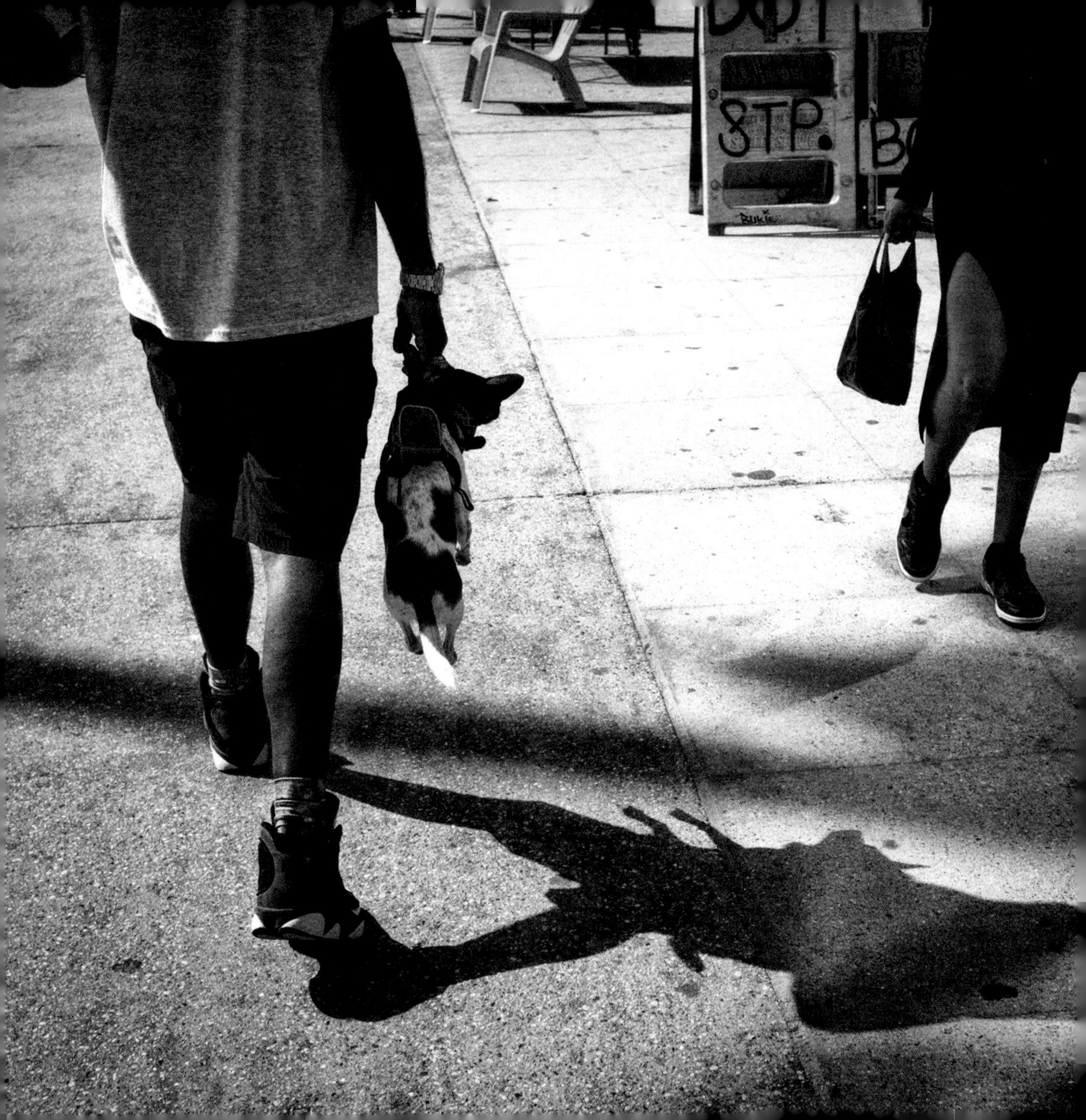
STP.

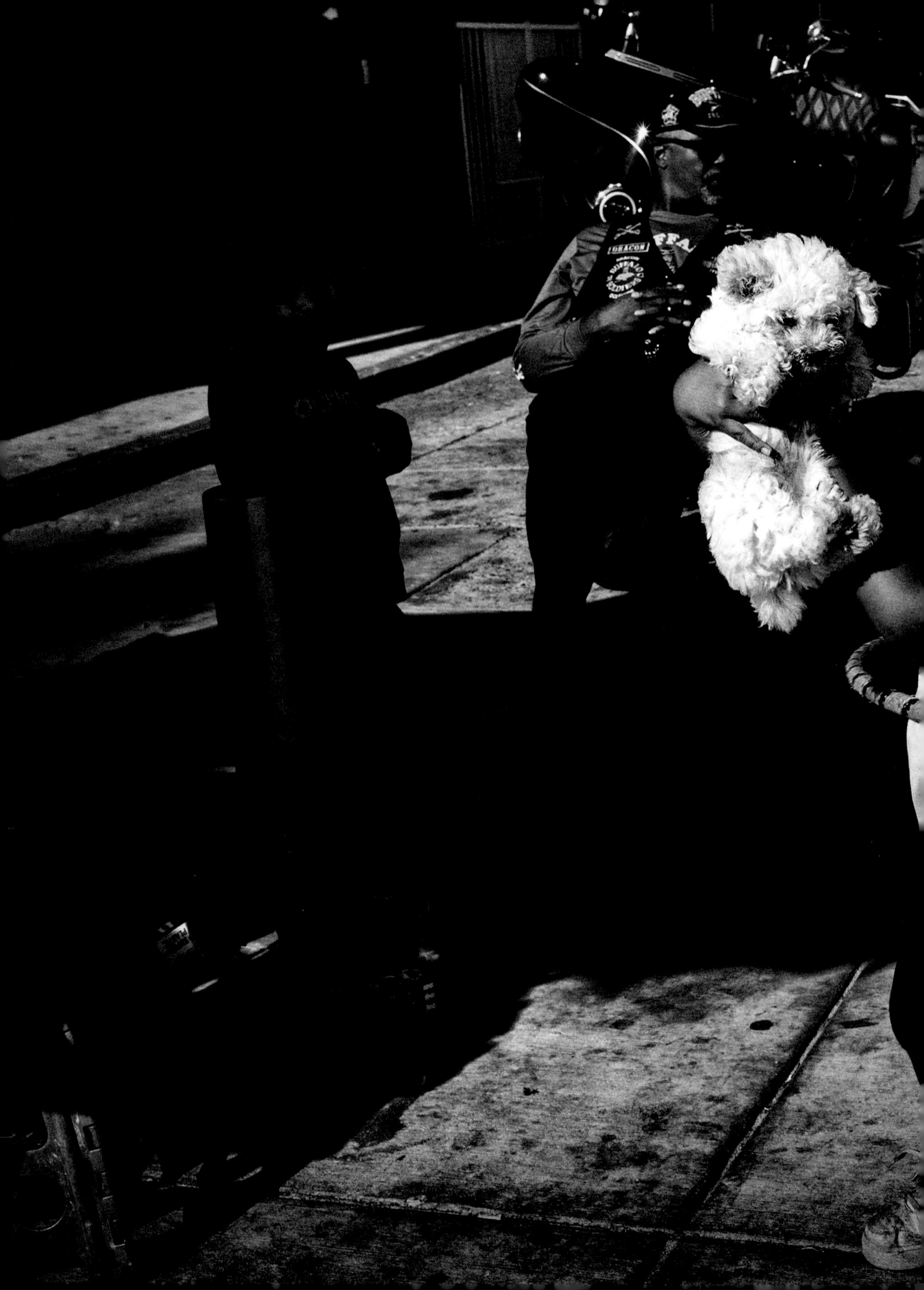
DEACON

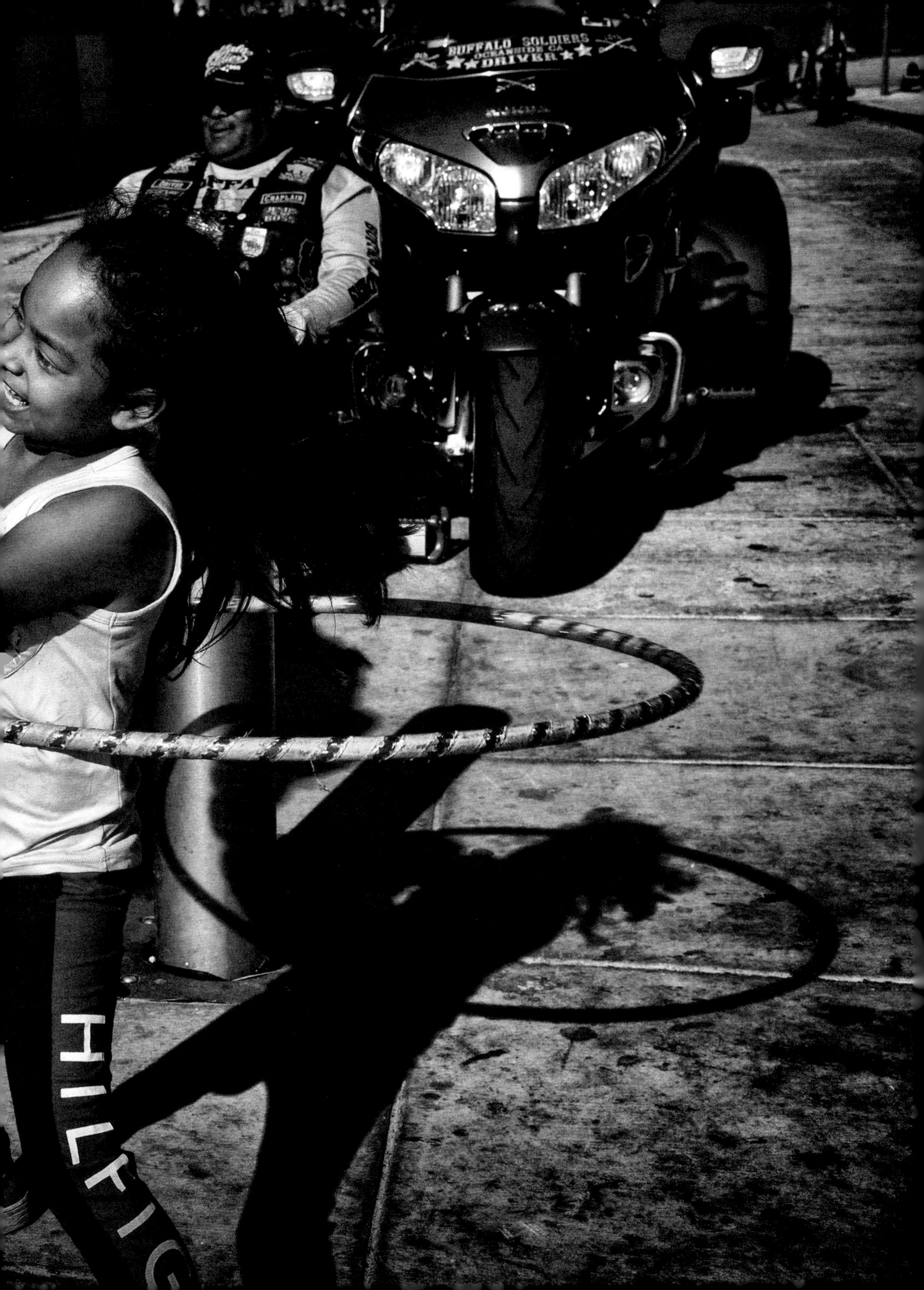
BUFFALO SOLDIERS
OCEANSIDE CA
DRIVER
CHAPLAIN
HILFIG

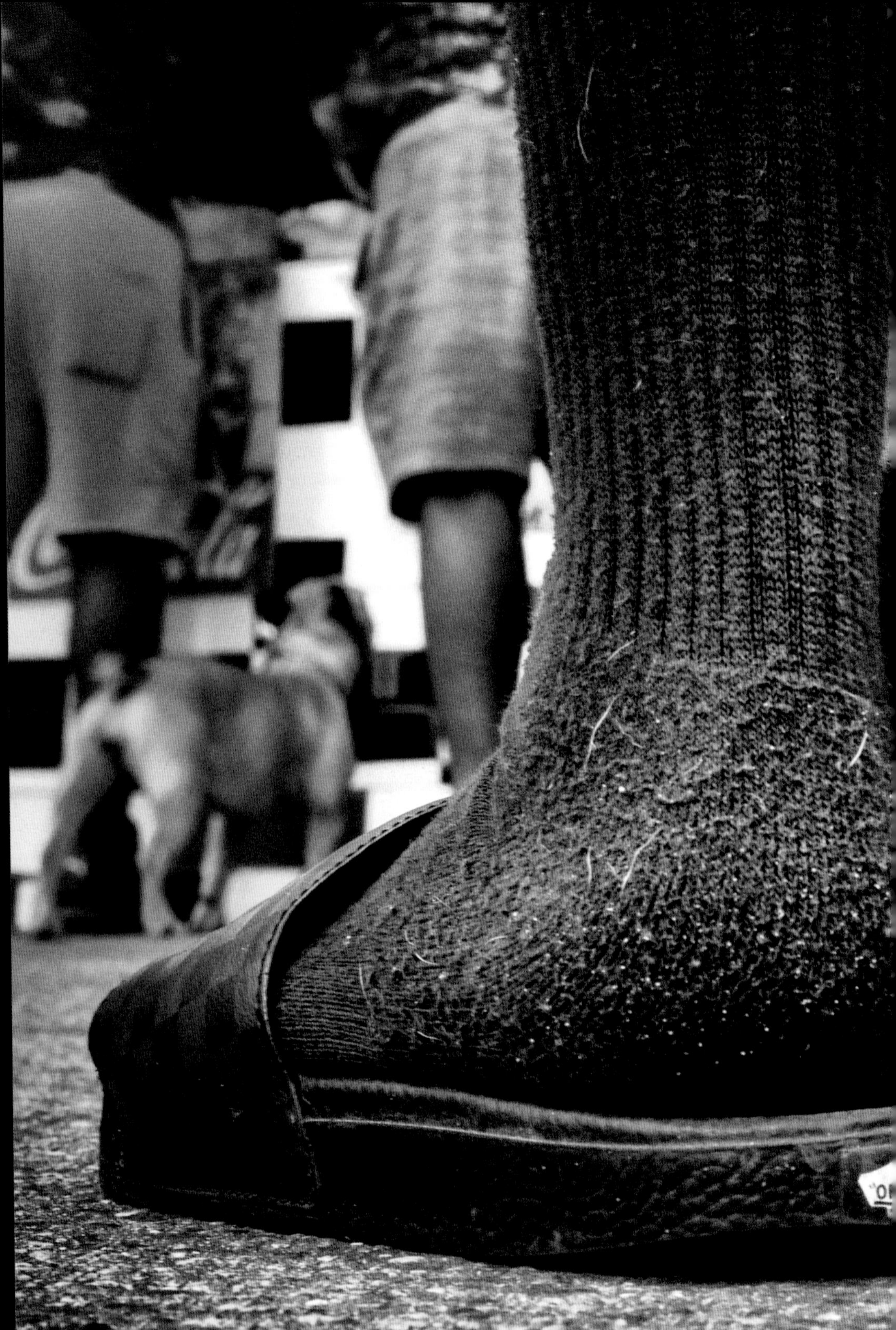

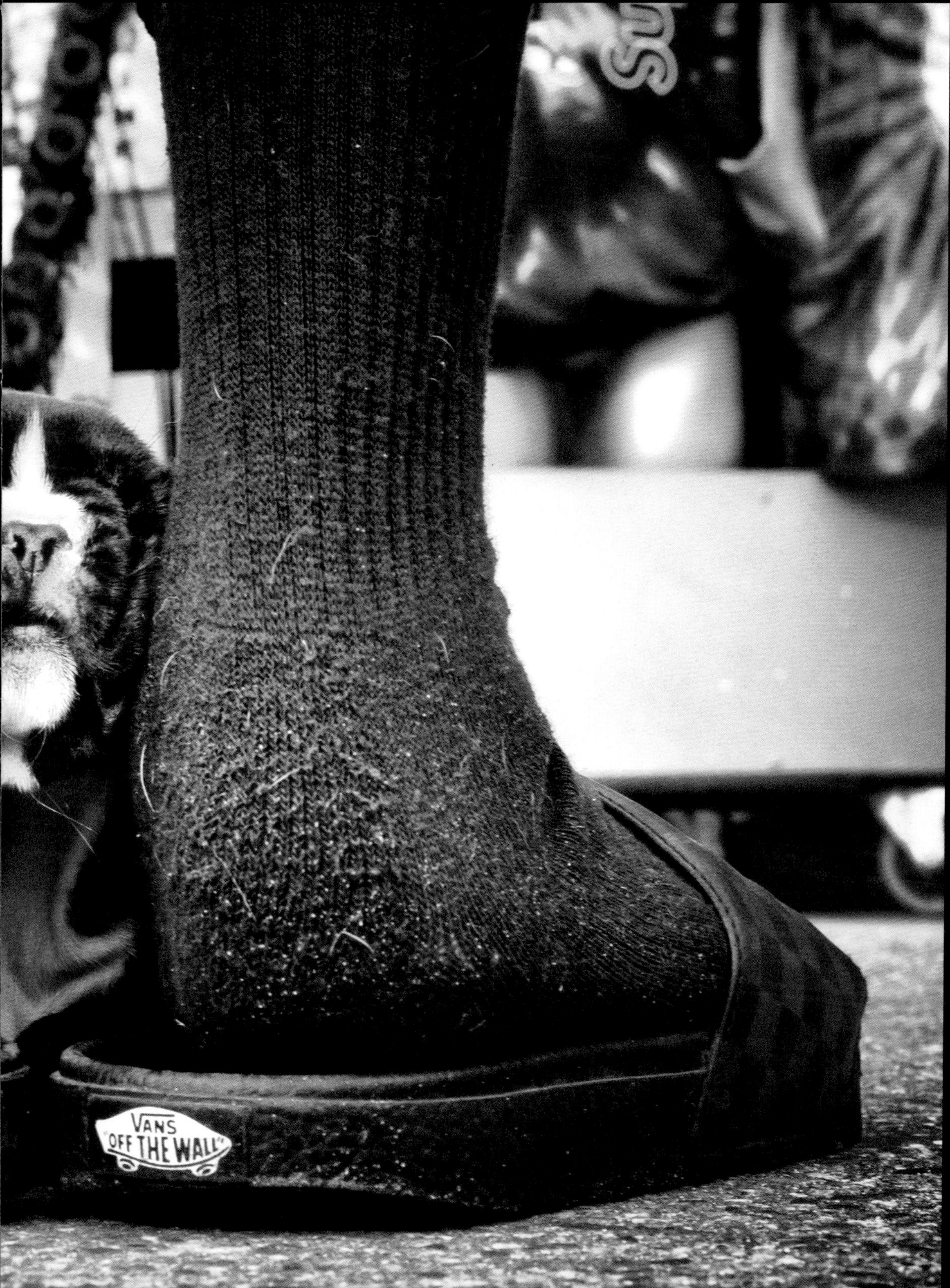
VANS
"OFF THE WALL"

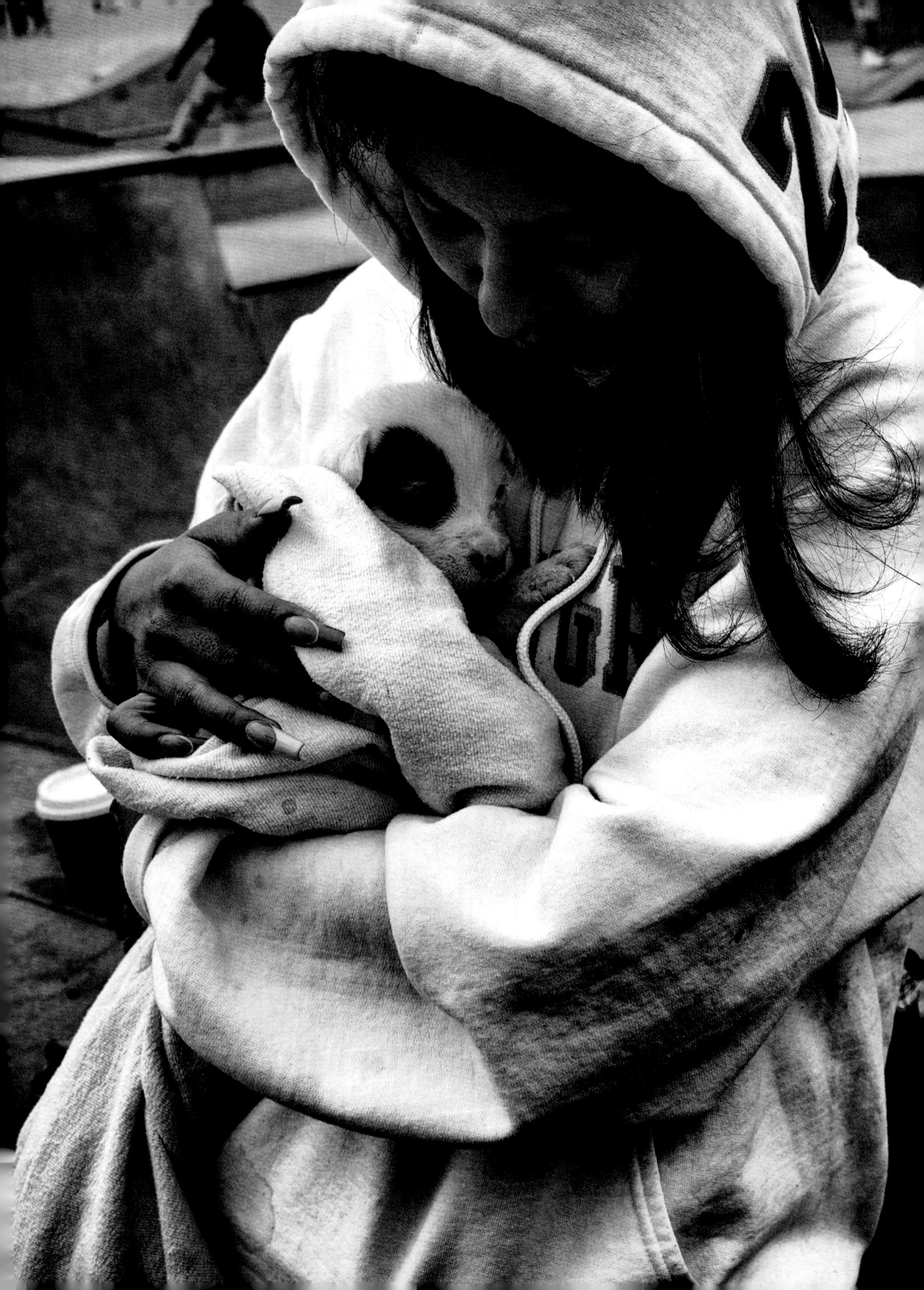

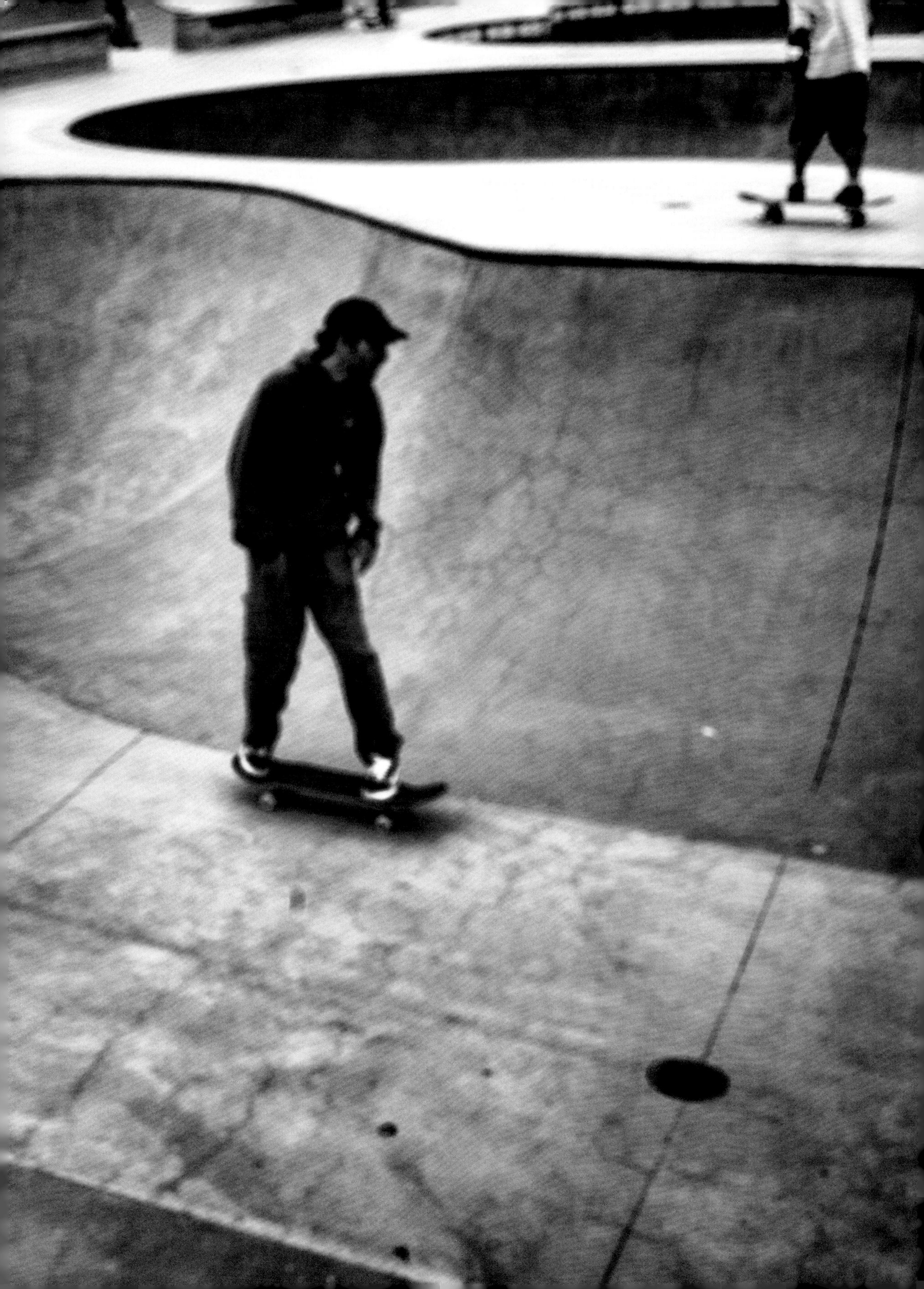

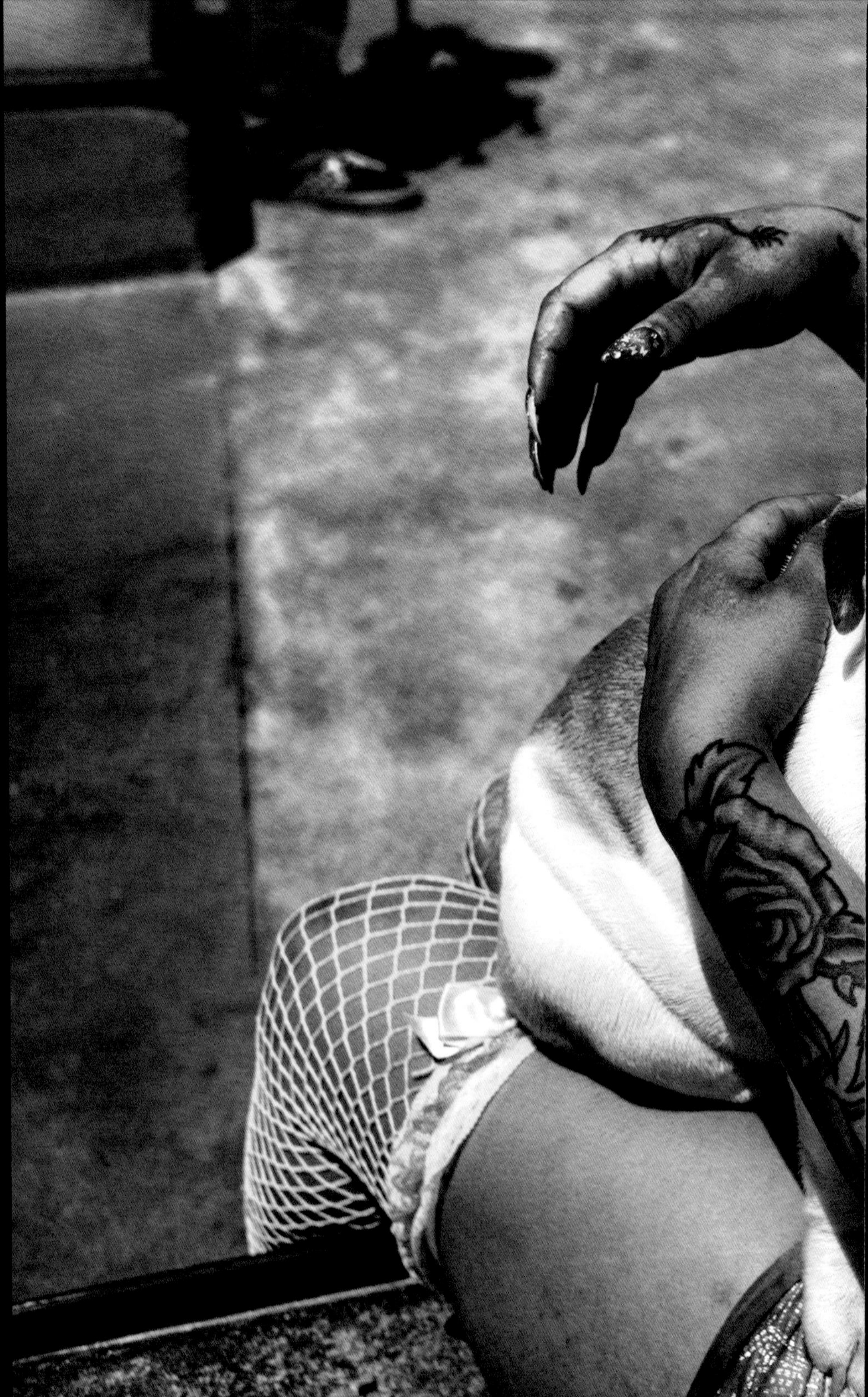

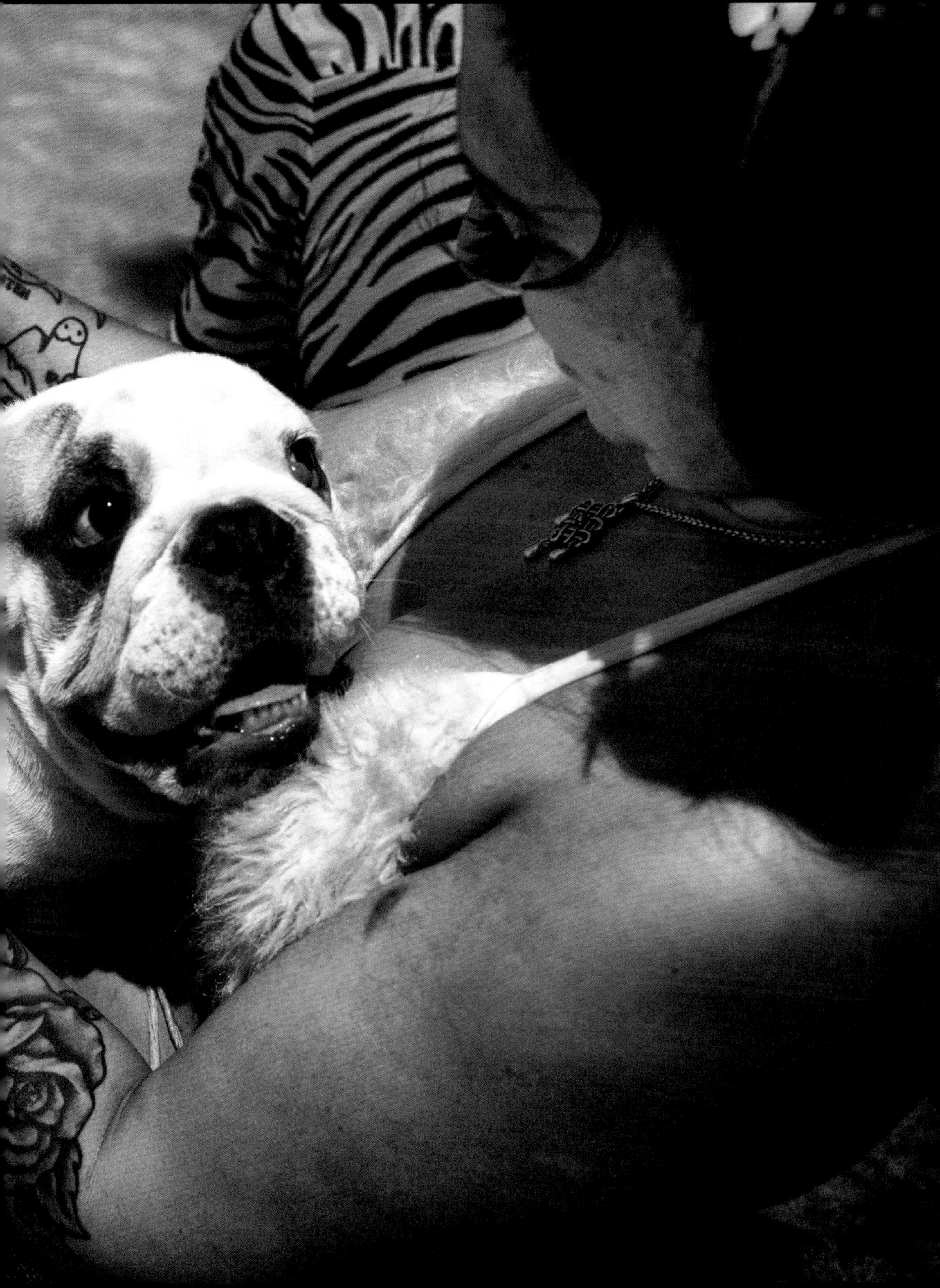

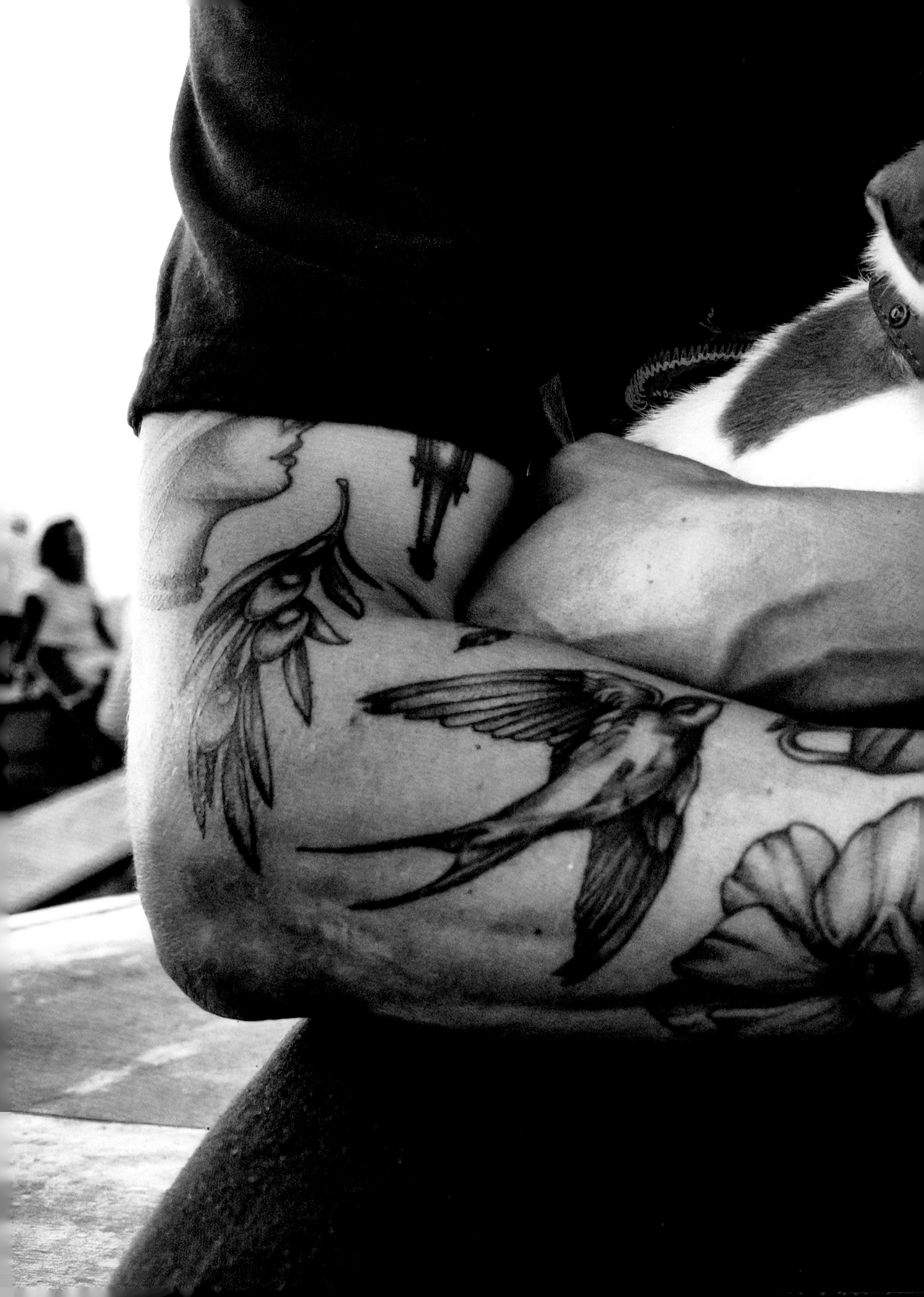

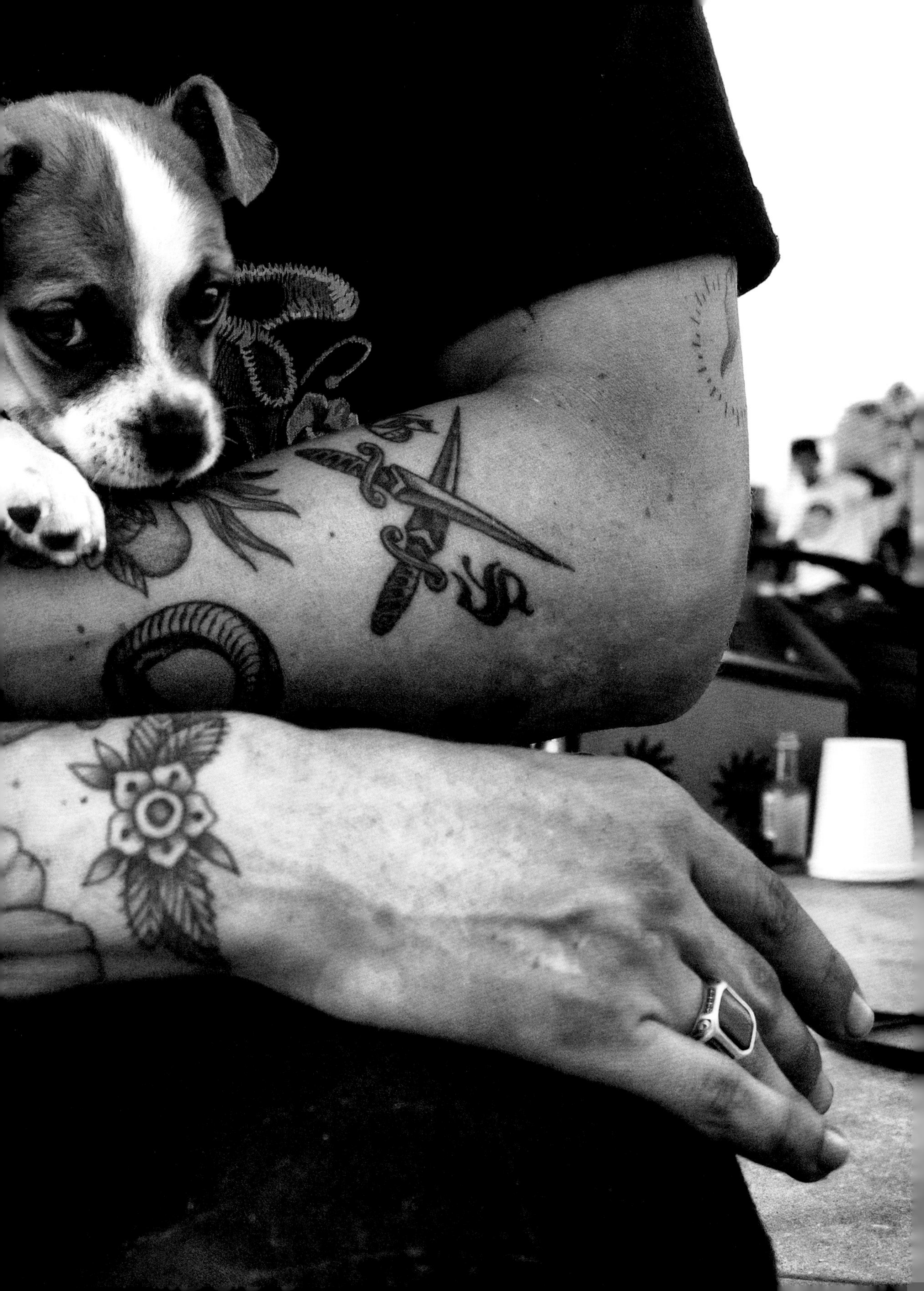

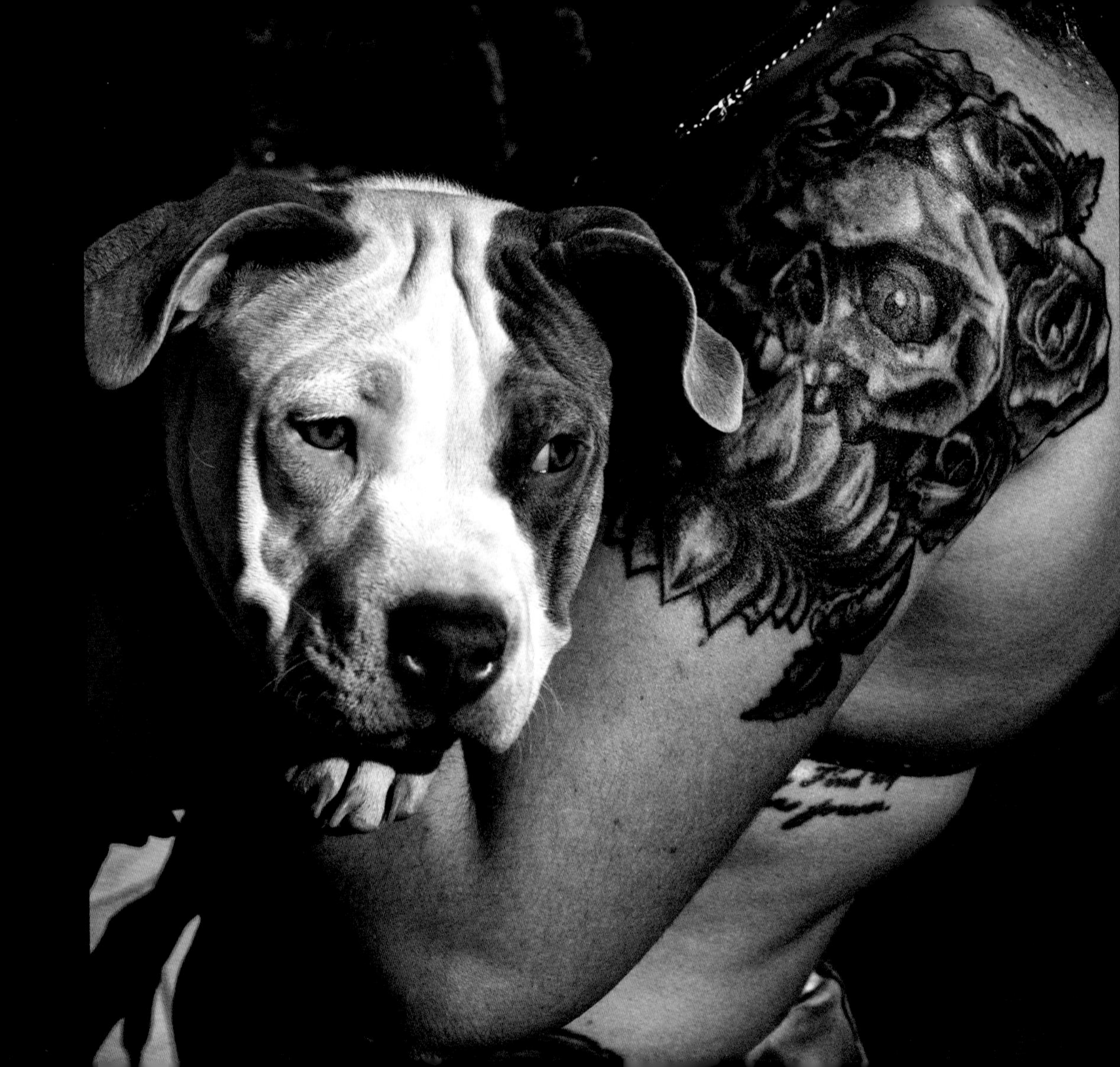

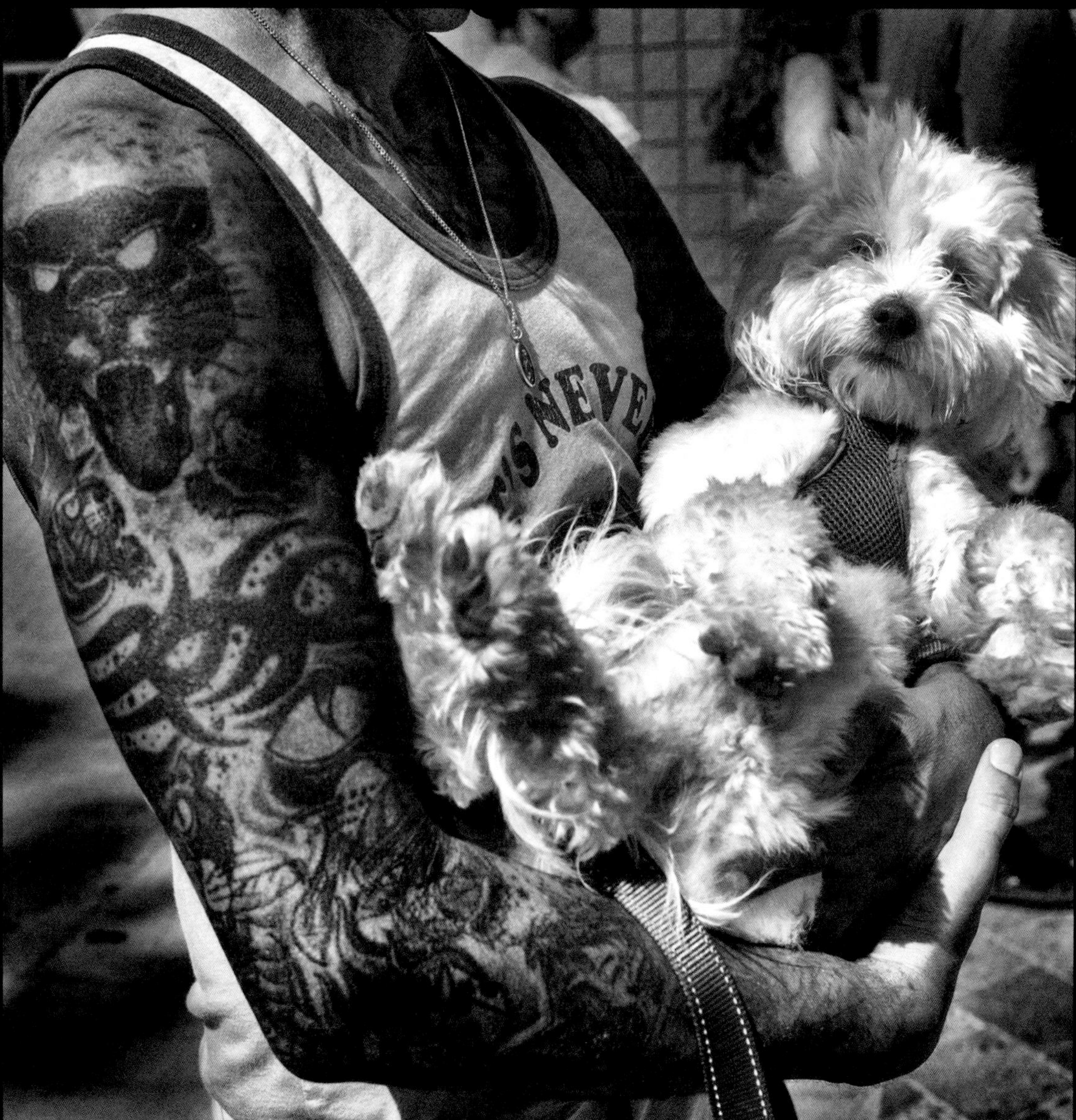

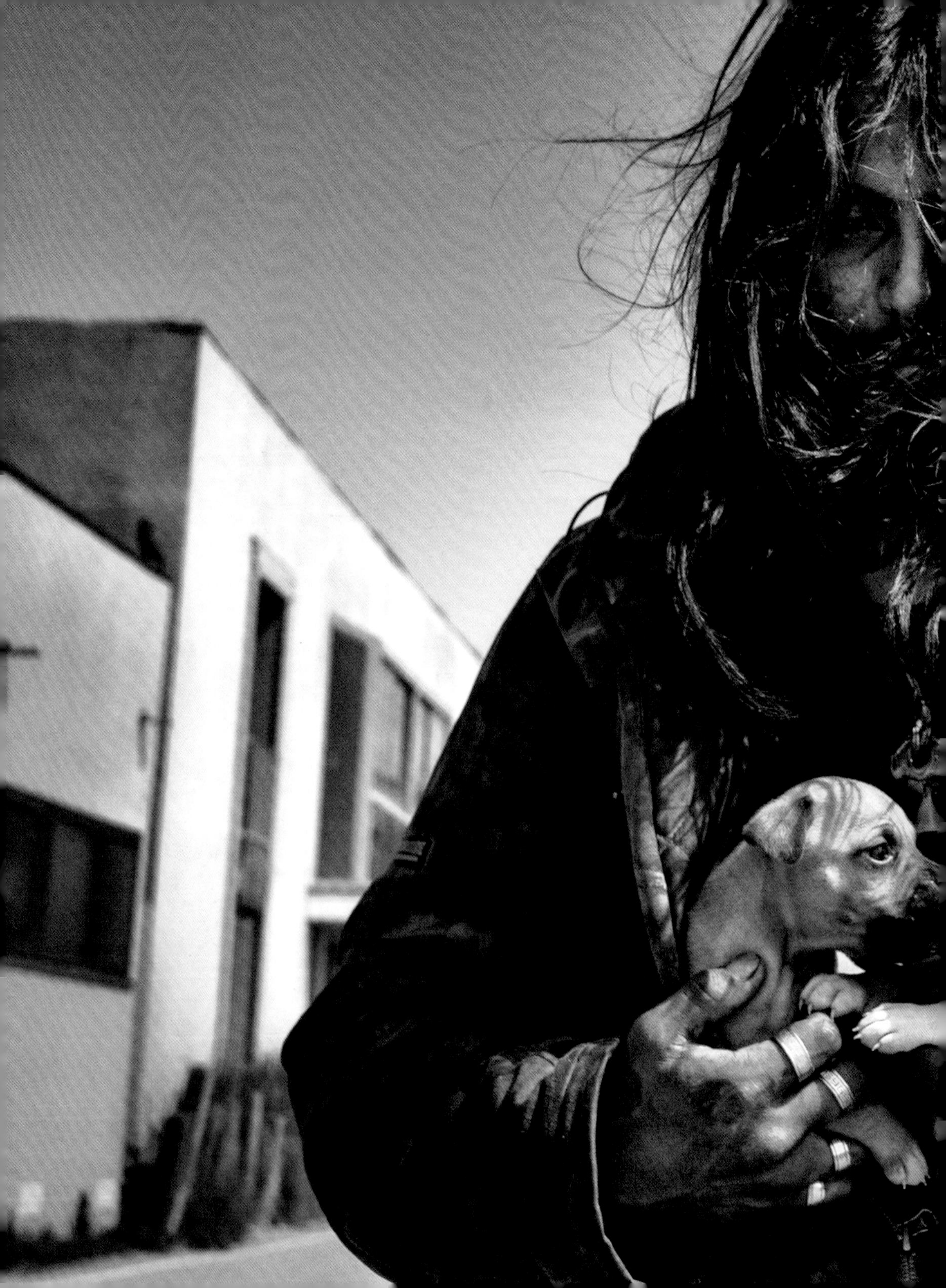

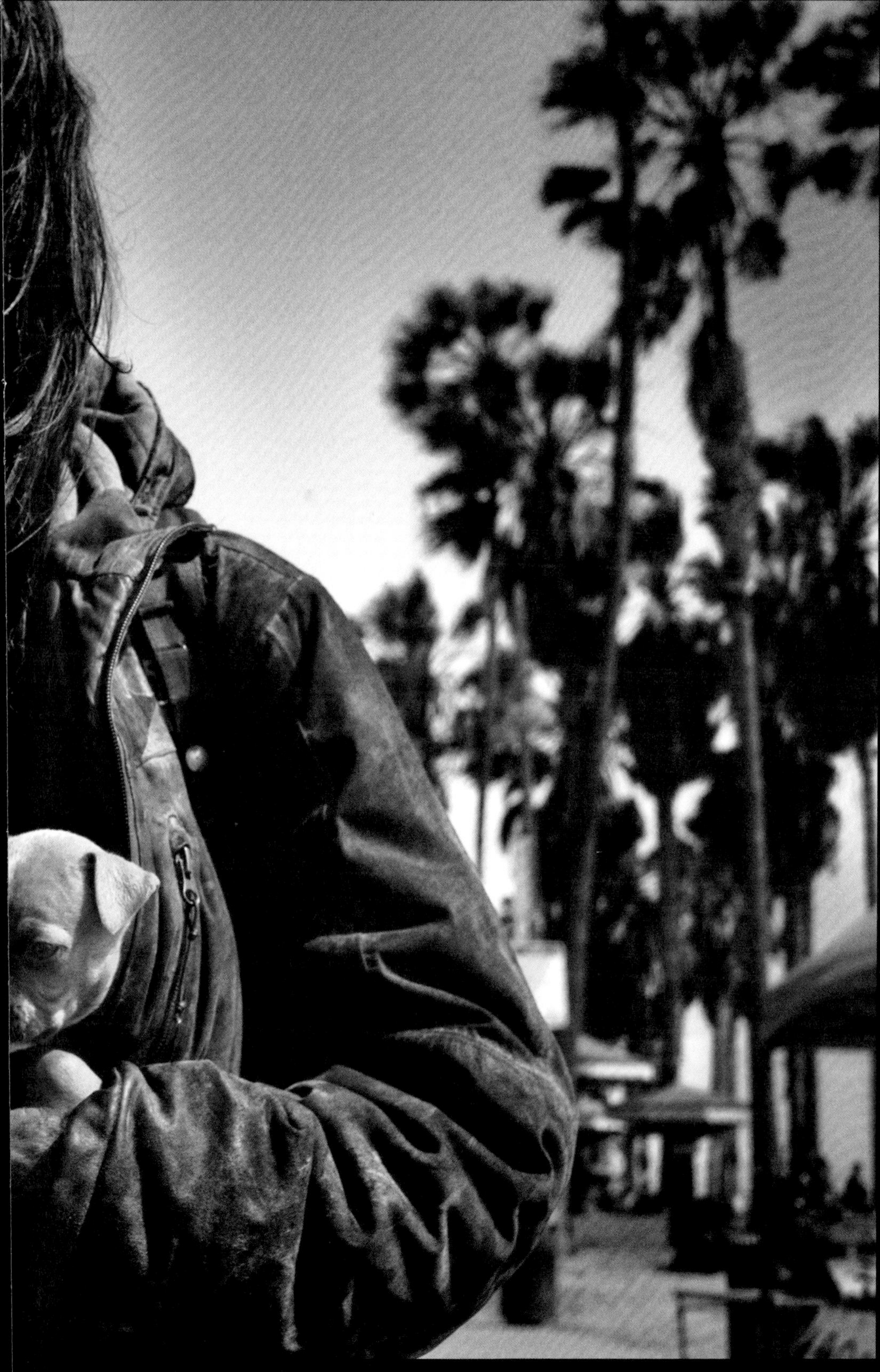

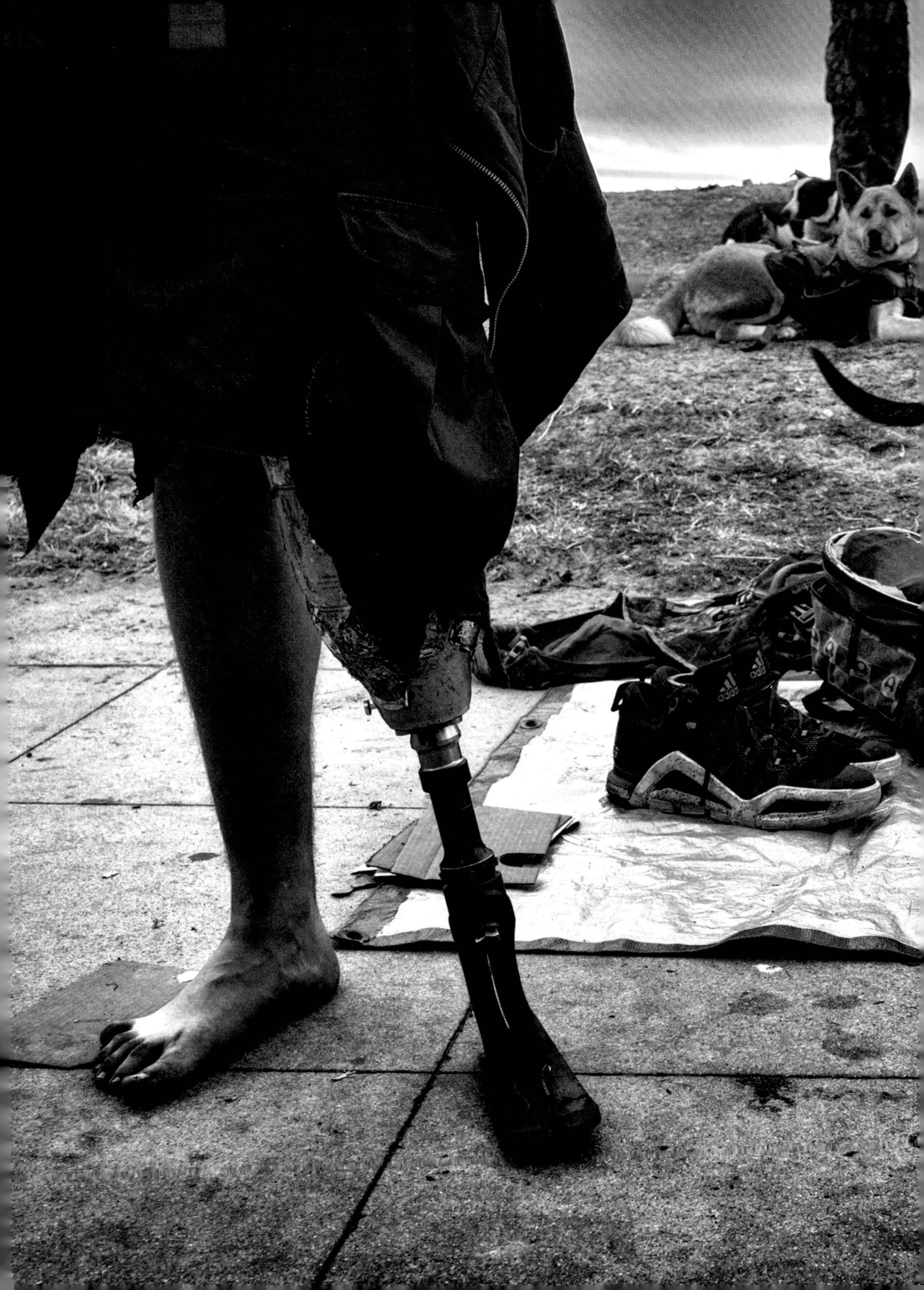
adidas

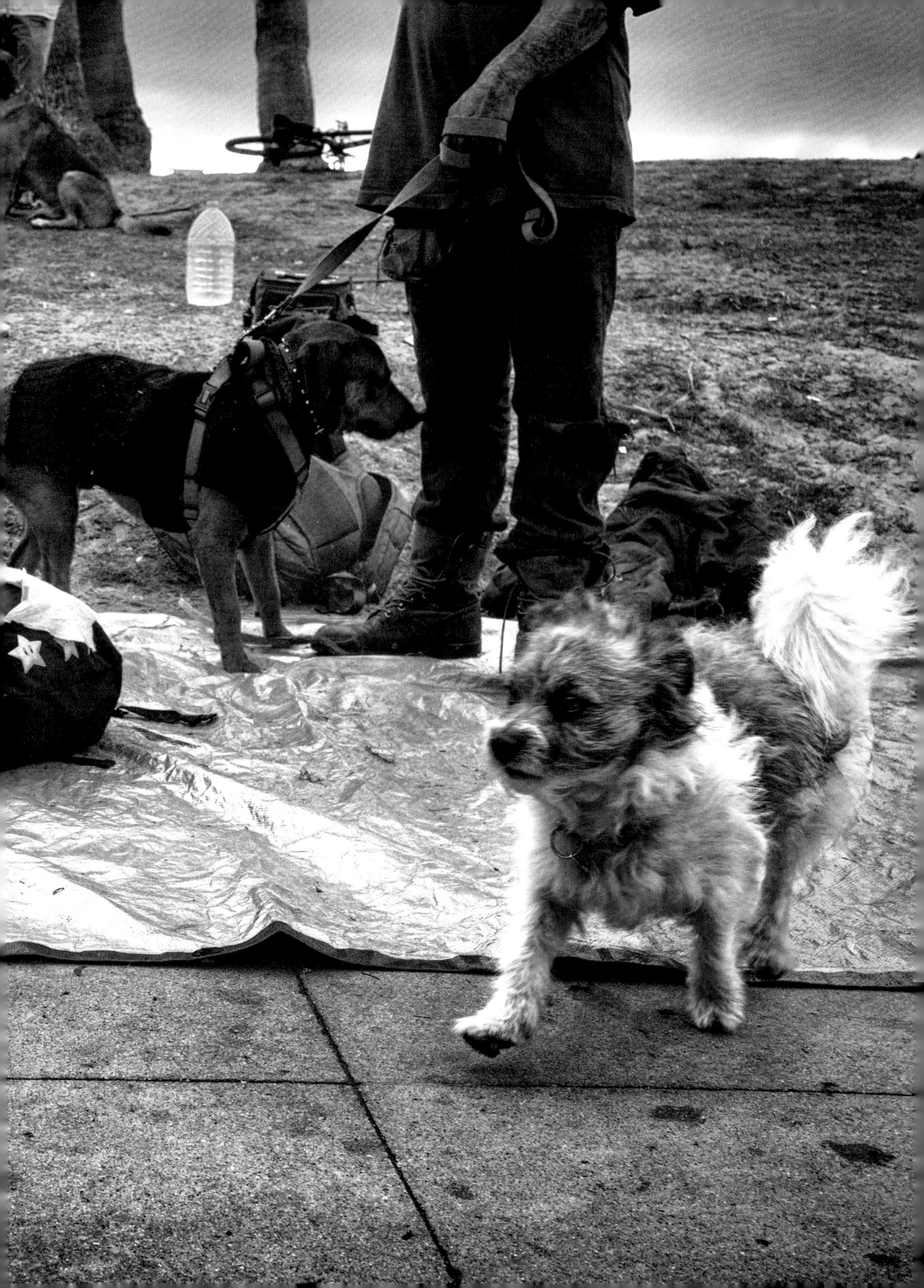

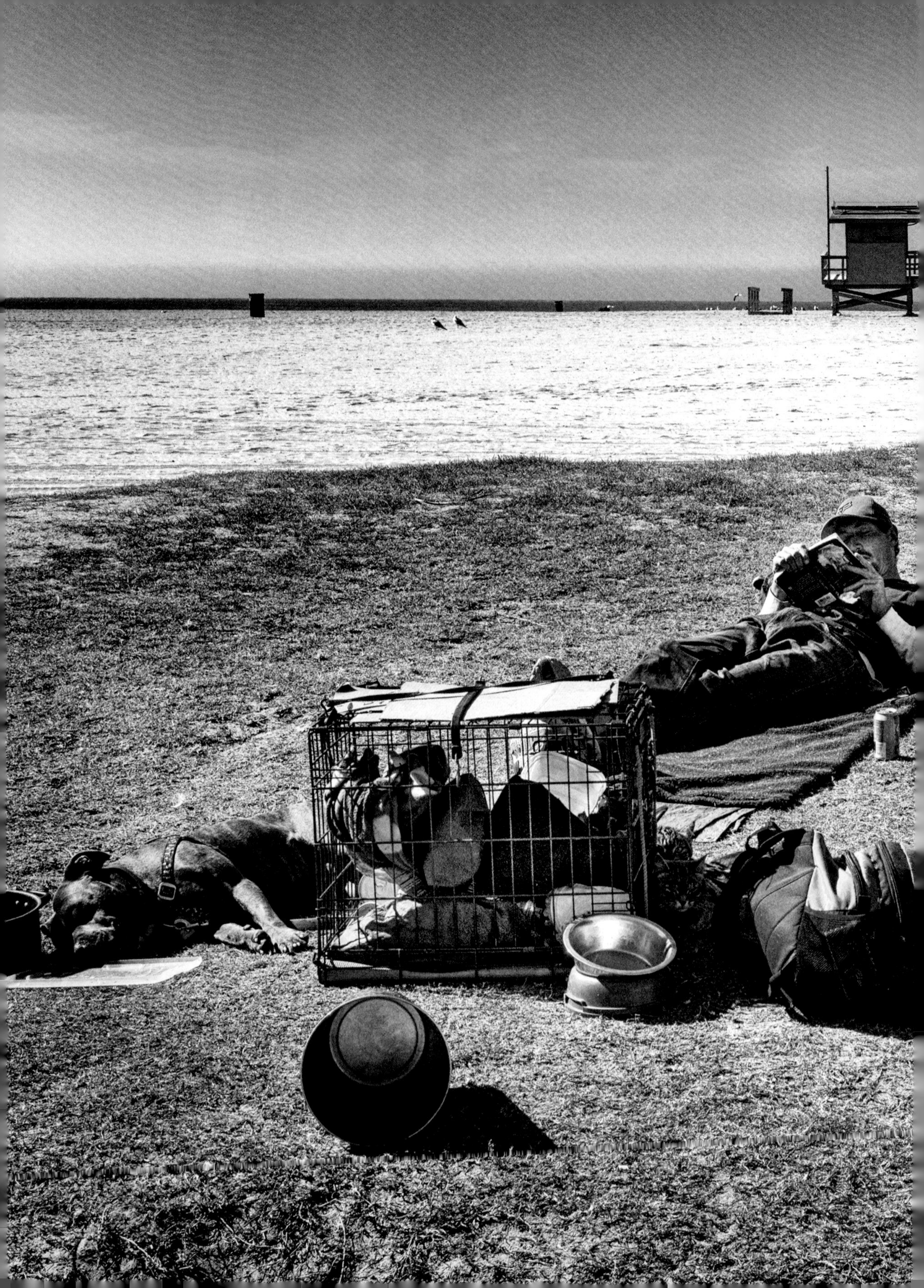

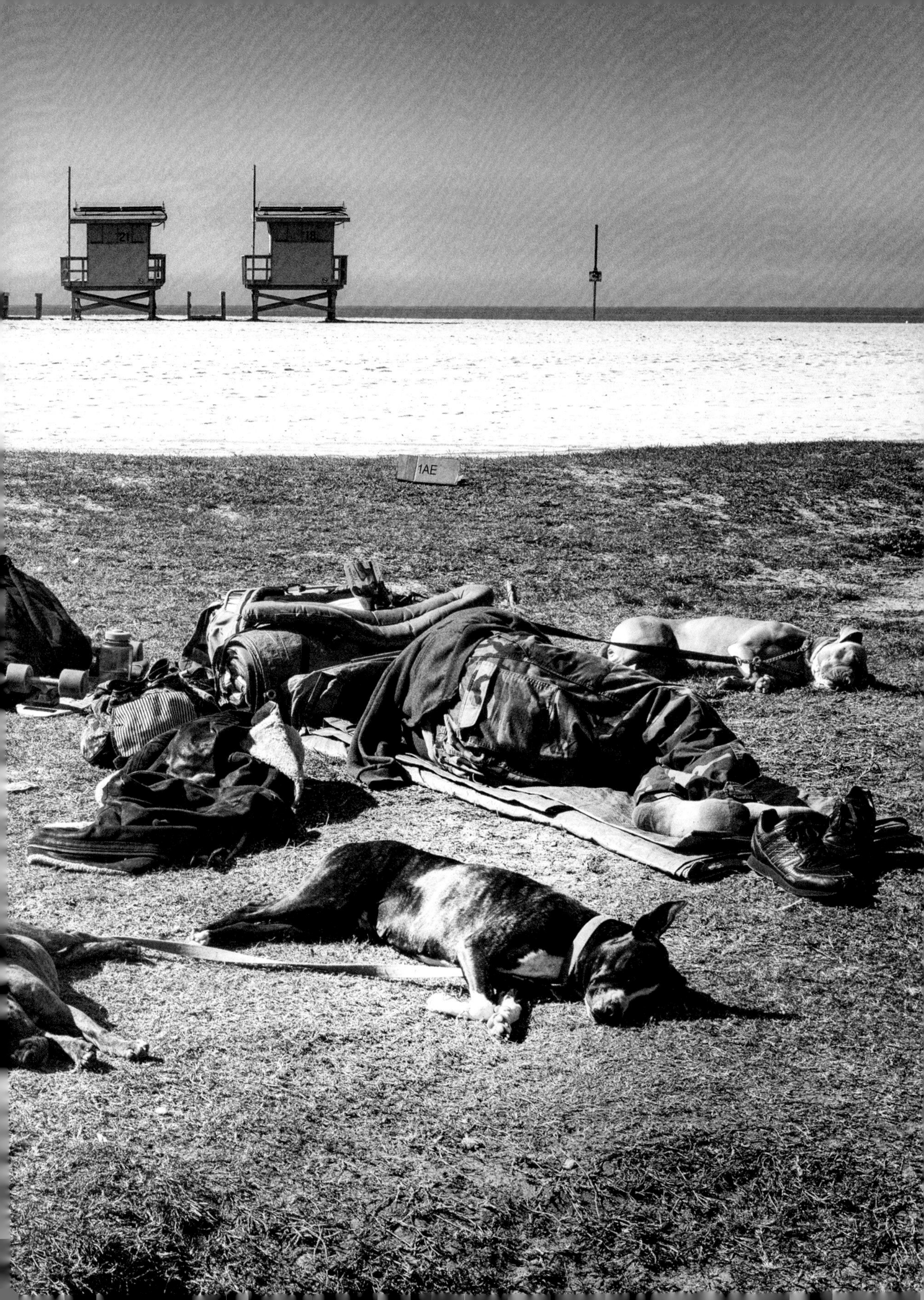
1AE

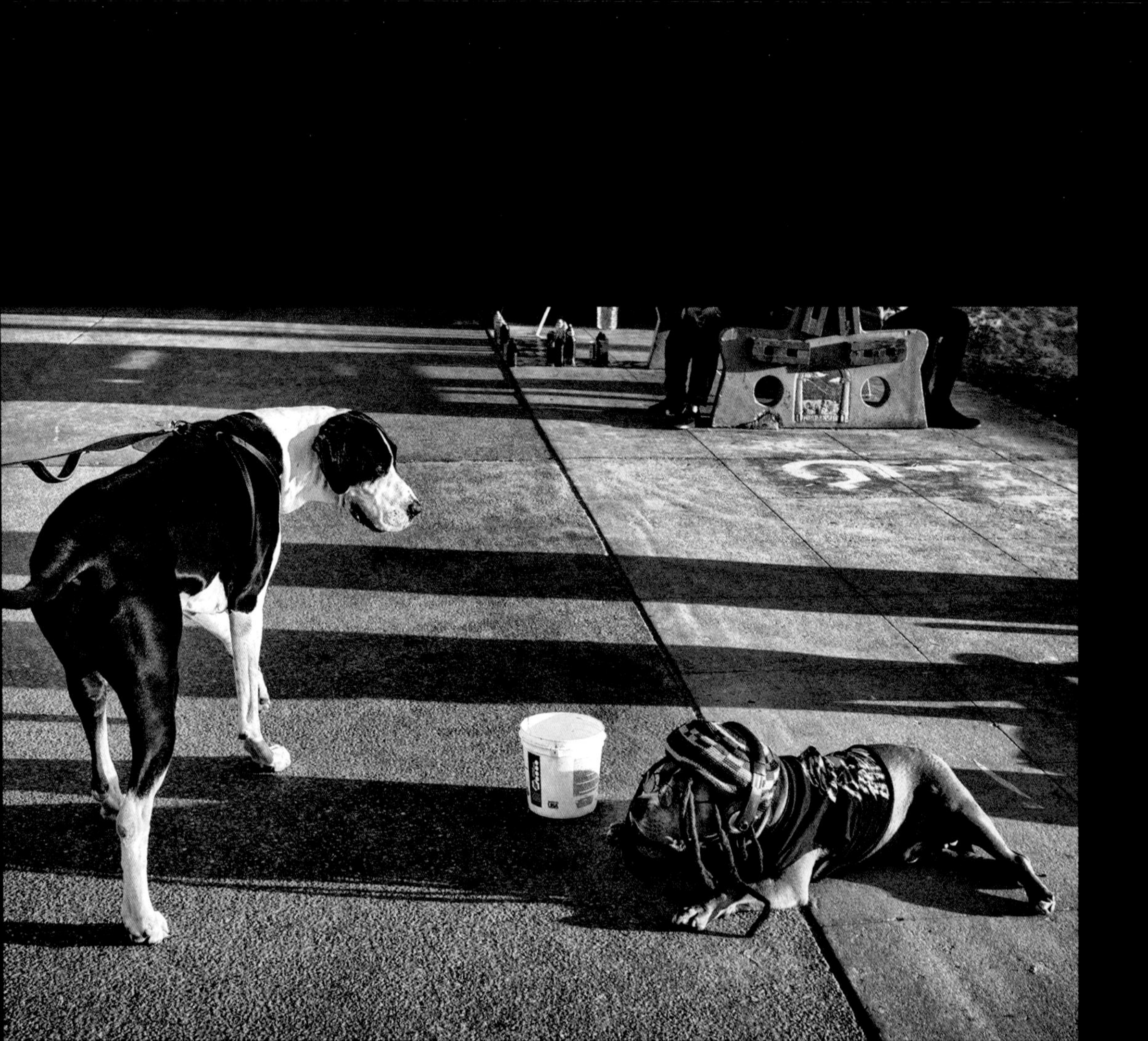

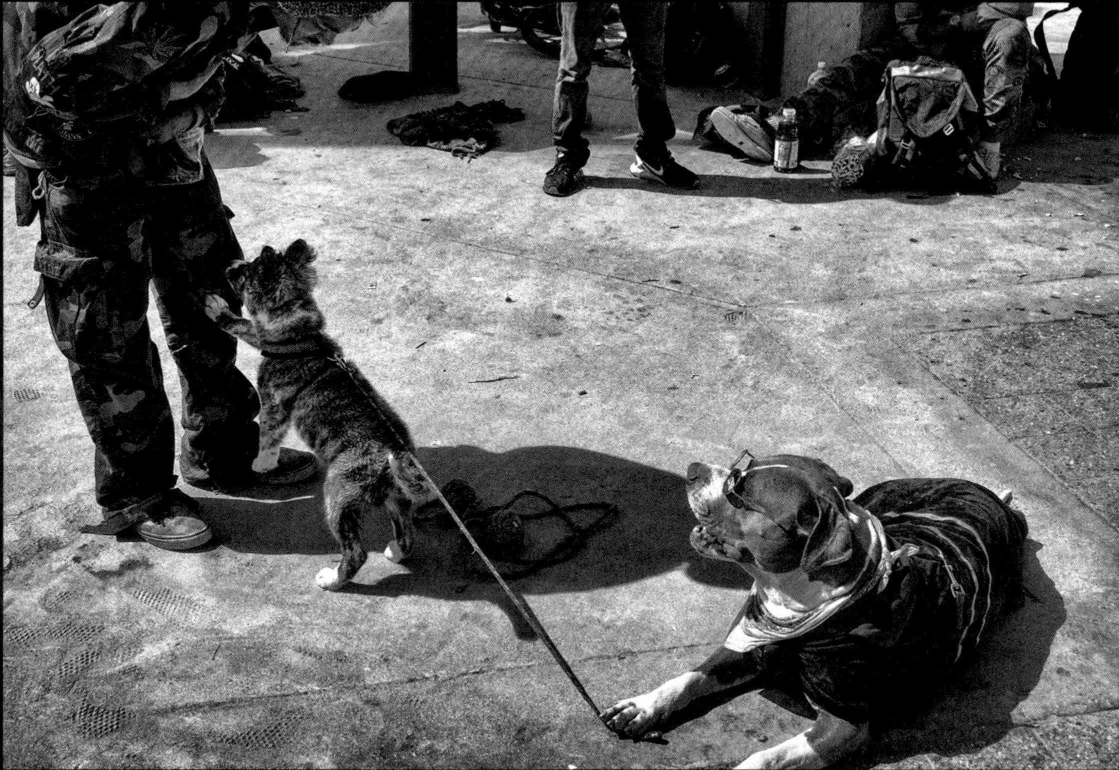

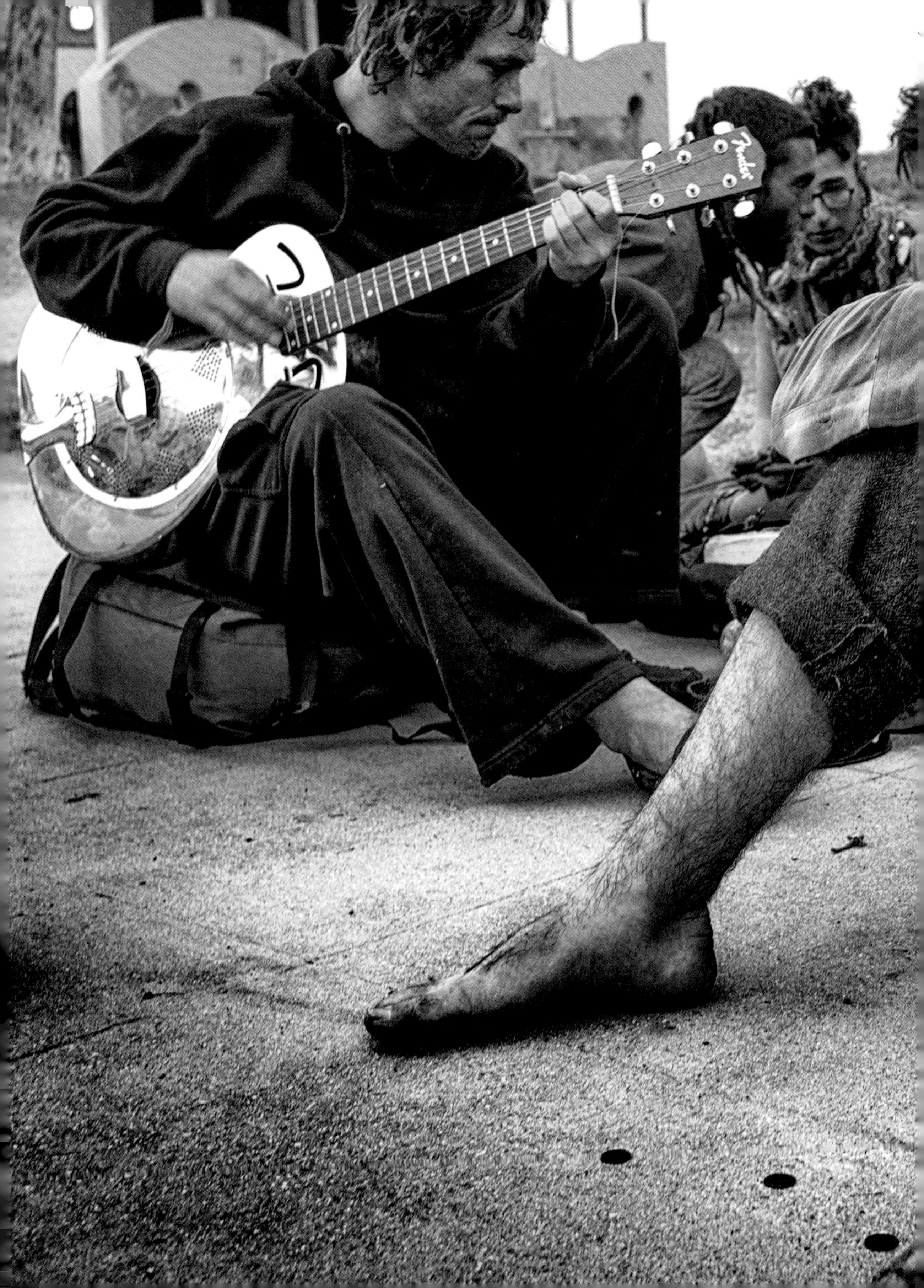
Fender

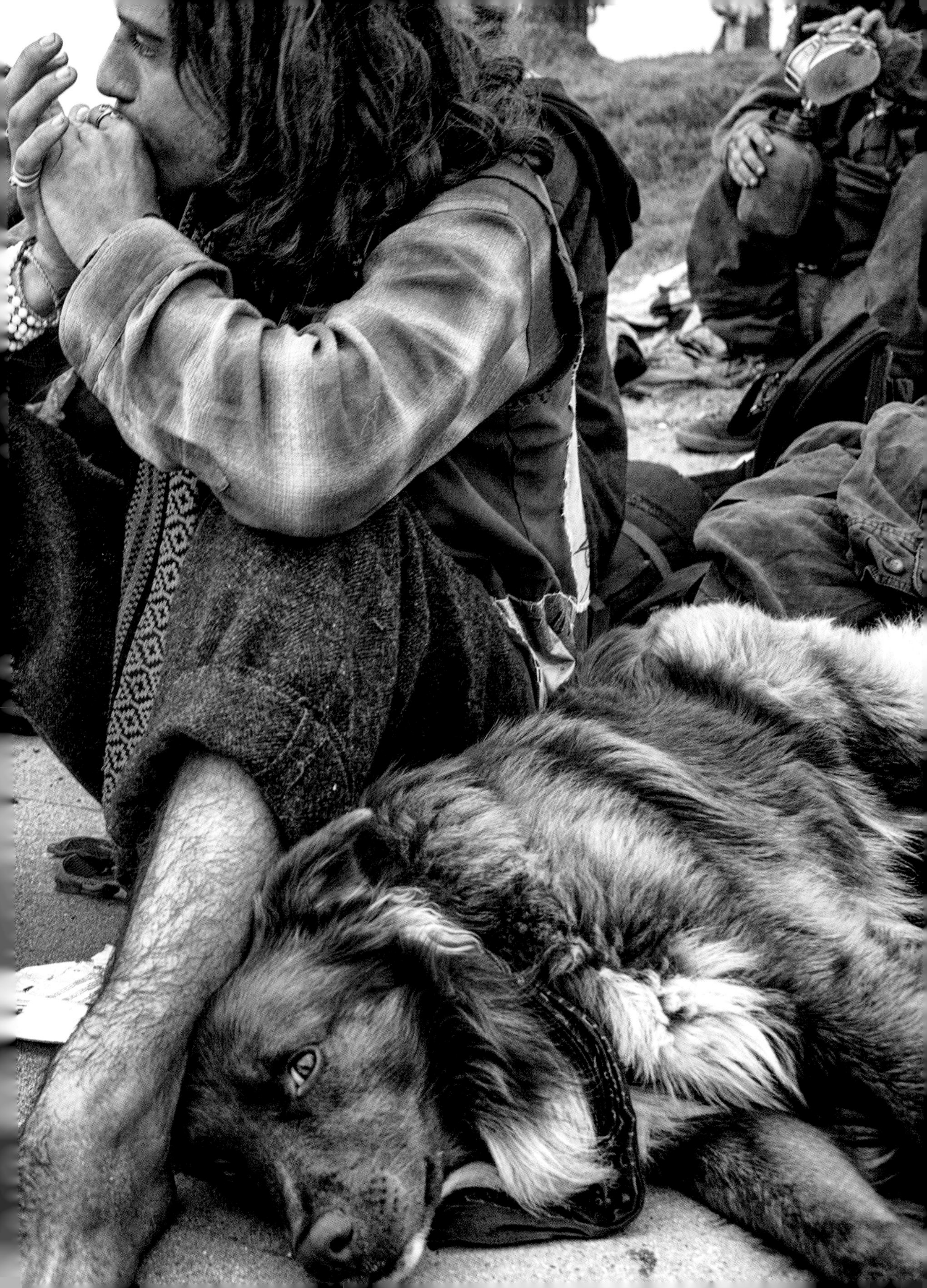

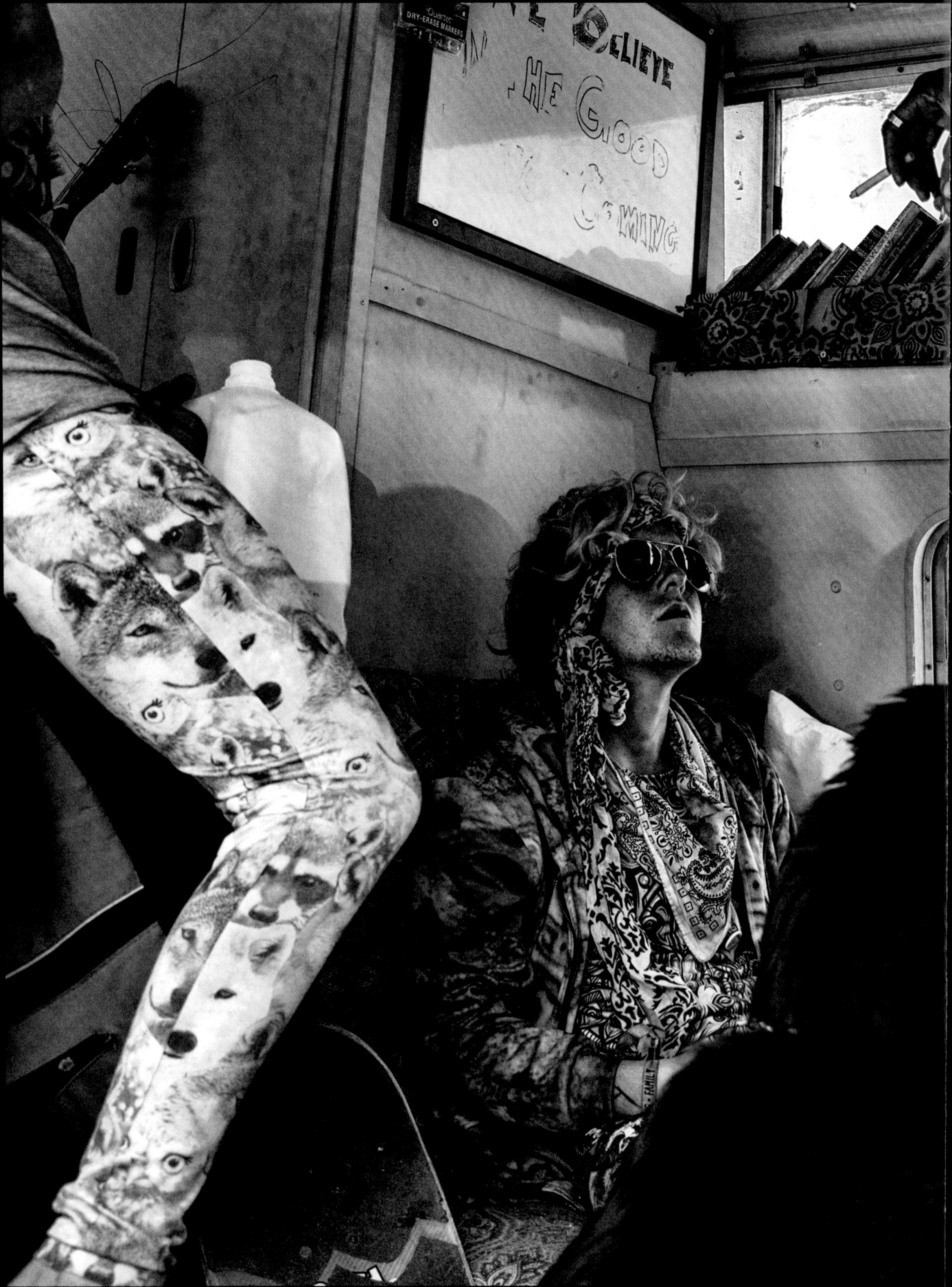
Quartet
DRY-ERASE MARKERS

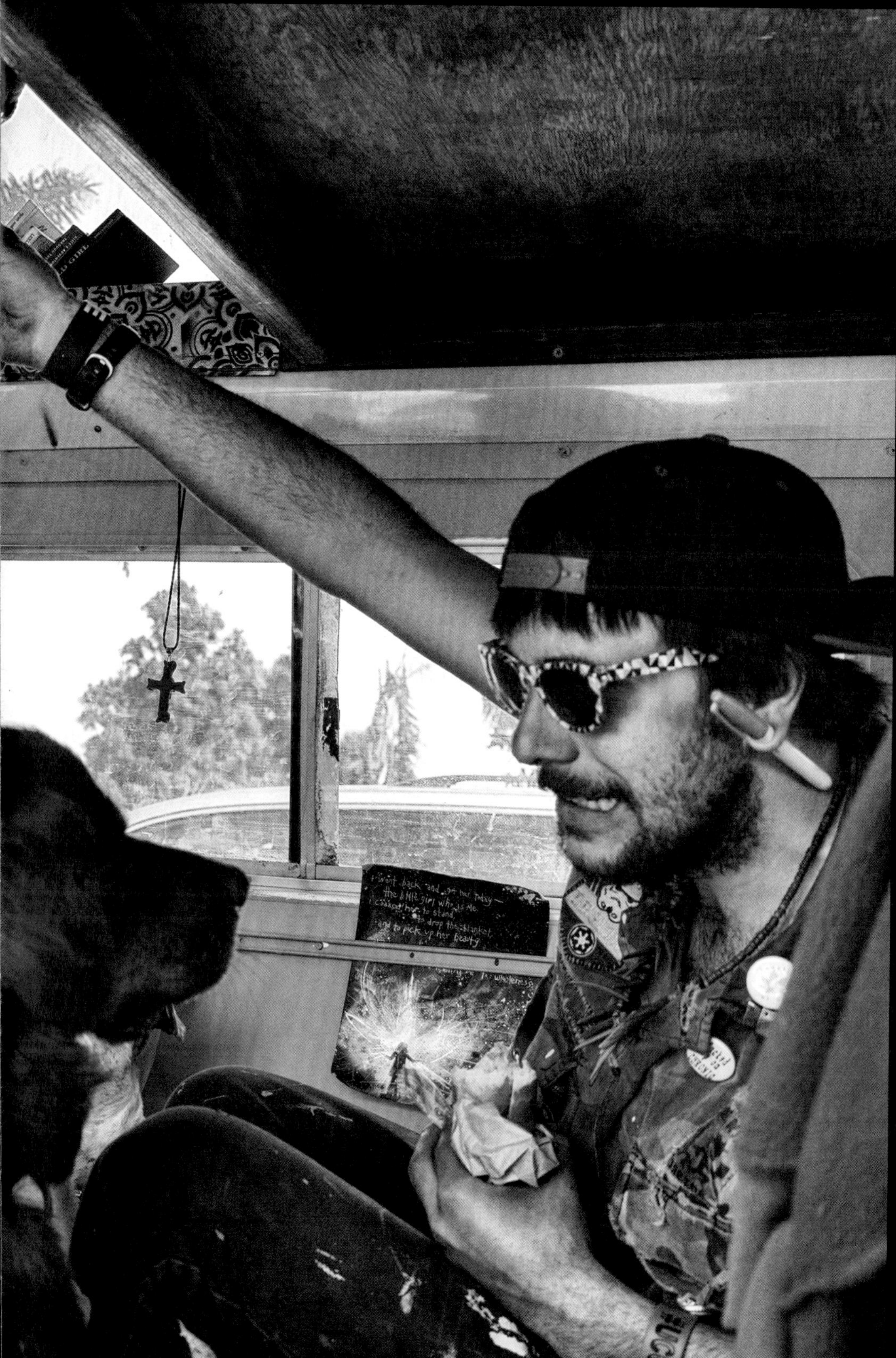
I went back and got her today—
the little girl who is me.
I coaxed her to stand,
to drop the blanket
and to pick up her beauty
wholeness

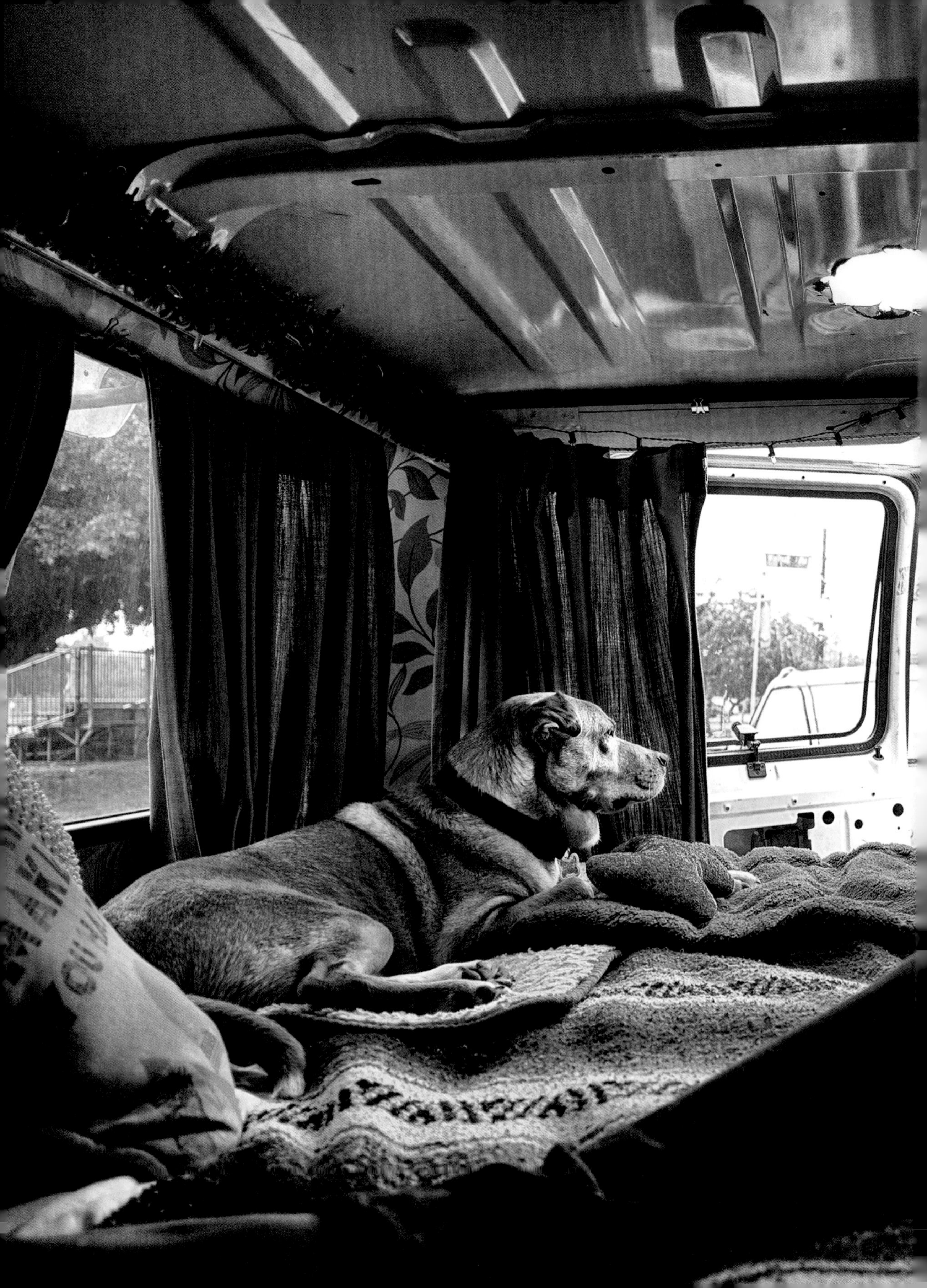

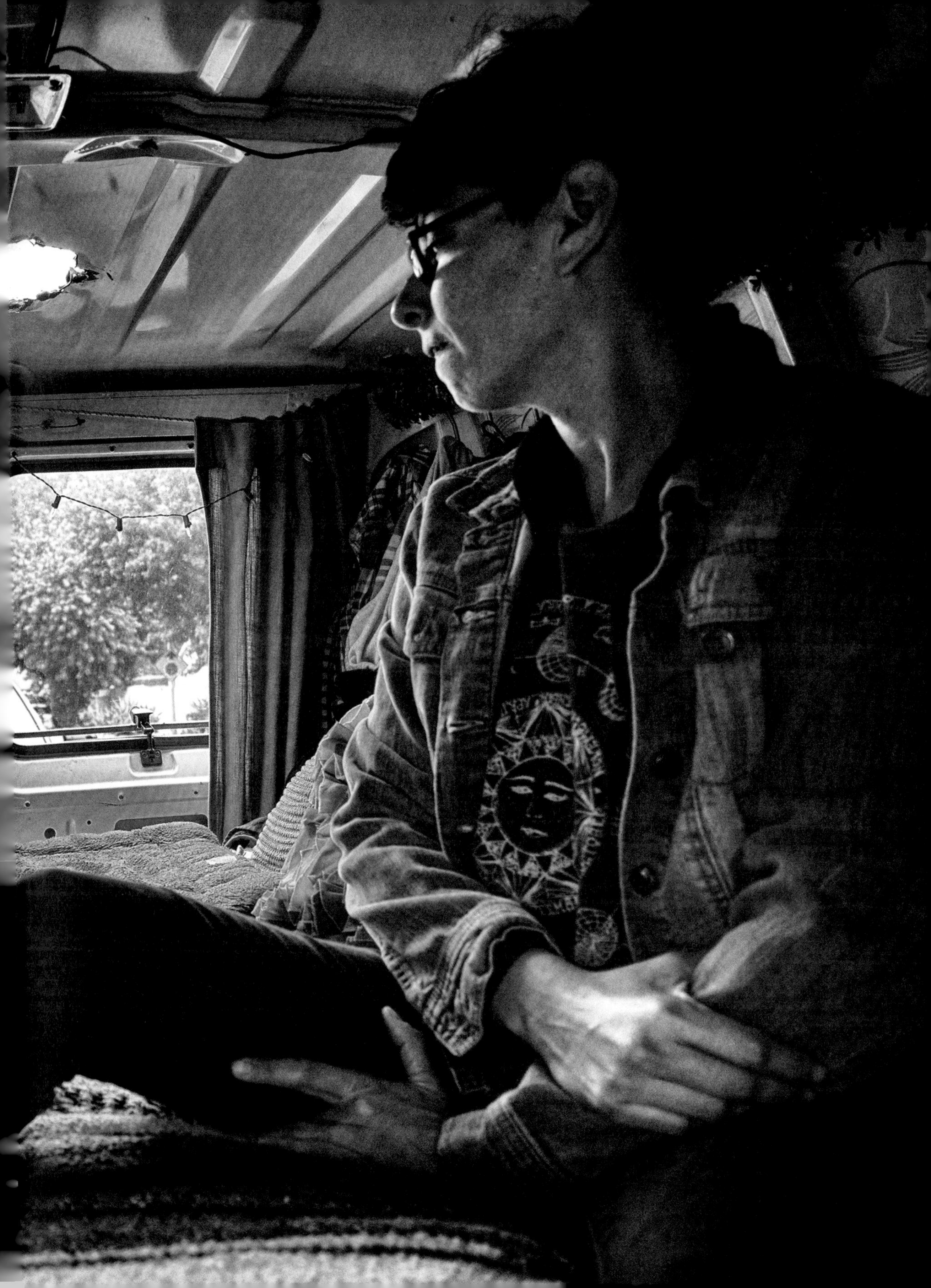

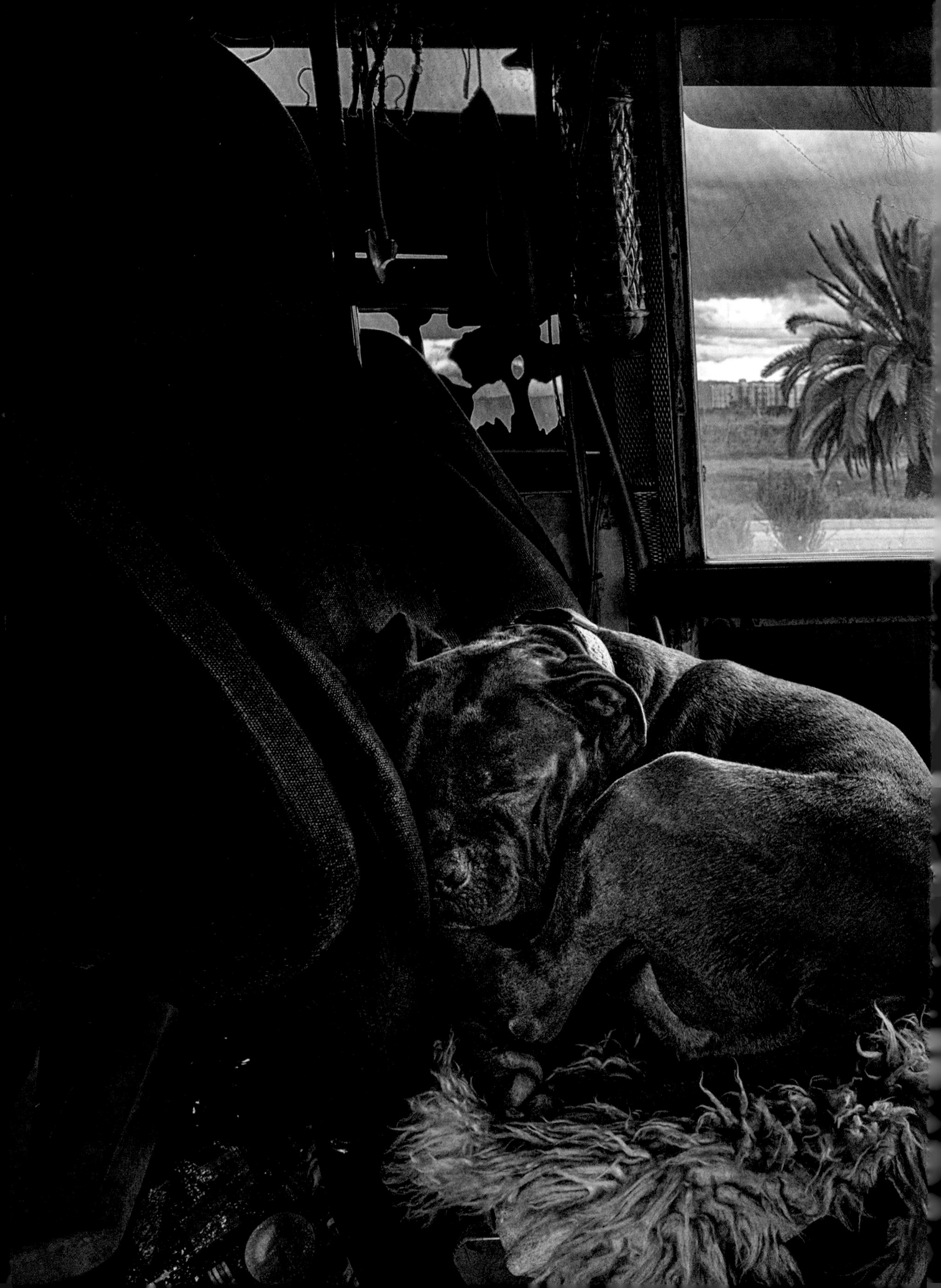

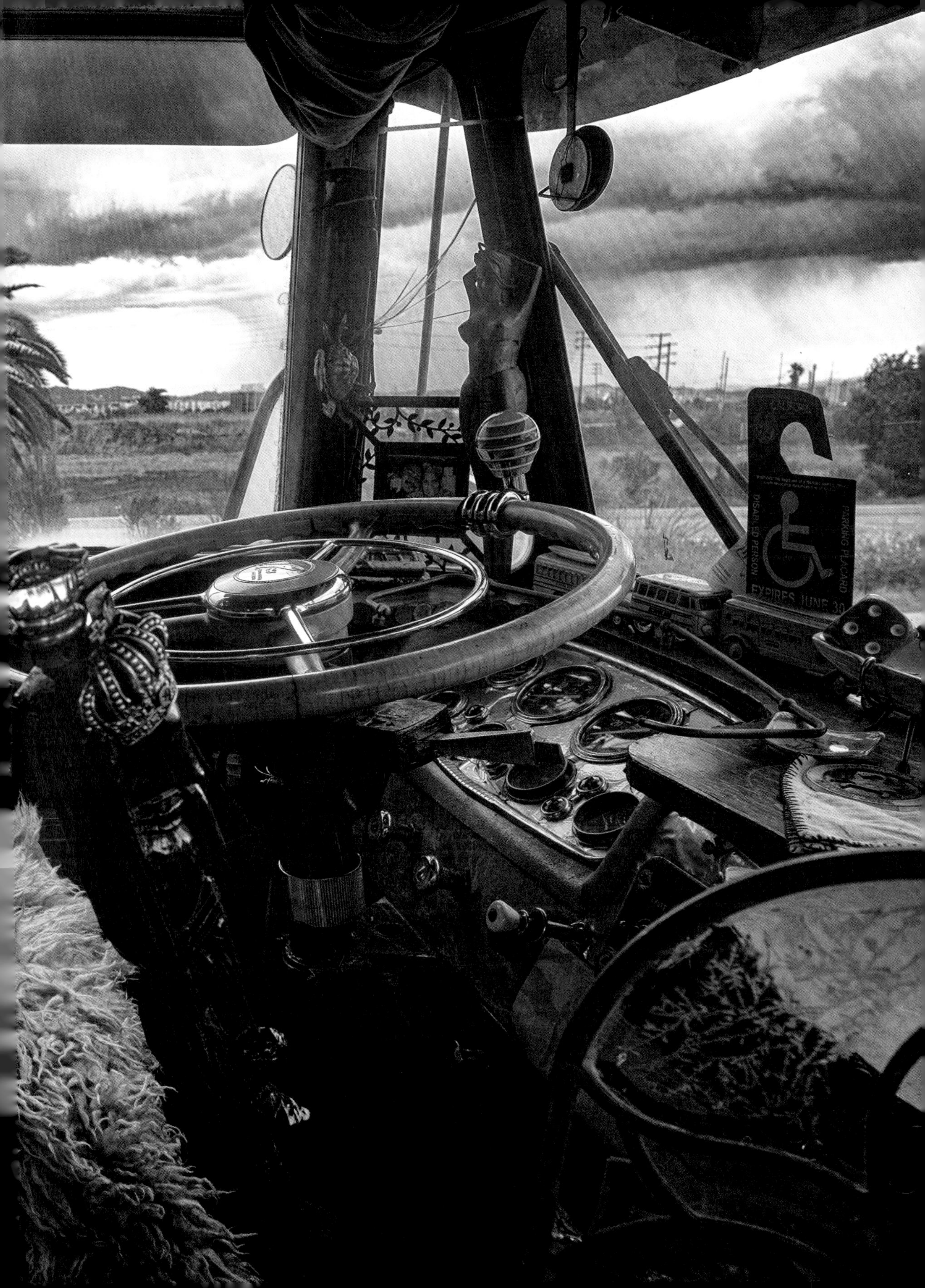
DISABLED PERSON
PARKING PLACARD
EXPIRES JUNE 30

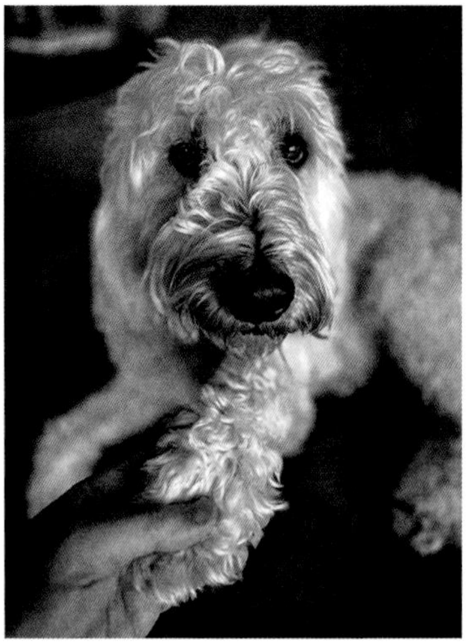

To my dog, Beau.
You inspire me every day to become the person you think I am.

Instagram: dotansaguy

EDITORS
Gail Fisher, Dotan Saguy

TEXTS
Dotan Saguy

COPY EDITING
George Macbeth

DESIGN
Kehrer Design (Loreen Lampe)

IMAGE PROCESSING
Kehrer Design (Erik Clewe)

PROJECT MANAGEMENT
Kehrer Verlag (Aydria Stadter)

PRODUCTION MANAGEMENT
Kehrer Design (Tom Streicher)

All images were made between 2015 - 2023 in *Dogtown*, Venice and Santa Monica, CA with a Leica Monochrom camera and a Leica 35mm lens.

Printed and bound in Germany
ISBN 978-3- 96900-143-1

Kehrer Verlag Heidelberg
www.kehrerverlag.com

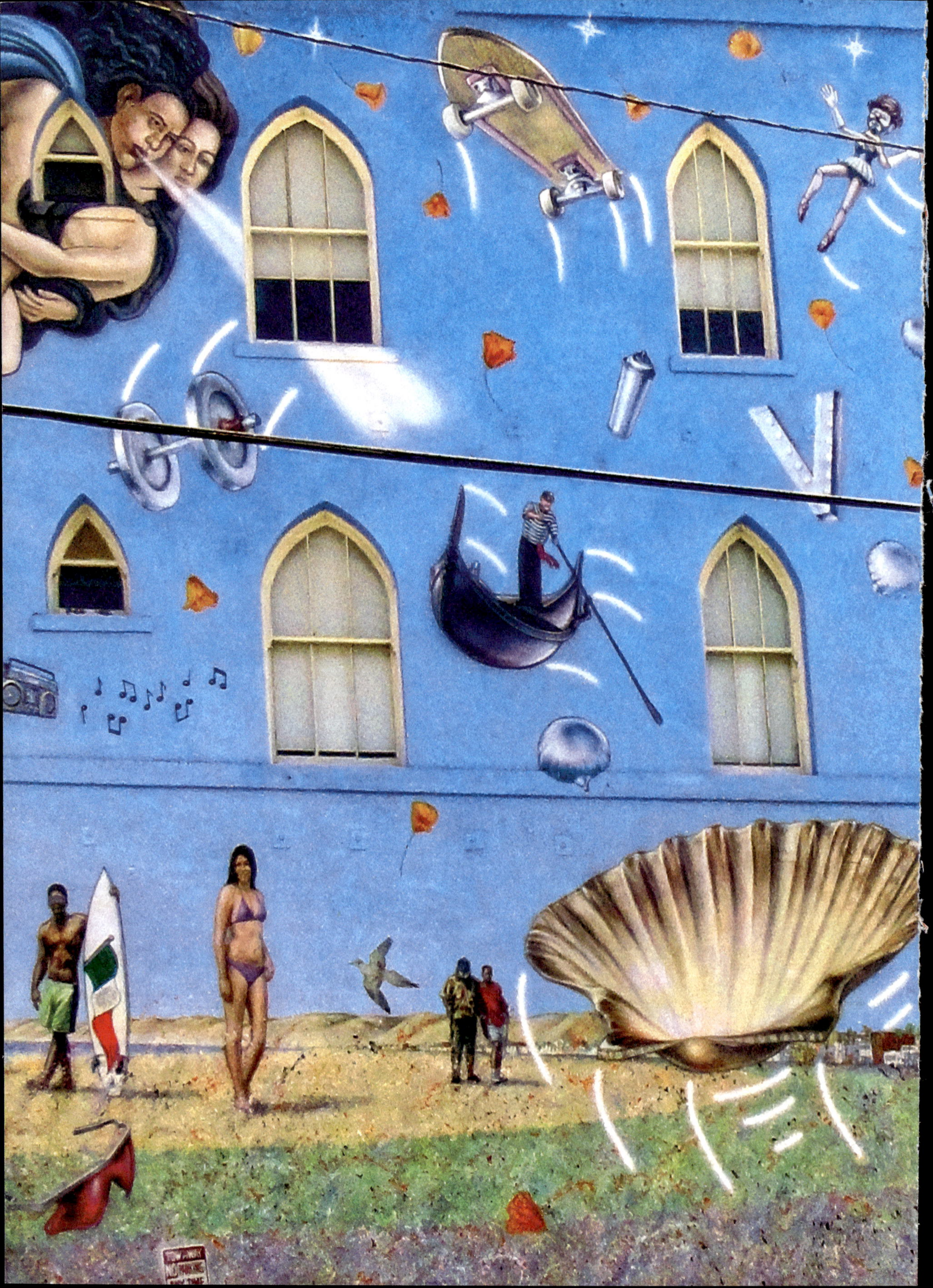